1994

Recasting the World

Parallax 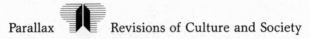 Revisions of Culture and Society

Stephen G. Nichols, Gerald Prince, and Wendy Steiner, Series Editors

Recasting the World

Writing after Colonialism

Edited by Jonathan White

The Johns Hopkins University Press
Baltimore and London

© 1993 The Johns Hopkins University Press
All rights reserved
Printed in the United States of America on acid-free paper

The Johns Hopkins University Press
2715 North Charles Street
Baltimore, Maryland 21218-4319
The Johns Hopkins Press Ltd., London

Library of Congress Cataloging-in-Publication Data will be found
at the end of this book.

A catalog record for this book is available from the British Library.

"No Ordinary Sun" is reprinted with the permission of Richards Literary Agency,
Auckland, from Hone Tuwhare, *Mihi: Collected Poems* (Harmondsworth: Penguin,
1987). "South of My Days" is reprinted with the permission of the publisher,
Angus and Robertson, Pymble, Australia, from Judith Wright, *Collected Poems:
1942–1970* (1971). "We Are Going" is reprinted with the permission of the publisher, Jacaranda Wiley Ltd., Brisbane, from Oodgeroo of the tribe Noonuccal,
We Are Going (1964).

To Francis

Contents

Preface

This collection of essays is concerned with the title notion of recasting realities through writing. It emerges largely from the context of a department of literature (in the School of Comparative Studies at the University of Essex) that, from its inception just over a quarter of a century ago, has not been tied to one national tradition, however widely interpreted. Indeed, in the form of area studies the department had tackled the postcolonial literatures of the United States and Latin America from its foundation and, more recently, other "new" literatures along with those two. The essays that follow are thus in the main the result of a framework for studying literature which is comparative and transnational. They are written by current or past members, former graduate students, visiting exchanges, and longtime associates of the Essex literature department. One is by a colleague from what has been, until the present change to university status on the part of many polytechnics, the only other university department of literature as such in Britain, that of the Open University.

Without the existence of the context I have outlined I could not have put together this volume. But far more help of other kinds has been forthcoming. I am grateful to my contributors for the hard work they have put into their individual essays, for being so mutually supportive and so constructive in their criticisms of what we were trying to achieve by way of a volume – nowhere more than in suggesting to me appropriate ways of introducing it. I would also like to pay a special tribute to several recent-year groups of Essex students, particularly those pursuing options in new literatures, cross-cultural studies, and the postgraduate diploma in literature, for their participation in developing the kinds of thinking represented here. Jeremy Tambling and his colleagues in the Department of Comparative Literature in the University of Hong Kong commented valuably on an early version of my own chapter. Sylvia Sparrow and Elizabeth Weall shared many initial tasks of typing and formatting essays. Their unstinting help was supplemented by that of my colleague Leon Burnett, whose programming wizardry at a later stage got me out of more scrapes than I would care to acknowledge. Our publishers too have been of the utmost assistance. For all their hard work and commitment I would like to express my special gratitude to, among many others at the Johns Hopkins University Press, the volume's copy editor, Elizabeth Gratch, and its production editor, Terry Schutz. Herbie Butterfield extended to me the unflagging support of his warm heart and hearth. Above all, I wish to say how invaluable to me during the putting together of this volume have been the help and friendship of Francis Barker.

Recasting the World

Introduction

Jonathan White

The title of this volume of essays, *Recasting the World: Writing after Colonialism,* was chosen with a politics in mind. It derives in part from Frantz Fanon's ensemble of ideas about going beyond colonialism, about which I have more to say. The contributors to this volume are mainly concerned with the specific place of "writing" within postcolonial histories. The notion that the world is available for writers to alter at will is quixotic. But that does not mean that texts of the kind we found ourselves drawn into studying are powerless to shape and influence postcolonial destinies. We have sought to avoid the idealist's trap of supposing that a clean end to colonialism is ever fully achieved and a subsequent reality, not colonial in kind, entered as a paradise in which writers freely disport themselves. No such paradises have come to pass.

And yet (together with many others) we continue to use the term *postcolonial,* which indicates an end to processes of colonialism and the subsequent existence of a different reality. This may seem a paradox – or worse, an intellectual confusion – on the part of many people. It is neither. Rather, our own and others' use of the term should be seen as part of a politics of ongoing creation of the reality it names, in the face of an ever-present counterreality. The name of that counterreality is imperialism, which, like the devil, has many guises.

There is, thus, a purpose behind our giving this volume a title that we hope marks an affirmative politics within that always double-stranded history, of the forces of decolonization in contention with those of imperialism. In conceiving the nature of the volume while workshopping early versions of chapters, we agreed it was important to name a time "after colonialism," since most of the writing under discussion (or, in the case of one chapter, cinema; in another, music) itself seemed interested in so much more than the old, closed world of oppression. However little such oppression had been definitively overcome, many of the texts studied seemed constituted as *ways of leaving it behind,* of coping with its terrors and creating conditions ripe for that "after" state, which we also therefore decided to look toward in the title of our own writing. As Nadine Gordimer has said, in an essay that bears on many of these issues: "The *transformation of experience* remains the writer's basic essential gesture; the lifting out of a limited category something that reveals its full meaning and significance only when the writer's imagination has expanded it. This has never been more evident than in the context of extreme experiences . . . central to the period."[1] Many of the essays of this volume have sought to understand more fully the workings of transformative powers unleashed by mere words on pages.

How was it that some texts seemed to possess those powers in larger measure than others? Was it from their understanding better the extremes of colonialism in the first place? Before being able to answer such questions we needed a larger purchase on what lay behind certain big words we were bound to go on deploying: *colonialism, decolonization, imperialism, independence.* As I have partly already indicated, it was the political theorist Frantz Fanon whose work seemed preeminently to have distinguished some of the goals and also the problems surrounding such concepts, managing thereby to describe many of the subtler realities that they were only names for. So here was a starting point.

Fanon based his theses about the nature of colonialism and decolonization on the society of Algeria undergoing revolution. He saw this revolution, which had begun in 1954 and which he did not quite live to see achieved in 1962, as providing possibilities for fundamental structural change: "This was the period during which men, women, children, the whole Algerian people, experienced at one and the same time their national vocation and the recasting of the new Algerian society."[2] The English term *recasting* (the original French was *refonte*)[3] is particularly felicitous, both in respect to Fanon's overall argument and for the multiple set of meanings it provides for us to tease out. The world in which colonial control is displaced, or from which it is forced to withdraw, requires new actors – another "species" of being, as Fanon had suggested,[4] as the formerly colonized replace the former colonizers – and so could be defined as "recast" in the theatrical sense, making for a new drama of emergent consciousness and eventuality.

But at such moments of revolution another recasting must go on – deep structural change, as a people seeks to shape its present and future. At this level of meaning the metaphor of recasting should no longer be understood only in terms of the art form of drama but also as one implying the reorganization of material form which occurs when an "old" reality is cast (as Marvell had said of a much earlier revolutionary moment) "into another mold."

In fact, as in the casting of metal, whether sculptural or industrial, this process of political transformation is fiendishly difficult to achieve successfully. Fanon saw the acute dangers of a neocolonialism in which there may indeed be a new cast of actors (a "national bourgeoisie" trained up by and left to dominate like their former colonial masters) in a real-life drama in which the fundamental structures of colonialism remain un-recast. Edward Said has put the case succinctly: "The new states are often ideologically in thrall to, and practical satellites of, their former colonial masters. Above all, the great transformation of which Frantz Fanon spoke, that after liberation, nationalist consciousness must convert itself into a new social consciousness, has not often taken place. In many new countries, dictatorships, fascist parties, brazenly neo-colonial regimes take power. Those intellectuals whose immediate predecessors fought the war of decolonisation awake to the reality that imperialism continues, in newer and more complex forms."[5]

In what sense is it possible to talk of "writing after colonialism" in a world in which no such after-state has even emerged? For in the postcolonial realities Said spells out we are left with a set of nightmare results frequently described in Fanon's own writings – as, for instance, in his account of an original colonialism so devastating that it has "settled itself into the very center of the . . . individual and has undertaken a sustained work of cleanup, of expulsion of self, of rationally pursued mutilation."[6] This, in the words of a later writer, Ngugi

Wa Thiong'o, is imperialism's "cultural bomb," whose effect is "to anni-
hilate a people's belief in their names, in their languages, in their environment, in their heritage of struggle, in their unity, in their capacities
and ultimately in themselves."[7] How, if Ngugi is not exaggerating,
might one even begin to envisage a project such as the one named in
the title of the text from which this last quotation is taken – namely,
that of "decolonising the mind"– let alone the still larger task of rescu-
ing whole peoples from imperialism's deadly, ever-new forms of enslavement?

There is simply no easy answer. Ngugi's own main solution – his ab-
juring writing in a colonial language and return to narrating in his
mother tongue, Gikuyu; reinstating "orature" to a cultural position
dominant over writing – seems not only belated but also incommen-
surate with the magnitude of the problem as he himself has defined
it. For if the reality of many postcolonial societies is that they have
been blasted apart by imperialism's cultural bomb, and the resultant
slough of neocolonialism is one in which its victims might endlessly
despond, then what ways forward, if any, are there?

So difficult a question – nothing less than how to overcome imperialism's worst legacies – needs canny and gradual answering. History
has repeatedly taught that there is no single, always effective way of
overcoming those legacies. They constitute a monolith, before which
teams of removalists may seem to have been provided with tools no
mightier than toothpicks. Writers, however, insofar as they can be
figured as a class, are not so much removers as introducers of things
not there before, especially of novel conceptualizations of reality,
"transformation of experience," as Gordimer put it. What in the face
of imperialism's vast legacies of oppression has been the response of
specific writers of the postcolonial condition?

The Caribbean poet Derek Walcott helps us (obliquely – but then
there can be none but obliquities in a task so difficult) both to see the
conundrum and to find a way out, initially through a very fine one-
line play on words:

> I decompose, but I composing still.[8]

The line is taken from a lyric-satirical fantasy entitled "The Spoiler's
Return." In this poem, as Dennis Walder in his chapter of this volume
also points out, Walcott reviews the present, postcolonial Caribbean
in the persona of the revenant spirit of a famous Trinidadian calypson-

ian of the preindependence 1940s and 1950s, Theophilus Phillip, known in his lifetime as "The Mighty Spoiler." In literal terms the spoiler decomposes because he's dead. But his spirit self is imagined wandering the places of his life, "composing still," in scissoring calypso couplets. It would be an exaggeration to claim that the single line quoted has much intended relevance to the exigencies of postcolonialism, when its literal meaning is so dominant. Nonetheless, we *can* legitimately extrapolate further meaning from so seminal a play on words and wield it as part of a larger argument.

Many such societies, by which I mean those in any way like the multiple Caribbean places of Walcott's poems, lay almost impossible burdens upon their peoples, so that Walcott's poetic activity of composing still can be considered as a form of ongoing political defiance in its own right. It is surely made possible only by plumbing the deepest resources of self-renewal and commitment, in the face of every prevailing individual and societal tendency to decompose. Creativity survives in the face of ongoing fragmentation and breakdown.

Indeed, the reality announced in Walcott's one-liner is possibly even more impressive than so far indicated. For the actions that are syntactically counterpoised are stark semantic opposites. We witness something like Blakean "contrary states of the human soul," in mutual if contradictory-seeming control of the poet/persona. Or rather, more exactly still, one of those contrary states, the tendency to decompose, over which we should say the dead spoiler/live poet—like any mortal individual—has little willed control, has had defiantly set against it, by a supreme act of will, an action that is its semantic "other." Such is their semantic alterity that the contrary states seem to take contrary inner trajectories, as though passing by each other in an adjacent space—or, still more strangely, moving through each other in an identical space—within the self, decomposing making inroads, even as "composing" issues forth. But what has such a discussion of individual quiddities to do with colonialism?

Perhaps quite a lot. If the cultural bomb of imperialism is what leads to the decomposing of societies, then we can figure, as a counterforce, *and part of an identical explosion,* a composing impulse with potential to achieve exactly opposite results. In such cases the old reality is literally torn apart by the contraries of imperialism and decolonization, shattering their way through each other in the same historical space and time. To reword that: opposing alternatives operate upon peoples, in identical spaces, within the same time-shocks of history. Their relative results depend a lot on happenstance, a lot on prior formations of power during the colonial period, and a lot on the individual and combined strengths of will of a people, when the rare and slender chances of overthrowing the effects of imperialism are offered.

There can be no overlooking the importance of writers in such histories. The question is what exactly, and with what counterforce, as individuals or as a class, they manage to be composing still in the face of imperialism's cultural bomb, as over extents of postcolonial time it goes on imploding within the souls of individuals and nations.

Consider a pair of more extended passages from Walcott's poetry, both from "The Star-Apple Kingdom," in each of which the historico-geographic formation of the Caribbean region is a spectacular "given," while they nevertheless hint that these islands' very creation was coterminous with and a consequence of their falling captive to multinational or at any rate big-power (British or American) economic control – in short, all the past and present forms of imperialism which subjugate them.

> One morning the Caribbean was cut up
> by seven prime ministers who bought the sea in bolts –
> one thousand miles of aquamarine with lace trimmings,
> one million yards of lime-coloured silk,
> one mile of violet, leagues of cerulean satin –
> who sold it at a markup to the conglomerates,
> the same conglomerates who had rented the water spouts
> for ninety years in exchange for fifty ships,
> who retailed it in turn to the ministers
> with only one bank account, who then resold it
> in ads for the Caribbean Economic Community,
> till everyone owned a little piece of the sea,
> from which some made saris, some made bandannas;
> the rest was offered on trays to white cruise ships
> taller than the post office; then the dogfights
> began in the cabinets as to who had first sold
> the archipelago for this chain store of islands.[9]
>
> What was the Caribbean? A green pond mantling
> behind the Great House columns of Whitehall,

behind the Greek facades of Washington,
with blotted frogs squatting on lily pads
like islands, islands that coupled as sadly as turtles
engendering islets, as the turtle of Cuba
mounting Jamaica engendered the Caymans, as, behind
the hammerhead turtle of Haiti–San Domingo
trailed the little turtles from Tortuga to Tobago;
he followed the bobbing trek of the turtles
leaving America for the open Atlantic,
felt his own flesh loaded like the pregnant beaches
with their moon-guarded eggs – they yearned for Africa,
they were lemmings drawn by magnetic memory
to an older death, to broader beaches
where the coughing of lions was dumbed by breakers.[10]

What we are given in the first passage of the poem is a comic opera history of present dominations over Caribbean economies by faceless "conglomerates," who have attained control by the peculations of neo-colonial politicos; in the second, a sadder comedy, of the Caribbean itself being engendered by a series of turtlelike tuppings among its various islands, "behind" the greater dignities of Whitehall and Washington – but all the time yearning back with historical memory for the Africa of her peoples' slave origins. Simplifying somewhat, what the two passages taken together as an account of the Caribbean offer is a contemporary metonym for, or, if this way of understanding the writing is preferred, a literary palimpsest inscribed over, the actual slave history of the region. What has been offered as the modern metonym of that history or as its overscribed palimpsest allows for vague memories of those slave origins and – and this is what is really impressive in the poetry – even for a yearning back to a time *before* the enslavement began, in an Africa behind its own "broader beaches," those important if by no means only launching points into the modern episteme of imperialism.

We get an impression of more than one "tone of voice" in such lines. An almost flippant insouciance lies in their inventive humor, at the same time that what is hauntingly spelled out by that inventiveness is nothing less than the horrors of perennial enslavement, in ever new, mutant forms. If there is a decolonized, free play of mind evident in all this, it is in Walcott's ability to provide ongoing ironic critique of those deadly imperial places and states of dominion which his comic inventiveness has quite literally "mapped out" as the islands and archipelagos of the region. The Caribbean is rendered in the poetry as spellbindingly beautiful—the colors of those bolts of various cloth of the first fantasy and the mixed pattern of islands trailing their engendered islets behind them of the second. But the acts of poetic realization of such beauty are coterminous with a reckoning of life anywhere in the region as a generic condition of enslavement under imperialism. These two antinomies are simultaneous and mutually interpenetrative realities. In just the same way there are not, *in fact,* two tones of voice, only the one. But it is a tone in which the tragic of imperialism and the comic of Walcott's insouciant mockery of it move in their opposite trajectories through the same space, simultaneously.

Consider a very different example of a decolonized play of mind: writing able to countershock through distilled understanding of imperialism's most destructive potentiality, that of nuclear weaponry. The Maori poet Hone Tuwhare prefigured by a generation New Zealand's own brave stance as a nation against nuclear arms testing and proliferation, in his poem of the early 1960s "No Ordinary Sun."

No Ordinary Sun

Tree let your arms fall:
raise them not sharply in supplication
to the bright enhaloed cloud.
Let your arms lack toughness and
resilience for this is no mere axe
to blunt, nor fire to smother.

Your sap shall not rise again
to the moon's pull.
No more incline a deferential head
to the wind's talk, or stir
to the tickle of coursing rain.

Your former shagginess shall not be
wreathed with the delightful flight
of birds nor shield
nor cool the ardour of unheeding
lovers from the monstrous sun.

Tree let your naked arms fall
nor extend vain entreaties to the radiant ball.
This is no gallant monsoon's flash,
no dashing trade wind's blast.
The fading green of your magic
emanations shall not make pure again
these polluted skies . . . for this
is no ordinary sun.

O tree
in the shadowless mountains
the white plains and
the drab sea floor
your end at last is written.[11]

Although much of Tuwhare's other poetry is regionally and culturally specific, in the above verses he takes the risk of using grand-scale natural typologies and a rather formal mode of direct address in order to spell out the ecological disaster of nuclear explosion. Without ever naming the atomic blast or protesting its perpetrators directly, he settles for such devices as circumlocution ("no ordinary sun"), which, instead of complicating the message, render it more simple and powerful. To adapt words from another poem protesting nuclear arms, Richard Wilbur's "Advice to a Prophet," Tuwhare "spares us all mention of the long-range weaponry" and instead "talks of the world's own change."[12]

To raise the issue of Tuwhare's being a Maori at this moment, however much other poems by him might evidence the double colonial bind of his membership of a minority but indigenous race, surrounded by the settler *Pakeha* culture, would be quite to miss the point of how far "No Ordinary Sun" needs – and manages – to transcend cultural specifics, because of the global relevance of its statement. To work in such large typologies and rely on timeworn vocative rhetorical strategies is to take great risks in poetry. When they come off, as here I think they do (consider only the sensory personifications of "ordinary" natural phenomena in the penultimate stanza, rhetorically contrasted with that "no ordinary" sun, and its chain effects of change on all that before was expected and given), then the forces of the "atomic club" of nuclear imperialism ignore them at their peril. For what is so fully evoked is destruction not at a regional, or cultural, but planetary level, liable to co-involve its very perpetrators. The grand typologies of tree, moon, wind, mountain, plain, and sea floor – all "othered" or "ended" by this "monstrous sun"– make us envision the planetary apocalypse as Tuwhare meant us to.

From their different locations as practicing poets both Walcott and Tuwhare, in bringing attention to the global dangers of multinational economic imperialism and the nuclear apocalypse, are voices from the "Empire," "writing back to the center," with warnings it would be folly to ignore. By "center," however, we should no longer understand Europe or the former colonial powers. Rather, it should henceforth be understood in moral and historical terms. News of what is important – central only in that sense – now comes to "us" from far-flung places, relative to wherever "we" may be (in Auckland reading Walcott, on St. Lucia reading Tuwhare, or in London writing about both). In terms of the institution of Literature the issues far transcend those of what "canon" of texts we teach. Whether and in what ways we open up the realms of what gets taught a little wider is, in other words, simply an inadequate way of framing questions of value, in texts such as these. We should be more exercised by the perils of *not* attending to the political value of what they may have to say.

Salman Rushdie's plea, "For God's sake . . . open the universe a little more"[13] – the line is borrowed from Saul Bellow's novel *The Dean's December,* in which a lone dog heard barking disconsolately in the distance is thought of as expressing the same anguish – if it is answered at all is answered in postcolonial writing. Our universe of values *is* pried open further by works that help us know better those global realities – the imperialisms of economic or nuclear domination (and the two are, of course, interlinked) – which oppress (colonize) us all.

The trouble with that way of putting the case, however, is that it doesn't adequately take stock of how far texts may count differently with the passage of time and with the continual change of political consciousness. Our inevitably differing cultural, racial, or geographical backgrounds inevitably go on influencing the perspectives from which we view things. The only remedy is the hard one, of thinking our way beyond personal limitations to understanding and beyond entrenched cultural parameters: trying to accomplish that – and aiding others to do so – is the main raison d'être of volumes such as this.

To develop these last points I wish to make one further comparison in terms of the cultural moments of writing and reception. The poems for contrast are both Australian but are written from utterly differing perspectives with respect to settler and Aboriginal cultures.

"South of My Days," from the first published volume of the Australian poet Judith Wright, *The Moving Image* (1946), is a stirring account of hardships faced in the early decades of a settler culture. Within little more than a decade of its appearance the poem had become a standard item in Australian secondary classrooms, where, along with another from that volume, "Bullocky," it served as a way of introducing a specific kind of appreciation of Australia. Here, combined with the harshness of landscape of this "clean, lean, hungry country," was a heroic (while yet, for the Australian temperament, acceptably demotic) portrayal of the suffering and sacrifices undergone by earlier generations in coming to terms with such a land.

South of My Days

South of my days' circle, part of my blood's country
rises that tableland, high delicate outline
of bony slopes wincing under the winter,
low trees blue-leaved and olive, outcropping granite –
clean, lean, hungry country. The creek's leaf-silenced,
willow-choked, the slope a tangle of medlar and crabapple
branching over and under, blotched with a green lichen;
and the old cottage lurches in for shelter.

O cold the black-frost night. The walls draw in to the warmth
and the old roof cracks its joints; the slung kettle
hisses a leak on the fire. Hardly to be believed that summer
will turn up again some day in a wave of rambler roses,
thrust its hot face in here to tell another yarn –
a story old Dan can spin into a blanket against the winter.
Seventy years of stories he clutches round his bones.
Seventy summers are hived in him like old honey.

Droving that year, Charleville to the Hunter,
nineteen-one it was, and the drought beginning;
sixty head left at the McIntyre, the mud round them
hardened like iron; and the yellow boy died
in the sulky ahead with the gear, but the horses went on,
stopped at the Sandy Camp and waited in the evening.
It was the flies we seen first, swarming like bees.

Came to the Hunter, three hundred head of a thousand —
cruel to keep them alive — and the river was dust.

Or mustering up in the Bogongs in the autumn
when the blizzards came early. Brought them down; we
    brought them
down, what aren't there yet. Or driving for Cobb's on the run
up from Tamworth — Thunderbolt at the top of Hungry Hill,
and I give him a wink. I wouldn't wait long, Fred,
not if I was you; the troopers are just behind,
coming for that job at the Hillgrove. He went like a luny,
him on his big black horse.
                            Oh, they slide and they vanish
as he shuffles the years like a pack of conjuror's cards.
True or not, it's all the same; and the frost on the roof
cracks like a whip, and the black-log breaks into ash.
Wake, old man. This is winter, and the yarns are over.
No-one is listening.
                    South of my days' circle
I know it dark against the stars, the high lean country
full of old stories that still go walking in my sleep.[14]

What is immediately arresting from the first line is the claim that
the particular region initially described — it is, in fact, the New England
of Judith Wright's birth, in northern New South Wales — is part of her
"blood's country." This suggests her family having lived for long generations already in the one place. Or, to say the least, that the region
had been so loved from early acquaintance with it that it had become
internalized into her very bloodstream. (This latter-day, highly specific
antipodean Wordsworthianism is certainly a part of the effect: an
early estimation of Judith Wright's poetry had remarked that, "though
in a sense the world is laid out before her to observe, it is yet to a
greater or a lesser degree as a part of herself that she observes it.")[15]
But there is a further hint in that remark of the first line, of lives having been given — blood *expended,* in other words — in her people's coming to terms with the land. This is the notion of appeasement of its
harshnesses through sacrifice, leading to rightful possession. Old Dan,
with his "seventy years of stories hived in him like old honey," is a living survivor from a more heroic, settler epoch; of droving ever-deplet-
ing herds of cattle across a third of the continent (Charleville to the

Hunter); of sandy camps en route and dried-up rivers on arrival; of bushrangers such as Fred Thunderbolt and the stagecoach era of Cobb and Co.

The poem – or one of a few others in roughly similar idiom or seeking to embody an equivalent settler narrative – would have constituted many an Australian child's first introduction to a deeply heartfelt common background – a sense of meaningful life-styles, made possible in an Australia variously won for its people through toil, adventure, and sacrifice.

What was not said about such poetry in the 1950s or 1960s, and scarcely appreciated by many until recently (the bicentenary of white settlement was a watershed of recognition), was the part it was playing in an ideology of conquest and possession of the land by the settler culture. Neither Judith Wright's nor any other white family's ancestors had held such places as their blood's country much before the seventy years of stories clutched around Old Dan's bones (that takes us back to the mid-1870s), since they simply were not there much before that – one further generation in the case of Wright's family, to be precise.[16] Dan's own earlier memories voiced in the poem are from the period of major settlement. So in a sense Wright's is a somewhat "shallow" historical claim, masquerading as deeper than it is by means of her indubitably heartfelt bond of feeling for the country of which she writes. This is the "unconscious" of the poem – its need to justify possessive claims on the land, born from the very recentness of white settlement, of sacrifice, and of coming to terms with something initially alien and unfamiliar. A large part of the work of the poem lies in its translating that still largely alien and unfamiliar country into realms that can be understood and appreciated. And this too was perhaps the unconscious reasoning behind teaching the poem to a generation at least of Australian children. Until familiarized to ways of appreciating so much that was harsh in their continent, they could not have been expected to internalize deeply felt regard for it all by themselves with anything like the blood feeling of Judith Wright's poem.

The above is not intended as a belittling of this fine poem but, rather, to show that it does hold a crucial place in the ideological justification of a settler culture, the cornerstones of which are adventurous toil and sacrifice and an acquired (but made to seem natural) love of an initially harsh-seeming and alien landscape.

Implicit in this ideology of justification is an omission or an occlusion. Nowhere in the poem is there mention of the land having been peopled before the coming of the drovers, the stagecoach, the bushranger, and the troopers. No displacement of others seems to have occurred, so the poem does not suffer from guilt. Either memory of another people is lost entirely at the moment of writing, or it is being so effectively occluded as to leave no detectable trace. This remark too might seem at first unfair to the author, Judith Wright. Since writing that first volume of poems, she has documented as almost no other Australian writer, white or black, the appalling "invasions" of tribal lands by white settlers and, as a corollary, the terrible displacements and erasures of Aboriginal culture by massacre, disease, and labor exploitation. It is arguable that her book *The Cry for the Dead* (1981) deserves to stand alongside *Bury My Heart at Wounded Knee* (1971), a work documenting the violent decimation of a different aboriginal culture. There is even in other poems of this same first volume—most notably in "Nigger's Leap: New England"—a haunted sense of the passing of an entire indigenous people (sharply marked as "they" in relation to the settler "we" of the speaking voice):

> Did we not know their blood channelled our rivers
> and the black dust our crops ate was their dust?
> . . . .
> Never from earth again the coolamon
> or thin black children dancing like shadows
> of saplings in the wind.[17]

But the point is that the poem concentrated on, "South of My Days," the one most anthologized soon after first publication, the one it is hardly an exaggeration to claim worked its way into the bloodstream of many present Australians in the processes of education, occludes all mention of a human presence before the heroic era of white settlement.

It is when we place it alongside a plainer, unstirring poem, one that seeks only to register the pathos of the other, occluded side of the story, namely Aboriginal displacement—the loss and disappearance of a culture, rather than, as in Wright's poem, the inception and strengthening growth of one—that we can feel some of the force in the contrastive history of settler and Aborigine. Here is the Aboriginal poet Oodgeroo Noonuccal's "We Are Going," published less than a score of years after Wright's poem (and originally under her "white" name, Kath Walker):

We Are Going   FOR GRANNIE COOLWELL

They came in to the little town
A semi-naked band subdued and silent,
All that remained of their tribe.
They came here to the place of their old bora ground
Where now the many white men hurry about like ants.
Notice of estate agent reads: "Rubbish May Be Tipped Here."
Now it half covers the traces of the old bora ring.
They sit and are confused, they cannot say their thoughts:
"We are as strangers here now, but the white tribe are the
     strangers.
We belong here, we are of the old ways.
We are the corroboree and the bora ground,
We are the old sacred ceremonies, the laws of the elders.
We are the wonder tales of Dream Time, the tribal legends
     told.
We are the past, the hunts and the laughing games, the
     wandering camp fires.
We are the lightning-bolt over Gaphembah Hill
Quick and terrible,
And the Thunderer after him, that loud fellow.
We are the quiet daybreak paling the dark lagoon.
We are the shadow-ghosts creeping back as the camp fires
     burn low.
We are nature and the past, all the old ways
Gone now and scattered.
The scrubs are gone, the hunting and the laughter.
The eagle is gone, the emu and the kangaroo are gone from
     this place.
The bora ring is gone.
The corroboree is gone.
And we are going."[18]

                    Oodgeroo of the tribe Noonuccal
                    (formerly Kath Walker)

Oodgeroo's poem is committed to communicating not so much a
recast world in any of the positive senses defined earlier but, rather,
what Sneja Gunew has elsewhere, in speaking of Aboriginal writers
using English, called the "outcast experience."[19] Language itself is

very much at stake at the moment in the poem when the remnant of the tribe would voice its condition. "Confused" and unable even to "say their thoughts"—nothing in their language makes possible a saying of something that has never before occurred (a kind of new instance of the old Sapir-Whorf law about limit conditions of particular language systems)—the tribespeople passively cede place to the poet, Oodgeroo herself, who, having highlighted this condition in outcast experience of the "unspoken because unspeakable," passes into an unmarked putting-into-English of what *would be* their communication if they could make it. In doing so she, of course, especially targets an audience that is *not* her own tribe but, rather, consists of users of the language of the poem: in other words the settler community, responsible for the displacing of the Aborigine and, in particular, for the negligent and ignorant cruelty of those acts of outcasting of one culture by another that are involved. The text itself is very sparing with use of explicit protest (e.g., "the white tribe are the strangers. / We belong here . . ."). This is the critical depth charge of a poem on the surface so seemingly pathetic and unprotesting, even self-canceling in the implied willingness of the Aborigines to disappear—its accusatory subtext! At this implicit level the poem is an ironic and bitter protest against the idea of the "vanishing savage," colonialism's next best alibi to the fantastic contention that no one was originally there.

A major issue of Oodgeroo's poem, at the heart of the question of cultural displacement, is the defilement of once sacred places. There is hideous irony in the fact of the newcomer white community's rubbish tip being sited on the Aborigines' old bora ground of sacred ceremonies, corroboree dance, and Dream Time. If Judith Wright's poem sought to sacralize Australian landscape and settler hardships for later generations, this poem definitively envisions the reverse process, of the same land being horrifically desacralized for the outcast and rapidly disappearing Aborigines. Only by placing the poems side by side can we see with full clarity how the sacralizing and desacralizing processes have at their core the same spun-out historical event: white settlement/Aboriginal displacement. The point I have been making is that the first of the poems only treats one strand of that dual event. I have not heard that the second ever became a noted poem for discussion and recitation in Australian schools, and I sincerely doubt that it did.[20]

Thus far I have plotted some of the issues of this collection, and of the postcolonial condition more generally, through poetry. This is not a common strategy. Yet discussing precisely poetry has served to focus and illuminate some of the central questions concerning the recasting of reality entailed in the processes of decolonization, or in any seeking to determine the present by focusing on an earlier, settler epoch. But, if there is a politics of interpretation implied in privileging writing (and, in particular, for the purposes of this introduction, poetry), there is also an institutional politics that must be addressed – a different, but related, and no less urgent agenda.

Throughout the world departments of English (so named) are increasingly teaching postcolonial or "new" literatures, in itself an excellent thing. But they are *wrongly named* for doing so. Even for those many literatures written in the English language, *English* as the umbrella term for the study in question seems (however unintentionally) like a continuation of imperial sway. Caribbean, Indian, African, Canadian, American, Irish, or Australasian literatures *in* English are no mere development of some hegemonically dominant "English" literature or culture. And, furthermore, no belated attempt to uprate the caliber of the "old canon" will ever make them seem so. Some few departments were founded on principles that implicitly or explicitly recognized this postcolonial reality. Again, our volume's title, and the essays contained within, seek to promote recognition of such a reality in many more places. We would be interested to see departments of English in which there were at least a debate about the need to recast the departmental name, in the light of our common object of study, increasingly no longer English but, instead, Literature – the practices, histories, theories, and purposes of "writing" in the modern world, itself living through the troubled, drawn-out aftermath of its epoch of colonialism.

The various chapters are in no sense intended as a survey. There have been useful recent volumes attempting to map a large terrain and its issues, none more notable than *The Empire Writes Back: Theory and Practice in Post-Colonial Literatures* (1989), by Ashcroft, Griffiths, and Tiffin. But the very disparateness of the points of emanation of the literatures in question and the fact that most of them are in the throes of an ongoing creative ferment mean that no one person can achieve critical understanding of these worldwide phenomena and set up as an "expert." There is simply no homogeneous totality, no mat-

ter how largely figured, to be expert *in*. For once the very notion of
expertise (in any case too often offered as a kind of imperialistic control over areas of interest on the part of the critic) lapses, for want of
an object of attention *discrete* enough to be held *fixed* enough for *long*
enough to act mandarin about! So, happily, a kind of "enforced democracy" of interests settles on any who would write on aspects of postcolonial literatures. Those who have worked on this volume have
appreciated the kinds of freedom to think out issues freshly which
not having to present ourselves as "overall experts" entailed.

Common themes and preoccupations have emerged nonetheless
and are all the more worth glancing at for their not having been programmed by any deliberately held, common mind-set concerning
what they would prove to be before we independently conceptual-
ized our contributions. Let me therefore as editor spend the rest of
this introduction tracing through, in necessarily synoptic form, one
thread of connection to have emerged. My doing so will also provide
the opportunity for discussing briefly the *separate* achievements of
the individual chapters.

Toward the end of the opening chapter of this volume, "Educating
the Savages," Jerry Phillips, searching for a judicious pathway through
the war zone of contemporary American literary studies, suggests
that the survival of humane education may require that there be initiated "difficult dialogues" (the term comes from an article by Johnella
Butler) "of cultural negotiation between opposing ends of the earth."
Phillips's chapter itself has conducted a dialogue between opposing
traditionalists and multiculturalists, mainly in the academies of a single country, the United States. Phillips traces back a specific American imperialism, and its attendant justification in the doctrine of
exceptionalism, to the early nineteenth century, showing how a writer
like Melville was caught between critique of and complicity in America's presence in the Pacific. But this in turn is used by Phillips as a
warning about the danger of mutant forms of the same imperial control, this time operating in the choosing and excluding of types of texts
today for study in America's universities, whose younger generations
of students are increasingly from complex cultural backgrounds. And
the issue is seen to be one of importance not only to the institution of
literature within educational structures but also to the whole question of relations between differing cultures in America, most espe-

cially to what Phillips decries as "the naked unofficial apartheid underlying the demography of most U.S. cities."

So, a difficult dialogue of one kind is broached in the first chapter. The parties shown to stand in need of it are located not at opposing ends of the earth but, rather, on the same contested intellectual ground, that of the setting of agendas for future syllabi in Literature in U.S. institutions of higher learning.

American literature is the largest and historically the longest post-colonial literature. Sally Keenan's chapter on *Beloved*, "Four Hundred Years of Silence," looks at the most extreme instance of oppression in American culture, namely slavery: slavery considered as an issue of the past but also urgently of the present. She shows us how Morrison takes up the challenge of a "psychological renegotiation" of a slave past and especially the problem of "living with impossible memories," using fiction to fill in what is sometimes irrecuperable to any more historiographical approach, ever aware of the threat of memories so terrible that they may disenable the present but also of "all the dead victims of slavery, reaching out to the living, demanding to be heard." Morrison's text delineates an area in which oppression by gender and the experience of colonialism intersect. Through a careful consideration of what we know and do not know about female resistance to slavery, and especially of the mother/child relations within American slave history and narratives, Keenan demonstrates Morrison's entirely new way of treating these issues, so as to break positively, step by canny step, through the many pain thresholds that must inevitably constitute the several stages of any such difficult dialogue between past and present in African-American experience.

Dennis Walder's account of the postcolonial order represented in V. S. Naipaul's writings concentrates on the novel *In a Free State* because it seems to him to represent Naipaul's largest consideration of the international context of postcolonialism. In view of Naipaul's reputation, especially among those critics who have discerned an unchecked mordancy or even racism in his treatment of postcolonial situations (suggesting that he too often seems to blame subjects for their states of subjection), Walder gives several point by point interpretations of Naipaul's implied attitudes to his material. The resultant readings, while not exonerating Naipaul from many of the charges that have been leveled against him, suggest how his most "difficult" writings – those in which Naipaul's own stances are hardest, but most necessary, to work out – do broach the crucial issues of who exactly is free and what conditions constitute freedom in a decolonized state. Not the least valuable aspect of this chapter is the way that it frames the question, by showing how the essentially postcolonial text *In a Free State* subtly rewrites the classic colonial text *Heart of Darkness,* about whether and in what ways residual colonial discourses present in the postcolonial era might be subverted or recast through writing.

The chapter that stands alongside Walder's is Peter Hulme's study of a Caribbean writer often seen as occupying the opposite political pole to Naipaul, namely George Lamming. Here the "difficult dialogue" broached is that between Lamming and his colonial inheritance, particularly as represented in metropolitan values encountered through reading classics of European literature. Like many other postcolonial writers, a key text Lamming had to negotiate was Shakespeare's *Tempest* – all the more so as it came closest to articulating at least some of the questions of colonialism which were at the forefront of intellectual debate in the 1950s and 1960s. Hulme's essay assesses the importance of Lamming's fraught meditations in fiction and nonfiction on *The Tempest,* in an attempt to understand his continual fascination with this play but also to ask whether Lamming's various reworkings of its central concerns might provide a model for others attempting to achieve the difficult passage from colonialism to postcolonialism. Hulme shows how Lamming's writings also conduct a dialogue with the dead in their urgency to construct what the writer has named as an "architecture of the future." (Readers might wish to compare Lamming's dealings with a past weighted with memories of the dead and Toni Morrison's already mentioned handling of a similar issue.) Part of what is challenging in these perspectives is the way Hulme's conclusion that "Britain too is a postcolonial country" is produced.

The most difficult of dialogues between cultures may need commensurate levels of reciprocity in order to maintain and develop themselves productively. This is recognized by Neil Lazarus in his chapter on recent trends in Afropop music. Although he regrets instances of kowtowing by African popular music to the political economy of Empire which underpins Western pop, he likewise deprecates any retreat on the part of Afropop into purist (and hence unchanging) traditionalism. Allowing for a hybridity of styles – mixing African with

Western – is seen as a potential and often real stimulus to Afropop's own progressive development but also a way of providing enough that is familiar and accessible to the committed Western enthusiast, amid so much else that is bound to be strange and at first inaccessible, as to maximize its political challenge. The "cultural dialogism" that he traces through recent trends of Afropop is offered in place of the cultural imperialism it is threatened by and which in its turn it constantly seeks to subvert. He reveals the lack of reciprocal musical dialogue between cultures in lyric modes that have opportunistically cannibalized African styles (outmoded ones at that, in the case of Paul Simon's *Graceland* album). By contrast, Lazarus considers recent developments in so-called "world music" which have flown in the face of, or even dismantled, the imperial economic bases of Western pop. His instances of the latter offer us real glimpses of how the given world of imperial domination has been (and might be further) recast.

In "Late Landings" Carolyn Masel finds that the depiction of landscape remains a major preoccupation in the literatures of both Canada and Australia, in both cases prompting and exhibiting the continuing anxieties of postcolonial inhabitants. A great deal of the contemporary literature of both countries exhibits an unresolved condition of perpetual belatedness, perceived in relation to the land. The land – and hence the matter of belonging to and being able to narrate stories out of a particular place (whether region or nation) – becomes an arena of conflict for writing, demonstrably so in the work of such authors as Mavis Gallant and Alice Munro. The old desires to possess the land, to settle it, to be at home in it, have modulated into a more metaphysical struggle: to speak authentically out of the landscape. And, although this authenticity, which so seems to require being striven for by settler or immigrant peoples, might be expected to be an uncomplicated right of the aboriginal population, it proves in the interesting example of Sally Morgan all the more difficult for individuals of such descent to achieve, in the face of their history of displacement from original contexts and loss of a sense of communal belonging. On the part of the majority settler culture the twin experiences of immigration and settlement not only constitute a recurring theme; they have also lent a shape and direction to a predominant pathway of narrative of each country. In certain cases this narrative pathway seems to undergo a reversal, as when writers take imaginative possession of the "Europe" of their ancestry. But doing this can be the sign of a personal aesthetic of incorporation so strong that it risks becoming an imperialism of the imagination, with virtually no limit set to the experiencing of different places and cultures. Masel sees the possibility of this form of aesthetic imperialism as a real danger. And she shows how difficult it is to judge whether particular texts merit critical censure for such a personal aesthetic (if not exactly politics) of "global" aggrandizement. After a wide-ranging comparative discussion of these and related issues in the work of Margaret Atwood and David Malouf, Masel ends by contrasting them with Elizabeth Jolley, many of whose characters are explicitly concerned with how to own, occupy, or use the land "properly."

Australians caught up in various problems of their "Australianness" is also Patrick Fuery's abiding theme in "Prisoners and Spiders Surrounded by Signs." Rather than concentrate on the land, however, he looks as well at an array of other signs and configurations used by Australians as ways of representing or seeing themselves. Australian culture is exercized by the need "to draw the new to the old twist," thereby excluding as much as it includes in its cultural frame and altering what it includes to harmonize with a preexistent order. Fuery's chapter delineates the interconnections between the many disparate elements of a national culture and seeks to develop a theoretical argument about what makes the particular Australian culture of his study at once postcolonial and postmodern. He ends on a somewhat disturbing note – the realization that, precisely in being both those things at once, there is a kind of restless relativism in "Australian identity," as it passes from one seductive paradigm to another.

The following chapter, "Politics and the Individual in the Modernist Historical Novel," is on the ways in which two highly political novels, which appeared within two years of each other, tackled the very different but equally fraught modern histories of South Africa and the Indian subcontinent. Rushdie's *Midnight's Children* and Gordimer's *Burger's Daughter* are both premised on the "coincidence" of protagonists born at the same time as the birth of the modern phase of the nation in question (1947 in the case of India, 1948 for South Africa). Each treats the entire nation's problems as they bear in on the lives of its protagonist. Furthermore, the two novels deal with much the same time span, through to the late 1970s, the time of their writing. How far has the burden of national histories been taken over from historians and shouldered by these novelists in order that its import reach a wider public? The answer seems to be: massively. That being so, there are major implications for the realms of education. For, if the intended import of these – however different – modernist texts is instructional, then not merely is their coming to be studied in literature courses an important realization of one of their aims but also the *ways we teach them* become especially debate worthy. This is one place in which the matter of the how and why of teaching postcolonial literatures, which the volume of essays has been seeking to answer throughout, is posed very directly.

Our volume ends with Jim Philip's study of one of the newer but richest seams of postcolonial text, namely, travel writing. Offering his chapter as a kind of epilogue to what has gone before, Philip reads travel writing – especially that of the group of writers published by *Granta* – in a spirit of personal journeying, consciously reminiscent of their ventures and styles. In a world whose distances have shrunk by means of new modes of travel and communication, Philip convinces us that the genre of writing which has most absorbed that dual fact, travel/communication, has its important role to play in any future "global cognitive mapping" (a concept borrowed from Fredric Jameson). Rather than being a mere "political tourism," travel writing of the kind studied is, suggests Philip, the ultimate expression of the postcolonial urge to recast the world, because it is, in the words of one of its practitioners most noted in this final chapter, the Polish writer Ryszard Kapuściński, "writing . . . about risk – about risking everything."

NOTES

1. Nadine Gordimer, *The Essential Gesture: Writing, Politics, and Places*, ed. Stephen Clingman (London: Cape, 1988), 298.
2. Frantz Fanon, *Studies in a Dying Colonialism*, trans. Haakon Chevalier (New York: Monthly Review Press, 1965), 62; French title *Sociologie d'une révolution* (Paris: François Maspero, 1968); original title, *L'an V de la révolution algérienne* [1959].
3. Fanon, *Sociologie d'une révolution*, 46.
4. Frantz Fanon, *The Wretched of the Earth*, trans. Constance Farrington (Harmondsworth: Penguin, 1967; original French title *Les damnés de la terre* [1962]), 27.
5. Edward Said, from foreword to *Selected Subaltern Studies*, ed. Ranajit Guha and Gayatri Chakravorty Spivak (New York: Oxford University Press, 1988), ix.
6. Fanon, *Studies in a Dying Colonialism*, 65.
7. Ngugi Wa Thiong'o, *Decolonising the Mind: The Politics of Language in African Literature* (London: J. Currey, 1986), 3.

8. Derek Walcott, *Collected Poems, 1948–1984* (New York: Farrar, Straus & Giroux, 1986), 432.

9. Ibid., 390–91.

10. Ibid., 393.

11. Hone Tuwhare, *No Ordinary Sun* (Auckland: Blackwood & Janet Paul, 1964); reprinted in *Mihi: Collected Poems* (Harmondsworth, U.K.: Penguin, 1987), 112, and in *The Penguin Book of New Zealand Verse*, ed. Ian Wedde and Harvey McQueen (Harmondsworth: Penguin, 1985), 277–78.

12. Richard Wilbur, *Advice to a Prophet* (London: Faber & Faber, 1962).

13. Salman Rushdie, *Imaginary Homelands: Essays and Criticism 1981–1991* (London: Granta, 1991), 21.

14. Judith Wright, *The Moving Image* (Melbourne: Meanjin Press, 1946); reprinted in *Collected Poems: 1942–1970* (Sydney: Angus and Robertson, 1971), 20–21.

15. H. M. Green, *A History of Australian Literature: Pure and Applied*, 2 vols. (Sydney: Angus and Robertson, 1961), 938.

16. Judith Wright's ancestors were very early settlers, first of all in the Hunter Valley region in the 1840s, then, in lean years, seeking successes further inland and a lot further north – the New England region of northern New South Wales and the south-tropical river regions of Queensland. All this is set out graphically in her first autobiographical work, *The Generations of Men* (Melbourne: Oxford University Press, 1959).

17. Wright, *Collected Poems*, 15–16.

18. Kath Walker [Oodgeroo Noonuccal], *We Are Going* (Brisbane: Jacaranda Press, 1964).

19. Sneja Gunew, "Denaturalising Cultural Nationalisms: Multicultural Readings of 'Australia,'" in *Nation and Narration*, ed. Homi K. Bhabha (London: Routledge, 1990), 111.

20. This comparison, which I have written as though each poet simply drew on her ancestral experience in writing her poem, omits one curious detail of literary history which has not gone unnoticed elsewhere. It seems likely that Oodgeroo conceived the idea for the rhetorical structure and even the theme of her poem from Judith Wright herself, who, again in that first volume of her poetry, *The Moving Image*, had begun a poem entitled "Bora Ring" with the line "The song is gone" and another of its stanzas with "The hunter is gone"– already thus early, in 1946, protesting the passing of Aboriginal culture. (The indebtedness to Judith Wright is glancingly noted in the *Australian Dictionary of National Biography* entry for "Kath Walker.") From this history alone it will be apparent that the point of comparing the two poems "South of My Days" and "We Are Going" has in no way been to suggest that the white poet Judith Wright evades issues of what happened and what goes on happening to Aborigines in their losing struggles to maintain the sacral experience of tribal culture. The point has been, rather, that in the institutions of white education in the postwar decades the dominant ideology unconsciously "chose" to promulgate only those poems by Wright which elided the historical "other side" of white settlement. Adjacent poems in *The Moving Image* and much of her subsequent oeuvre make anything but such an elision.

1   Educating the Savages

Melville, Bloom, and
the Rhetoric of
Imperialist Instruction

Jerry Phillips

We, on the other hand, are for giving the heritage neither to
the Barbarians nor to the Philistines, nor yet to the Populace;
but we are for the transformation of each and all of these
according to the law of perfection.—Matthew Arnold, *Culture
and Anarchy*

Civilization or, to say the same thing, education is the taming
or domestication of the soul's raw passions—not suppressing or
excising them, which would deprive the soul of its energy—but
forming and informing them as art.—Allan Bloom, *The Closing
of the American Mind*

> Abhorred slave,
> Which any print of goodness wilt not take,
> Being capable of all ill! I pitied thee,
> Took pains to make thee speak, taught thee each hour
> One thing or other: when thou didst not, savage,
> Know thine own meaning, but wouldst gabble like
> A thing most brutish, I endow'd thy purposes
> With words that made them known.
> —William Shakespeare, *The Tempest*

On one side we have Prospero, Robinson Crusoe, and Kipling's white man; on the other we have Caliban, Man Friday, and the "wretched of the earth"; in its classic formulation the moment of imperialism is also the moment of education. Imperialism—a system of economic, political, and cultural force that disavows borders in order to extract desirable resources and exploit an alien people—has never strayed far from a field of pedagogical imperatives, or what might be called an ideology of instruction. Christianity, Progress, Democracy, or whatever is the prevailing imperialist version of history demands of certain cultures, nations, or "chosen" races that they subject those who fall radically short of the ideal state. Subject peoples are "savage," "infantile," "untutored," "backward," or simply "underdeveloped"; as the imperialist encounters them, a model of their "uplift" is always thus entailed. Unashamedly ethnocentric, frequently racist in its implications, the rhetoric of imperialist instruction has all too often served as a bridgehead between extremely different cultures.

Consider the words of Captain John Moresby, the nineteenth-century Pacific explorer. Moresby understands that New Guinea and Polynesia afford "a hundred commodities," riches that Great Britain is determined to extract. Extraction will take place; that much is certain. And, as Moresby sees it, in return for the extracted riches Great Britain has an immanent (Christian) "duty" to protect, instruct, and reform the native races it comes into contact with by "teaching [them] the ways and uses of . . . civilization." John Bull will not find it too difficult to lead the islanders into "membership with the human family," for, unlike the natives of the West Indies, who have been "degraded by generations of slavery," the Pacific Islander exists in a perfect state of nature, an original condition implying all kinds of cultural infancy. Thus, Britons are the "tutors of the childhood of [those] races that lie directly within [their] influence." Britons must lead the savages "up to moral and intellectual manhood."[1]

The idea of infancy carries great significance for the imperialist. Infants are dependent, powerless, and speechless; they are paradigms for cultures that cannot represent themselves. Infants are particularly receptive to the example of their elders; they can be made to imitate their parents. Infants are a model for all pupils. Moresby captures this complex of beliefs in one extraordinary sentence: the savages of the Pacific "offer an almost virgin page on which we are free to write the whole moral code."[2] I do not know of a more appropriate image for imperialism's self-conception. If the savage mind is a "virgin page," then civilized instruction is high cultural writing visiting itself upon a barbaric tabula rasa. The passing on of culture through script is a perennial concern of those who wield discursive authority; as Jacques Derrida and Michel Foucault remind us, not infrequently, this process becomes nothing less than an authoritarian control of what can constitute standards of truth. Note that Moresby's authorial metaphor culturally monopolizes what counts as "the moral code"; it implies that the islanders are amoral, that they lack moral vision. True morality is a code, and left to themselves, we are to suppose, the islanders could never break that code in order to apply its dictates to their lives. This leads us to yet another tenet of the rhetoric of imperialist instruction: those we are forced to subject are, to all intents and purposes, functionally illiterate; not having been written upon by history, we have to attend to the fact that they cannot write or read. Scores of travel works and anthropological treatises tell us that savages are "unlettered." Savages, as Montaigne famously put it, have yet to learn their ABCs.[3] To be savage is to be *analphabétique.*

The venture of script upon a supposed blank page: colonialism and imperialism took place – or so the story goes – in countries that could not read. As I write, the postcolonial society argues with itself over the vexed issue of what exactly it should read. The argument occurs on a complex social terrain definitive of the postcolonial society. Postcolonial societies exhibit these abiding features: racial, ethnic, and linguistic diversity. A society steeped in multicultural practices, in human differences, must also be a creature that faces, each and every day, cultural struggles for what counts as an index of citizenship and political struggles for the contents of national culture. In this sense the postcolonial society can be home or abroad: I use the term to refer to a country (not always one that was colonized but sometimes one that was a colonizer) which exhibits the features that I have mentioned.

As demonstrated by the belief, held by some white parents, that state schools in Britain are becoming increasingly "Islamicized" or by the belief, held by some African Americans, that their contributions to the national culture have been less appreciated at every level of the education system, debates about culture in the postcolonial society are inseparable from the realities of race and racism, religion and secularism, power and oppression.

The nation's cultural core encapsulates its ideals of citizenship, community, family, religion, and economy. The great debate about the core has as its progeny debates about core curricula and national canons. This I take to be in keeping with the idea that education lies at the core of a society's self-perception, that society's values are transmitted through a core or tradition of instructive texts. The scene of cultural battle in the postcolonial society usually looks like this: on the one hand, the dominant group—call them the traditionalists—argue that the genius of the nation, its informing values and ethics, derives from a select body of works; these works must thus occupy center stage in any program of education. For the traditionalist culture is a script. On the other hand, their opponents—call them the levelers—argue that education should reflect the cultural diversity of the nation, rather than a set of ideas supposedly crystallized in specific cultural scripts. The levelers contend that ethnic and racial elitism should not be encouraged; they stress that the playing field should be leveled. I will take the United States as my particular example of the postcolonial society and endeavor to trace traditionalist and leveling concerns in a novel by Herman Melville and a treatise on education by Allan Bloom. My analysis will focus on the imperative to interpret the self—write about the self—in what is taken to be a context of radical cultural backwardness, a context that demands to be read. I shall call this imperative civilized literacy in the face of the state of nature.

In the early decades of the history of the United States political independence from Great Britain stimulated a quest for its cultural and ideological counterpart. If British models of government, community, and law were made redundant by the revolution, then it followed that the accompanying ideas of civility must also be modified. No less so than postcolonials today, American writers and artists were not slow to take up the challenge. From Cooper to Emerson, from Jefferson to Whitman, a significant amount of literary production—the moment of reading, writing, criticizing, and publishing—was devoted to the task of defining a civilian identity for the purpose of postcolonial nationhood. Underlying such an ambitious project is a double contention: we are what we read; we should read about who we are.

Herman Melville believed in the nationalistic mission of United States literature ("American writers should studiously cleave to nationality in their writings"),[4] but I submit that Melville's writings frequently call into question their own Utopian trajectory. I turn to *Typee: A Peep at Polynesian Life* (1846) to advance my thesis.

Typee is a weave of fact and fiction. As a sailor aboard a whaleboat, Herman Melville visited the Marquesas Islands in July 1842. Disillusioned with his despotic captain, he deserted ship at the island of Nukihiva, where he spent a month in "indulgent captivity." *Typee* is the record of his real-life story. In many ways anticipating the typical ideological gesture of the modern travel writer (e.g., Claude Lévi-Strauss, Paul Theroux, or Bruce Chatwin), who transforms his experience of alien places into a political allegory of the wider social concerns of home, Melville's literary treatment of his stay on Nukihiva is nothing if not highly self-conscious. Melville recognized that his Marquesan experiences afforded a ready-made drama for reflecting upon the imperialist ethos of adventure and its relevance to the critical perceptions of a developing writing self. Thus, for no small reason reading and writing about Self and Other are central concerns of *Typee*.

The protagonist Tommo, the dissident adventurer who jumps ship and ends up as the captive of the "bloody-minded Typees" (69),[5] functions as a critical consciousness whereby themes of nationhood, race, culture, history, and nature can be deftly entertained.[6] Tommo is an American who flees his culture because he finds it ethically wanting but then employs the ethical standards of this same impoverished culture to judge the exotic asylum to which he has fled. He is the typical Melville narrator: undecidability is his natural element. Indeed, it is the notion of a state of nature which most troubles Tommo.

For Tommo the state of nature has two faces, one hostile, the other benign: the former refers to an environment of lawlessness, inhumanity, and war; the latter to an environment of peace, plenty, and felicity. Throughout his captivity Tommo cannot make up his mind about which face is really a mask. Either way, however, his conception of an original condition of existence bereft of history, free of cultural inscription, is strictly literary in nature and canonical in its essentials. The hostile face of the state of nature is a fiction primarily associated with Thomas Hobbes but finds its best literary expression in *The Adventures of Robinson Crusoe*, a book that Tommo is clearly wedded to. The index of nature's snarling face in *Typee* is, of course, cannibalism. The benign face of nature is primarily associated with the writings of Jean-Jacques Rousseau; as regards the issues of health, sexuality, property, and communality, *Typee* reiterates many of the arguments of the *Discourse on the Origin of Inequality*. The final destination of all this repetition is the phrase the "Happy Valley" (179). Melville borrowed this phrase from Samuel Johnson's *Rasselas: Prince of Abyssinia,* and Tommo applies it to the Typees' territory to dramatize his sense of their Utopia.

Writings about the state of nature determine the way Tommo reads Typee culture, and thus they determine the way he writes about it. On the one hand, the Typees are proof that progress is not conducive to happiness; they enjoy sexual and familial harmony. The comparative argument holds that Europeans and Americans do not. But, on the other hand, the Typees are backward in the extreme: they do not work; they do not understand history, not even their own history; they are superstitious, facile, and childish; they barbarously write upon their bodies; and they delight in consuming human flesh. In short, the Typees are an example of those who somehow need to be set an example. Like a child caught between divorced parents, Tommo vacillates between a primitivist rhetoric of defense and a rhetoric of imperialist instruction. Not without difficulty, the two rhetorics converge in a single passage: "Let the savages be civilized, but civilize them with benefits, and not with evils; and let heathenism be destroyed, but not by destroying the heathen. The Anglo-Saxon hive have extirpated Paganism from the greater part of the North American continent; but with it they have likewise extirpated the greater portion of the Red race. Civilization is gradually sweeping from the earth the lingering vestiges of Paganism, and at the same time the shrinking forms of its unhappy worshippers" (266).

According to Melville, the worldwide performance of colonialism — its radical essentials are displayed on the North American frontier — raises a blood-red curtain on the realities of ethnocide and genocide, appalling iniquities that have long attended the civilizing mission as the venture of script. Melville's critique of empire is within and without the trope of savagery as a "virgin page." From the confines of within savages are "heathens"; savages are children; savages need Christianity. Thus, "let the savages be civilized." From the standpoint of without the blank page, however, the last thing that the islanders need is "civilization." In principle the colonialists should put education before "extirpation"; in practice extirpation seems to be the order of the day. In other words, the "Anglo-Saxon hive" murders the very class of children which God and History have supposedly instructed it to instruct. The failure to live up to the Word collapses the rhetoric of uplift. No barbarism is greater than that of the civilizing mission.

Melville's inside-out critique is precisely made so by ambivalence concerning the state of nature (more than civilization, less than civilization) and ambivalence toward Christian expansionism (better than heathenism, worse or certainly no better than heathenism). In its articulation and yet undoing of the rhetoric of imperialist instruction *Typee* seems to contend that we cannot use one cultural standard absolutely to judge another. If we do so, we do so at our own – and certainly at others'– peril. The renunciation of an absolutist or supremacist cultural standard has devastating consequences for Tommo's claim to civilized literacy in the face of what he takes to be nature. His ability to read, interpret, understand, and criticize Marquesan signs and rituals is not as God-given as he is initially wont to assume. Eventually, Tommo reaches the point at which he realizes that, although many aspects of Marquesan culture fall within his purview, he actually comprehends very little of what he sees (244). In this sense his captivity becomes a lesson in cultural humility.

Picture a mature political science professor sitting in his office reading Plato. He enjoys the liberties and material comforts made possible by the hard work of others. The labor of others had provided libraries, classrooms, a university – a fair haven from which to view the world. And in what does privilege culminate? A "pettish, bookish, grumpy, reactionary complaint" against feminists and black nationalists, young people and a dark age called "the sixties"[7] – in short, *The Closing of the American Mind: How Higher Education Has Failed Democracy and Impoverished the Souls of Today's Students* (1987).[8]

Bloom's criticisms of higher education extend far and wide (from sexual mores to guns on campus); I shall only concern myself with those that have a direct relevance to the subject of national canonicity versus multicultural education. No less than *Typee*, *The Closing of the American Mind* is an educational treatise in the form of a captivity narrative.[9] In a combative style, steeped in platitudes, aphorisms, and generalizations, Bloom relates a somewhat ponderous tale of illiteracy, intolerance, vanity, servility, nihilism, and cowardice. The hero of his narrative is reason. Reason, or true intellectual openness, faces a death sentence in the university. The extermination of reason is called for by the despotic forces of relativism. A sort of jack-of-all-trades mind-set, relativism entertains "all kinds of men, all kinds of life-styles, all ideologies" (27). The only thing that relativism does not countenance is the person who, in the name of the disinterested pursuit of truth, opposes relativism's pedagogic or political operation. To those who seek to privilege one interpretation or one cultural standard over another relativism simply says no. Thus, says Bloom, masquerading as a style of openness, relativism is really a form of closure: it makes reason a captive; it makes the truth the slave of its own biased agenda; it encourages intellectual conformism. In short, relativism is a cousin of thought control.

As Bloom defines it, relativism is a leveling tendency tuned to the frequency of tyranny. His defense of reason, relativism's natural enemy, reads something like this: reason is the heroic and disinterested pursuit of truth; the pursuit of truth defines philosophy, the Great Books, "the West" (39); the Great Books (read Plato, Aristotle, Shakespeare, etc.) are no longer treated as great – apart from the crude and biased readings of them which now prevail (read feminist and leftist critiques, etc.) – and lesser works are increasingly the educational order of the day. The failure to pursue the "truth" has produced an entire generation of students who are spiritually (and sometimes practically) illiterate. *The Closing of the American Mind* contends that the universities are betraying their charters, betraying their intellectual missions, and the more they do this, the more they betray the promises of modern democracy.

Bloom's narrative is compelling not so much for what it says but for the way it says it. His story of cultural decline is shot through with colonialist metaphorics. Indeed, a good image for the overall feel of the book is the last colonial, the last white man, holding onto civilized values in the face of a horde of barbarians. Consider the vocabulary of a typical denunciatory passage: "Much of the great tradition was here [in the United States], an alien and weak transplant, perched precariously in enclaves, vulnerable to native populism and vulgarity. In the mid-sixties the natives, in the guise of students, attacked" (324). It does not require a great stretch of the imagination to appreciate that, in another time and place, this might easily be an Englishman lamenting the collapse of Indian allegiance to the British Crown. Throughout *The Closing of the American Mind* Bloom implies that the language of the last colonial is the only language that makes sense in a society in which students read the journal of an indigenous Guatemalan Marxist woman before they read Dante, in which universities generally provide the culture for breeding the savage mind.[10] Thus, it seems natural for Bloom to write: "Civilization has seemingly led us around full circle, back to the state of nature" (109). The noble savage of yesterday, the typical American student who, though barbarous, was eager to learn (48), has become the ignoble savage of now and tomorrow, the student whose only interests are easy sex and rock music.[11] Once the university was a Paradise Island of Reason; now it is a wilderness full of "barbarism and darkness."

As much as in *Typee*, the rhetoric of imperialist instruction runs deep in Bloom's argument. His diatribe against higher education is premised on the idea of underdeveloped or unscripted students: "University officials have . . . to deal with the undeniable fact that the students who enter are uncivilized, and that the universities have some responsibility for civilizing them" (341). Like Moresby and Melville, and like E. D. Hirsch, Bloom sees culture as a script that, when learned, permits one to call oneself civilized. As a cure for the intellectual diseases of pluralism, liberalism, and philistinism, Bloom offers the trusted antidote of a reasoned education in the classics of the Western tradition.

It is not difficult to see that Bloom's model of savage and civilized education is really a contemporary version of Matthew Arnold's memorable distinction between culture and anarchy; nor is it difficult to see how Bloom's rhetoric of instruction resolutely opposes multicultural education. The specter of multiculturalism occupies a position in Bloom's text which is analogous to the position that tattooing occupies in *Typee:* they both involve the issue of modes of writing; they both suggest a civilized fear of "going savage." A multicultural education would, in Bloom's terms, be a covenant with the devil of relativism. Multiculturalism leads to anarchy because it elevates our differences, whereas, in contrast, the Great Tradition deals with the nature of our social ties. Therefore, Bloom's defense of the old, his celebration of the classics, amounts to a defense of "the social contract" (27). Bloom is the teacher become missionary become guardian of the state.

Bloom's defense of reason, his disavowal of a multicultural pedagogy, is, in one sense, a very native defense of a postcolonial ideal whose history has been nothing less than tortuous: the myth of the melting pot. In his *Letters from an American Farmer* Crèvecoeur writes, "Here [in the United States] individuals of all nations are melted into a new race of man."[12] We know that the fires of acculturation burnt more fiercely for some races or nations than they did for others. Bloom accepts the idea, however, that U.S. nationhood requires or even demands the boiling away of old cultural identities. Those who would maintain a distance from this requirement (who do not show respect for the Great Tradition, who practice separatism) risk jamming up the works, as it were. Witness what Bloom has to say about African Americans: "Blacks are not sharing a special positive intellectual or moral experience; they partake fully in the common culture, with the same goals and tastes as everyone else, but they are doing it by themselves. They continue to have the inward sentiments of separateness caused by exclusion when it no longer effectively exists. The heat is under the pot, but they do not melt as have *all* the other groups" (93).

So much of what is wrong in Bloom's critique of the state of nature is implicit in this passage. Note that Bloom's rhetoric of instruction turns itself inside out: the ideal of the melting pot finds expression in the image of the cooking pot, a traditional image of cannibalistic savagery, as *Typee* informs us. The irony of using an emblem of savagery to belabor uncivilized behavior is appropriate in an argument so lacking in sensitivity, proportion, and consistency. Bloom takes it to be axiomatic that there is an unproblematic "common culture" in which "everyone" has "the same goals." He downplays the importance of minority or alternative cultures; he blinds himself to the question of power in not recognizing that dominant cultures like to call themselves shared. Bloom also takes it to be axiomatic that African American students needlessly segregate themselves. He argues that they are on the wrong moral wavelength. He underestimates the power and prevalence of distrust, enmity, and racial tension. He ignores the questions of comfort, support and safety. In putting the onus on African Americans to reform race relations Bloom fails to appreciate the degree of intransigence that they face. Finally, Bloom takes it to be axiomatic that "all other groups" have allowed themselves to be melted down into regular Americans; thus, he conveniently ignores those groups, such as indigenous peoples, who do not fit into his picture. Just what is Bloom carping on about?

It seems to me that Bloom's criticisms of the university are not really about the university but, instead, about the nature of U.S. society in general. This might not be so telling if his criticisms weren't so selective. Apart from a few passages expressing dismay over the proliferation of master's programs in business administration, there isn't a word in *The Closing of the American Mind* about the corporate penetration of academic studies, about the direct political service that the universities provide to the military-industrial complex.[13] There isn't a word in the text about the coarsening of young people's minds by what Richard Hoggart has called the "shiny barbarism" of advertising,[14] the continual making and remaking of the consumer. And, finally, not a single word passes Bloom's lips on the naked, unofficial apartheid underlying the demography of most U.S. cities. Bloom sees the end result of this fraught urban reality in the social makeup of campus life and then has the temerity to lay the problem at the door of African Americans. Only an ivory tower professor could criticize the university without criticizing the wider world in which it performs.

Reading *The Closing of the American Mind,* one gets the impression that the wider world of politics is simply, for Bloom, an inconvenience that interrupts seminars on Plato. But like all Utopian schemes, Bloom's model of civilized education sees itself as having radical meaning for the entire globe. Consider the coda with which he concludes: "This is the American moment in world history, the one for which we shall forever be judged. Just as in politics the responsibility for the fate of freedom in the world has devolved upon our regime, so the fate of philosophy in the world has devolved upon our universities, and the two are related as they have never been before. The gravity of our given task is great, and it is very much in doubt how the future will judge our stewardship" (382).

Here, then, is the true god of Bloom's worship: the continuation of U.S. economic and political "stewardship" of the world. As Bloom sees it, "the fate of freedom," the fate of U.S. hegemony—and thus, by extension, the fate of so-called Third World peoples—is inextricably bound to the defense of reason, the defense of the Great Tradition, within the university.[15] In a nutshell his point is this: as long as Americans read the right books, they will know who they are; knowing who they are, they can continue to determine what others should be. Thus, Plato and Shakespeare have the power to shape lives, to direct forces, to mobilize interests, and to control destinies.

Melville, too, believed in "the American moment in world history." In *White-Jacket* he writes: "We Americans are the peculiar, chosen people—the Israel of our time; we bear the ark of the liberties of the world. . . . God has predestinated, mankind expects, great things from our race; and great things we feel in our souls. The rest of the nations must soon be in our rear."[16] Melville's characterization of the American highlights the central myth of United States postcolonial nationalism (a myth that Bloom is not embarrassed to promote): the myth of American exceptionalism. This myth, that the United States is first in the moral table of nations and therefore has a responsibility to bring all other nations to its godly level, is most familiar to us in the form of the story that Uncle Sam has a grave mission to spread or safeguard democracy.

I claimed above that Melville's literary nationalism often removes its own ideological grounds. Consider the example of *Typee*. Tommo comments upon the cruelty, rapacity, and hypocrisy that mark the French annexation of the Marquesas Islands. For Tommo the work of Empire, as performed by the French, is nothing less than a "cavalier appropriation" of someone else's shores. And, yet, Admiral du Petit Thouars, the villain of the piece, is only following in the footsteps of Captain David Porter, the U.S. naval commander who had visited, renamed, annexed, and made war upon the Marquesas Islands three decades earlier.[17]

During the 1812 war between the United States and its former colonial master, Great Britain, Captain Porter of the USS *Essex* was given the task of harassing British whaleboats in the Pacific. In the course of his mission Porter landed at the Marquesan group; the act of taking possession, imperialism's baptismal ceremony, he describes as such: "On the 19th November [1813], the American flag was displayed in our fort, a salute of seventeen guns was fired from the artillery mounted there, and returned by the shipping in the harbour. The island [Nukihiva] was taken possession of for the United States, and called Madison's island, the fort, Fort Madison, the village, Madison's Ville, and the bay, Massachusetts Bay. The following declaration of the act of taking possession was read and signed, after which the prosperity of our newly acquired Island was drank by all present."[18] Language and liquor, the salute and the signature, make Nukihiva a ward of the United States; the British, claiming virgin space in Africa, could not have done it better. In Porter's version of events, through the symbolic action of renaming, the political father of democracy, President Madison, suffers the savages to come unto him. As no one else can, the American president will lead the savages to a brighter, new day.

As Melville is intent to point out, however, Porter's naked imperialism challenges and ultimately collapses the ideological underpinnings of the discourse of American exceptionalism. Those from "the land of the free" cannot deprive others of their lands without generating contradiction. In other words, American declarations of possession run directly counter to the American *Declaration of Independence,* for that document is surely the first, and among the greatest, of anticolonial arguments, in which the principle of self-determination becomes all. Thus, if the *Declaration of Independence* is the Magna Charta of modern democratic politics, then Porter and Madison, the captain and his president, are really enslavers in the guise of liberators, warmongers in the guise of peacekeepers, or wolves in sheep's clothes. The doctrine of "inalienable" human rights and the application of imperialist property rights to an alien setting are inherently incompatible. Porter repeats the violence and mendacity of Mendana before him and anticipates the violence of du Petit Thouars. In no sense at all is Porter's mission uniquely beneficent. From a Marquesan point of view all imperialists look very much the same. Now, with its celebration of democracy but faced with the inescapable truth of U.S. imperialism, where must American literary nationalism go? A traditionalism like Bloom's is condemned to fall short on answers.

More than a million copies of *The Closing of the American Mind* were sold in the four years following its original publication. How do we make sense of this figure, a phenomenal figure in the marketplace for what is supposed to be an academic book? I submit that one way to read *The Closing of the American Mind* is to see it as a symptomatic text about openings. As we move into a brave, new world, a socioeconomic order increasingly dominated by delirious flows of people, information, resources, and capital, in which the question of the border looms large, a specter haunts the United States: the specter of pronounced multiculturalism. Consider some telling statistics. One in four Americans is a person of color. In 1985 whites constituted just under 80 percent of the U.S. population; by the middle of the next century they will constitute something like 50 percent; it is estimated that of the labor force entering the marketplace in the year 2000 only 9 percent will be white males. In 1965 the proportion of European to non-European immigrants to the United States was nine to one; by 1985 this ratio had been reversed. The typical immigrant of today comes from East Asia or Latin America.[19] It is against the background of this extraordinary cultural revolution – numerous new threads added to the social fabric—that one can begin to make sense of the success of Bloom's book.

I suspect that many of Bloom's readers discover in the margins of his text a United States with which they can still identify, if only in its inevitable decline. The United States of Allan Bloom's undergraduate days at the University of Chicago (his temporal measure of how bad things have become) seems to have been a society in which one did not have to apologize for being an elitist or a traditionalist or Eurocentric to the core. Today such sentiments are strictly out of vogue: elitism has become snobbery, traditionalism has become pigheadedness, and Eurocentrism is now dismissed as a racist pose. Today students march to the tattoo that Western culture has got to go.[20] Bloom sees all this as lamentable, for such criticisms deny our heritage: they do not allow us to be proud of who we were or who we are. And here, indeed, is the rub that makes his book a register of the cultural transformation of Uncle Sam.

It seems to me that Bloom's complaints about declining cultural standards, about how the difficult questions will soon be impossible to ask, represent the last stand of an ideal of national core culture. Bloom speaks for all those who feel that U.S. culture is being stewed into something unpalatable. Not for nothing is nostalgia his paramount tone. Nostalgia also plays a significant role in *Typee:* Tommo's flight from the valley is in large measure due to his inability to forget "'Home' and 'Mother'" (328). For Tommo home and mother are permanent points of reference; they give meaning to a problematic wider world, and in this sense they closely resemble Bloom's vision of the ideal Alma Mater. Nostalgia names the memory of what we once were in the light of what we have become; in both *Typee* and *The Closing of the American Mind* it accounts for what Ishmael Reed calls "the strange and paranoid attitudes toward those different from the Elect."[21] In short, nostalgia is the order of the day for those in the United States who would defend their country's European heritage in the face of a sustained multicultural assault. For what is nostalgia but the rose-colored memory of an original condition of felicity before the walls caved in?

This essay advances the thesis that not only is traditionalism suspect; it may even be redundant. What, then, is to be done? The first thing that needs to be said is that postcolonial society cannot spirit or think away its differences. The cultural, racial, and linguistic diversity of a social landscape is, for better or worse, something that we have to confront. Whether or not we recognize it, in one way or another we are all members of a limited "imagined community" (to use Benedict Anderson's apt phrase).[22] In the widest sense we all belong to "ethnic minorities." Of course, in the best of all imaginable worlds none of this would matter. But, alas, this is the world of the French National Front, the British National Party, and the Ku Klux Klan, and in that context we must temper our appeals to one cultural standard over another with wisdom and sensitivity and with ethical considerations at the fore.[23] Now it would be foolish to claim that multicultural literacy can do everything that needs to be done; as regards racial tension, ethnic animosity, and religious conflict, powerful social and material forces will doubtless persist in having their say. I would simply assert that traditionalism has got us where we are, and where we are is not all bad (I wouldn't dispute that the Great Books retain their power to move) – but what proof is there that a serious multicultural approach to education would necessarily do worse?

I reject Bloom's arguments because I see in them a recipe for continuing divisiveness. But I agree with his general sentiment that things can improve. In answer to Bloom's critique of the multicultural agenda I would offer three contentions: first, that multicultural education does not represent a drop in academic standards; second, that multicultural education enriches a student's "soul"; third, that multicultural education is a liberal arts education at its best. With regard to point one: this is not the place to undertake a full-scale discussion of reason and relativism, but let me say, somewhat schematically, that multiculturalism does not necessarily entail a relativistic worldview. It may well be true that Plato is among the greatest of political philosophers and Shakespeare among the greatest of poets, but to counter the skeptical Saul Bellow, who awaits an "African Proust," it does not then follow that outside the so-called Western tradition we cannot find anyone who is "great."[24] I agree with Bloom: we should judge a work by the quality of its ideas, the beauty of its style, the range of its insights and feelings, and its applicability to our world. But I see nothing in any of these criteria that guarantees we must read the work of English or French writers to the exclusion of, say, Peruvian, Kenyan, Indian, or Polish works. In short, "sweetness and light," or "the best that has been thought and known,"[25] can be found in other places than those designated as the West (witness Naguib Mahfouz, George Lamming, Derek Walcott, Maxine Hong Kingston, Elias Khoury, Ngugi Wa Thiong'o, and Gabriel García Márquez). Concerning point two, I believe that a multi-cultural perspective can help students develop a profounder understanding of the diverse and sometimes dangerous forces at work in the world. Phenomena such as starvation, militarism, and terrorism are not God-given, nor are they easily understood. If, for instance, Chinua Achebe's novel *A Man of the People* enlightens European or United States students to the complexity of postcolonial Nigeria, then, in my view, an important task will have been performed. And, finally, as regards my third point, I believe that, insofar as a multicultural education can teach me to respect my neighbor, I take it to be a fulfillment of the moral mission of the liberal arts. That is to say, Bloom sees multiculturalism as necessarily opposing the appropriateness of powerful social ties, but I would argue that multiculturalism can instruct us about why our ties don't work. And in that sense it can be a cohesive ideology.

Underlying my three contentions is a basic premise: culture is not a finite process that can simply be reduced to a script; culture is a patchwork of languages, practices, values, rituals, memories, and desires. Culture treated solely as a script is an abstraction: scripts are performed in specific and relatively stable dramas; scripts do not require that the actors care for what they assert. Such is not the case with culture. Culture twists and turns to the specific interests of those groups and individuals who live it. In short, scripts impose upon their speakers, whereas culture, especially with regard to education, can (and should in a democratic society) respond to a community's human needs. Finally, a script comes to a halt; culture is a polyvalent, promiscuous creature that is very difficult to kill.

Instead of the monologism implied in what is ironically called the Great Conversation — that is, the tradition of the Great Books: great white men talking to one another — we should move to establish what Johnella Butler calls "difficult dialogues," models of cultural negotiation between opposing ends of the earth.[26] We should do this for two reasons. First, because, in the words of Patrick Hogan, "our understanding of Virgil or of Shakespeare may be deepened and rendered more sensitive by our appreciation of other cultures, other works, other traditions. Breadth of study, if sincerely and rigorously undertaken, does not inhibit but expands our understanding of particular fields."[27] A powerful example is provided by Martin Bernal, whose controversial study *Black Athena* challenges a conception of Western culture which Bloom, for one, takes wholly for granted.[28] Another powerful example occurs in Pacific literary history. In *Typee* Melville writes of the advent of "death-dealing engines" (180) in the Pacific world. In our day the Solomon Island poet Celo Kulagoe writes:

> A mushroom sprouts from
>   an arid Pacific atoll
> disintegrates into space
> leaving only a residue of might
>   to which for an illusory
>   peace and security
>   man clings.[29]

Juxtaposing Melville to Kulagoe in this manner opens up our eyes to an entire poetic tradition of lamentation which intimately relates to the excesses of imperialist power. It affords us a model for reading the politics of respective styles. A third example of Hogan's argument, that multiculturalism can deepen our understanding of the canonical, is provided by volume 1 of the *Heath Anthology of American Literature.* The anthology includes material from indigenous America and brings other groups that have traditionally been marginalized, such as African American and women writers, out of their obscurity and into the critical fore. The effect is to challenge the perception of United States literature as the sole product of New England white males. I conclude with the second reason that we should inaugurate a difficult dialogue between distant cultural positions: for too long we have not listened to what others have to say.

NOTES

I would like to thank Mary M. Gallucci of the University of Connecticut for the helpful criticisms that she made of this essay.

1. John Moresby, *New Guinea and Polynesia: Discoveries and Surveys in New Guinea and the D'Entrecasteaux Islands, a Cruise in Polynesia, and Visits to the Pearl-Shelling Stations in Torres Straits of HMS "Basilisk"* (London: John Murray, 1876), 300–301.
2. Ibid., 301.
3. Michel de Montaigne, *Essays of Montaigne*, ed. William Carew Hazlitt, trans. Charles Cotton (London: Navarre Society, 1923), 5:17.

4. Herman Melville, "Hawthorne and His Mosses," *The Portable Melville*, ed. Jay Leyda (New York: Viking Press, 1952), 413.

5. All quotations from the novel are from the Penguin edition, *Typee: A Peep at Polynesian Life* (Harmondsworth: Penguin, 1972).

6. See Jerry Phillips, "Cannibalism, Comprehension and Critique: The Split Narrative of *Typee*," *Herman Melville and the Politics and Poetics of Adventure* (Ph.D. diss., University of Essex, 1990), 369–413.

7. Robert Paul Wolff, "Book Review: *The Closing of the American Mind*," *Academe* (September–October 1987), 64–65; reprinted in Robert Stone, ed., *Essays on the Closing of the American Mind* (Chicago: Chicago Review Press, 1989), 18–22.

8. Allan Bloom, *The Closing of the American Mind: How Higher Education Has Failed Democracy and Impoverished the Souls of Today's Students* (New York: Simon & Schuster, 1987).

9. Interestingly enough, Bloom wholeheartedly rejects the cross-cultural critique of home which the writing of exotic adventure often encourages. Witness what he has to say about Margaret Mead, the "delinquent traveler" become anthropologist: "sexual adventurers like Margaret Mead and others who found America too narrow told us that not only must we know other cultures and learn to respect them, but we could also profit from them. We could follow their lead and loosen up, liberating ourselves from the opinion that our taboos are anything other than social constraints. We could go to the bazaar of cultures and find reinforcement for inclinations that are repressed by puritanical guilt feelings. All such teachers of openness had either no interest in or were actually hostile to the Declaration of Independence and the Constitution" (33). The concluding generalization about the dissident adventurer is, to my mind, a patent falsehood. Melville was a "teacher of openness," but his misgivings about the two great social contracts of U.S. democracy were not simply based upon a libertarian idealization of "the Primitive" but also upon the (well-grounded) belief that U.S. society was from the beginning a fallen entity. Slavery, industrial capitalism, and the war of extermination against the Native Americans testified to that. In other words, he saw the ideals of democracy as frustrated by the economic system and the territorial acquisitiveness of the Young Republic. Such a perspective seems beyond the intellectual horizon of Bloom.

10. Few better cases could be mustered to demonstrate what the traditionalists find wrong with multiculturalism. No right-minded culture would replace Dante, one of the great Western poets whose work expresses universal themes, with the sectarian reflections of an obscure "Third World" writer. The self-evident status of this interpretation is amply conveyed by Robert Stone: "Evidence of the refurbishing of Western Civilization courses can be seen in an article from *The Wall Street Journal* which describes the purge of several great books from the curriculum of Stanford University [home of many student protests about the lack of cultural diversity in course offerings] in December 1988. Dante's *Inferno* was replaced in the curriculum by *Yo Rigoberta Menchu*, the autobiography of a Marxist female Guatemalan Indian. No wonder that Bill Honig, the Superintendent of Public Instruction for the State of Cali-

fornia, in 'What is Right About Bloom?' is alarmed. Honig argues that because there is now so little concern for ethics and the ideas of great men in our schools, we risk cultural suicide" (Stone, ed., *Essays*, 332). Honig's dramatic equation, that life is synonymous with "the ideas of great men," is a classic example of traditionalist reasoning. Saul Bellow or England's Roger Scruton could not have put it better.

11. Of yesterday's savages Bloom writes: "Young Americans seemed, in comparison [to young Europeans], to be natural savages when they came to the university. . . . American intellectual obtuseness could seem horrifying and barbarous, a stunting of full humanity, an incapacity to experience the beautiful, an utter lack of engagement in civilization's ongoing discourse. . . . But for me . . . this constituted a large part of the charm of American students. . . . For Americans the works of the great writers could be the bright sunlit uplands where they could find the outside, the authentic liberation for which this essay is a plea" (48). Yesterday's savage was an enticing white page, a heathenish blank that inspires missionary zeal. Today's natural savages are clean slates that refuse to be written upon, heathens that refuse to be converted. The typical American student of the post-1960s era moves the philosopher away from lyricism and ever nearer the shores of despair. Bloom dedicates his book to his students, but his portraits of students are nothing if not critical. Consider a typical example: "Sated with easy, clinical and sterile satisfactions of body and soul, the students arriving at the university today hardly walk on the enchanted ground they once did. They pass by ruins without imagining what was once there" (136). This passage bears interesting comparison to an incident described in *Typee:* Tommo marvels at the great stone monuments that reside in Typee Valley; he is somewhat shocked when he discovers that none of the Typees know "anything about them" (217). The idea that savagery is a condition of not knowing one's history is thus central to both Bloom's and Tommo's reflections.

12. J. Hector St. John de Crèvecoeur, *Letters from an American Farmer* (Harmondsworth: Penguin, 1986), 70.

13. See John Trumpbour, ed., *How Harvard Rules: Reason in the Service of Empire* (Boston: South End Press, 1989); Jonathan Feldman, *Universities in the Business of Repression: The Academic-Military-Industrial Complex and Central America* (Boston: South End Press, 1989); and David Noble, "The Multinational Multiversity," *Zeta Magazine* 2, no. 4 (April 1989): 17–28.

14. Richard Hoggart, *The Uses of Literacy: Changing Patterns in English Mass Culture* (Boston: Beacon Press, 1961).

15. In this context it is worth noting that Bloom was codirector of the John M. Olin Center for Inquiry into the Theory and Practice of Democracy at the University of Chicago. Establishing a "think tank" is, of course, one of the easiest ways for a corporation to penetrate academia. Olin and other conservative foundations provide the material basis for the ideological defense of both corporate interests and the national security state. On such issues as Central America, terrorism, or "supply-side" economics (welfare state cutbacks, tax breaks for the rich to stimulate investment, etc.) foundations put up the money, in the form of fellowships and grants, while academics put on the

show. See Jon Weiner, "More Dollars for Necon Scholars," *Nation* 250, no. 1 (1990): 12–14.

16. Herman Melville, *White-Jacket; or, the World in a Man-of-War* (Evanston: Northwestern Univ. Press and the Newberry Library, 1970), 151.

17. See David Porter, *Journal of a cruise made to the Pacific ocean, by Captain David Porter, in the United States frigate Essex in the years 1812, 1813, and 1814*, 2 vols. (Philadelphia: 1815), 2:1–145; and Melville, *Typee*, 62–63.

18. Porter, *Journal*, 2:82.

19. The statistical data on the cultural transformation of the United States is drawn from William A. Henry, "Beyond the Melting Pot," *Time*, 9 April 1990, 28–33. Subtitled "America's changing colors," most of this edition of *Time* attempts to address the question of "What will the United States be like when whites are no longer the majority?"

20. "Hey hey ho, hey hey ho, Western 'civ' has got to go" was the refrain used by students of color at Stanford University protesting the lack of cultural diversity in the undergraduate curriculum. Their protest focused on the fact that a survey course in Western culture was obligatory, whereas courses in multiculturalism were optional and marginal. Since 1988 other campuses have witnessed Stanford-type protests. See Susannah Abbey, "Diversity: The Demand in Curriculum Reform," *The Guardian: An Independent Radical Newsweekly*, 17 October 1990, 13.

21. Ishmael Reed, "America: The Multinational Society," in *The Graywolf Annual Five: Multi-cultural Literacy*, ed. Rick Simonson and Scott Walker (St. Paul: Graywolf Press, 1988), 159.

22. Benedict Anderson, *Imagined Communities: Reflections on the Origin and Spread of Nationalism* (London: Verso, 1983).

23. It need hardly be said, in the light of the Salman Rushdie incident in which liberal-minded but shortsighted attacks on "Islamic Fundamentalism" played right into the hands of Fascist terror groups like the National Front and the British National Party, that our appeals to harmony, or free speech, or standards of decency, should be consistent with a conception of human rights which transcends any particular culture. In other words, we do not have to resort to cultural elitism to make vocal our disapproval of abuses. An abuse is an abuse regardless of the specific names by which it is known.

24. For a cogent discussion of Bellow's disdain for the multicultural position, see Lillian S. Robinson, "What Culture Should Mean," *Nation* 249, no. 9 (25 September 1989): 319–21.

25. Arnold, *Culture and Anarchy*, 70.

26. Johnella Butler, "Difficult Dialogues," *Women's Review of Books* 6, no. 5 (1989): 16.

27. Patrick Colm Hogan, *The Politics of Interpretation: Ideology, Professionalism, and the Study of Literature* (New York: Oxford Univ. Press, 1990), 212.

28. Martin Bernal, *Black Athena: The Afroasiatic Roots of Classical Civilization; The Fabrication of Ancient Greece, 1785–1985* (New Brunswick, N.J.: Rutgers Univ. Press, 1987).

29. Celo Kulagoe, "Peace Signs," *Lali: A Pacific Anthology*, ed. Albert Wendt (Auckland: Longman Paul, 1980), 213.

2   "Four Hundred Years of Silence"

Myth, History, and
Motherhood in Toni
Morrison's *Beloved*

Sally Keenan

Until recently studies of postcolonial and Third World literatures have not customarily addressed themselves to the writing of
Native or African Americans.[1] On reflection this must appear surprising, given the extreme forms of "colonialist" subjection which have
marked their respective histories: genocide and slavery at the hands
of European imperialist powers. This lack of attention can be explained in part by the complex character of the United States's emergence as a nation, in which it played the role both of the colonized,
fighting a war of independence from European control, as well as that
of the colonizer of an indigenous population and of African slaves.
That the inclusion of Native and African American histories in postcolonial discourse has not been axiomatic in the past signals a failure
to address the processes of colonization on which the foundation of
the United States rests. That it is a postcolonial society can no longer
be in question. Furthermore, in the United States, as elsewhere, the
post- of that term should not be regarded as a sign that the processes
of colonialism have ended; rather, their legacy continues to exist as a
lived reality for many citizens.

The writing of African American women, which has been so prolific
over the last two decades, has done much to highlight the postcolonial condition of the contemporary United States. Moreover, this body
of writing has made a significant contribution to the revisioning of

North American history, a recasting of our understanding of the past which resonates beyond the borders of that continent. Toni Morrison's *Beloved* provides an exemplary instance of this revision.

When *Beloved* won the Pulitzer Prize in 1988 Morrison's work finally received the recognition by the literary establishment which many writers and critics in the African American community believed it had long deserved.[2] Was this a sign that black American women writers had finally made the move from the margins to the center of North American cultural and intellectual life which had been promised by the success of Alice Walker's *Color Purple* five or so years before? Or are Morrison and Walker merely token figures used by the literary/publishing establishment to provide not only a highly profitable product but also the illusion that the publishing world in the United States does not still exercise discrimination against the work of large numbers of writers from the so-called margins of North American culture? I suspect that Morrison herself, although no doubt pleased with the accolade of a Pulitzer Prize, might agree that there is an element of tokenism here, having described the sense of responsibility she feels as an editor in a New York publishing house who often finds herself insisting on the acceptance of work by black writers, against a belief that there isn't room in the catalog for more than one or two. But then Morrison, despite her success, would not agree that she has moved from the margins to the center of cultural life, for, as she has said, "There's nothing remotely marginal about being a black woman."[3] Such an assertion, I believe, lies embedded in her novel's dramatic evocation of what it might have meant to be both a slave and a mother.

Even before winning the literary establishment's most prestigious prize, *Beloved* had assumed a central place within current writing by African Americans which insists on an examination of U.S. culture and history, one that takes account of the processes of "internal colonization."[4] I believe, however, that Morrison's novel can also be read as contributing in a wider sense to contemporary postcolonial discourse, as it offers a perspective on African American history and literature which refuses to place its origins in the institution of slavery but, instead, situates that history within the larger context of the African diaspora. It is significant too that the novel has rapidly become established in the academic curriculum at the very moment that a debate is raging concerning the traditional canon of literature studies in U.S. universities and the value of Western culture foundation courses for undergraduates is coming under attack.[5]

In this essay I want to examine what I consider to be both timely and different about Morrison's *Beloved*—that is, its placing of the issue of motherhood and female resistance to slavery at the heart of an exploration of the processes of memory, recovery, and representation of African American history and the dilemma that has long faced African Americans of finding a language to speak and write about their past. Morrison's narrative, I will argue, exposes with painful clarity that the ambiguities of connection and separation between the slave mother and child bear some correlation with the contradictions that mark the relationship of African Americans to their history. If, in psychoanalytical terms, the mother as source, or origin, is problematic and irrecoverable, so too African Americans, perhaps above all peoples, have learned through their particularly fractured past that history is problematic and often irrecoverable. I do not wish to suggest that the idea of motherhood can function as some kind of all-embracing metaphor for that history—far from it—but that the mythologizing that black women as mothers have been subjected to is a crucial part of the mythologizing of African American history as a whole, whether that be the enabling myths that have helped black culture to survive or the disenabling mythologies imposed by white culture and threatening to that survival. If feminist writing and postcolonial writing are said to "have strong parallels,"[6] Morrison's text delineates an area in which they intersect. At the same time *Beloved* extends the limits of previous histories and autobiographical writings on slavery through its exploration of the ways subjectivity might be established and inscribed by those who have been denied its possibility.

At the opening of *Beloved* Baby Suggs, the grandmother of an ex-slave family, has finally laid down the burden of her "intolerable" life and retired to bed. "Suspended between the nastiness of life and the meanness of the dead, she couldn't get interested in leaving life or living it." It is clear in these opening pages that all the inhabitants of her home at 124 Bluestone Road are also suspended between the past and the present, the living and the dead, the presence of the latter most vociferously signified by the baby ghost who haunts the house, furious "at having its throat cut" before it was two years old. The ghost has chased off Baby Suggs's grandsons, and the memory of the manner of its death has cut the family off from their community of freed and former slaves.

Morrison's narrative pivots around the contradiction implied in living with impossible memories, the need to remember and tell and the desire to forget, memories with an inexhaustible and monstrous power to erupt and overwhelm the mind but which must somehow be laid aside if life is to continue; it is a life that is structured around each "day's serious work of beating back the past." Denver, however, the last living child remaining in the family, born outside slavery while the mother, Sethe, was on her fugitive's flight to freedom, desires to know "all what happened," the story of the past having been told and retold in part but always cut off at a point in the narrative "beyond which [her mother] would not go." Her sister, the baby ghost, Beloved, represents the insistent claims of that forbidden or hidden part of the family's history, and Beloved, as both text and figure in the text, becomes in the course of the narrative a complex metaphor for black America's relationship with its enslaved past. If Beloved's spectral return into the slave family represents within the narrative the eruption of that which has lived on as memory but has remained unspoken, the text, *Beloved,* signals a current discursive renegotiation with their history by African Americans which amounts to a contestation of the ways that past has been erased by or subsumed within the historical discourse of the hegemonic culture. The writer Sherley Anne Williams says, "Afro-Americans, having survived by word of mouth – and made of that process a high art – remain at the mercy of literature and writing; often these have betrayed us."[7] It has become an imperative for black Americans in the post–civil rights period of the 1970s and 1980s to write their own histories, in order to negotiate that difficult relation between past and present, a necessity of the postcolonial present that Morrison's ex-slave protagonists are depicted as negotiating in the colonial past.

It is a curious coincidence that two novels of slavery by African American women writers, Morrison's *Beloved* and Sherley Anne Williams's *Dessa Rose* should be published within a year of each other in the mid-1980s and that both are based on sketchy fragments of recorded history concerning the rebellion and escape of female slaves in the nineteenth century. Both novels can be read as part of the important contemporary feminist enterprise of recovering women's lost or unrecorded history; they can also be read as part of that momentum among writers and critics within the black community to look back across the span of their history in the United States in an effort to revision a story that has been made virtually invisible, a repetition of the effacement that had been enacted within the institution of slavery. But neither text makes any particular claims to performing the functions of an empirical history. Both, in fact, considerably alter the narrative trajectories of their source material.[8] Morrison's text, in particular, draws attention to its decidedly fictive quality by constantly transgressing the bounds of even realist fiction, emphasizing a desire to step beyond the problematic parameters of historical record in order to address the question of how to think, speak, and write an unmanageable or lost history.

The critic Hazel Carby calls *Beloved* "a remarkable exploration and revisioning of the limits of conventional historical narrative strategies for representing slavery."[9] In discussing the conventions of the genre, Carby writes, "In formal terms, a narrative of slavery has three conventional conclusions: escape, emancipation, or death. Antebellum slave narratives conventionally ended with escape to the North. In historical sagas like *Jubilee,* emancipation is central. In novels based on rebellions, death is the conclusion."[10] She adds that in contemporary novels of slavery these conventions have been rewritten. She cites Ishmael Reed's *Flight to Canada,* in which the escaped slave returns to the plantation; *Dessa Rose,* wherein the escapees flee West rather than North; and David Bradley's *The Chaneyville Incident,* in which the flight ends in death, another form of escape.

Morrison's revision of the genre is most immediately discernible in the historical present of her narrative, 1873, eighteen years after the protagonists' escape. Although the events of that escape are woven into the narrative structure as memory and story, they do not constitute the denouement of the story but, rather, in a sense its beginning, the escape not just a road to freedom and narrative conclusion but also the means of a liberty dearly bought and still being paid for by the escapees. Thus, escape from slavery as both narrative motif and historical event is represented not as a resolution but, instead, something that is subject to a continual psychological renegotiation by those who survived its traumatic effects. Morrison's chosen historical moment for her story is also significant in this regard; she situates her characters in the Reconstruction period, when the institution of slavery was finally beginning to crumble, thus locating them at a crucial juncture both historically and psychologically between enslavement and emancipation. They are, as the figure of Baby Suggs highlights, physically and notionally free but not psychologically free. They have just managed to escape from the fact of slavery but have not been released from its effects. Situating her characters thus, Morrison is able to explore not only what it was to be a slave but also what it meant to live with the psychological continuation of the experience of slavery.[11] Her exploration of that liminal condition between the then of slavery and the future of freedom acts as an analogue to the relationship of contemporary African Americans to their past – the need, that is, to recover and recall their history and the need to escape the cycle of oppression and violence it tells and in which many remain entrapped.[12]

The other sign of *Beloved*'s revisionary quality, which it also shares with *Dessa Rose,* is that the fugitive is not only a woman but she also gives birth to a child during the escape. This striking conjunction of escape and childbirth indicates a shared interest in questions that until very recently have not been examined, even within the plethora of historiography and literature concerning slavery in the United States – that is to say, the remarkable absence of an adequate discourse that could address slave women's forms of resistance to slavery on the one hand and the meanings women attached to motherhood within slavery on the other. The image of the black mammy, the slave woman who rules the kitchen and the nursery of the plantation mansion with a rod of iron but who is nonetheless devoted to her white master's children and acquiescent with her own enslavement, is a cartoonlike figure who has been popularized in fiction and on the Hollywood screen; she is, moreover, a figure whose relation with her own children is generally effaced. There have been historical narratives that addressed the issue of slave women's relation to their children and their attempts to resist or escape from slavery, such as Margaret Walker's *Jubilee* and André Schwarz-Bart's *A Woman Named Solitude.* It is only in the last few years, however, that a scholarly discourse addressing these issues is in the process of evolving through the work of women historians and literary critics.[13] This work has also ensured the recovery of autobiographical writing by slave women, once thought to be nonexistent, which testifies to the link between maternity and resistance to slavery.

In her history of women under slavery in the United States, *Ar'n't I a Woman?* Deborah Gray White offers a succinct summary of the directions taken in the historiography on slavery and the debates surrounding it in the 1960s and 1970s. White argues that Stanley Elkins's well-known thesis in *Slavery: A Problem in American Institutional and Intellectual Life,* published in 1968, determined the limits of much of the ensuing debate. In arguing that slaves in the United States were so undermined by the overwhelming power of their masters that they assumed a childlike, or "feminine" passivity, Elkins provoked a counterattack by male historians, both black and white, who, at a time when the black power movement was at its most militant, set out to prove that male slaves had remained the dominant force within their own households and, therefore, within slave culture at large. The work of John Blassingame, Eugene Genovese, and Herbert Gutman, as important and productive as it has been in terms of the source material unearthed and the way in which it countered some of the racist assumptions underlying much previous research, tended to ignore or at least minimize the role of women in an attempt to represent men as the primary resisters to slavery. White concludes that "the male slave's 'masculinity' was restored by putting black women in their proper 'feminine' place."[14] Regarding the difficulties she encountered in her own research, White says: "Slave women were everywhere, yet nowhere. They were in Southern households and in Southern fields but the sources are silent about female status in the slave community and the bondwoman's self-perception. . . . In fact, the material sheds little light upon the way sex and race shaped her self-concept."[15] This lack, the result of the double oppression of sexism and racism, forced White to rely largely on the interviews with ex-slaves compiled by the Works Progress Administration (WPA) research that revealed that slave women were not "submissive [or] subordinate" and "were not expected to be so" within their own culture.[16]

Black women in the United States, of course, have not only been subjected to this silencing of their history; they have also been subjected to a pervasive mythology, historically circulated within white U.S. culture, which has represented them within a fixed set of stereotypes. In 1987 Hazel Carby reiterated what Angela Davis first pointed out in 1971, that the source of stereotypes about black women can be traced back to the institution of slavery.[17] Davis and, more recently, Joyce Ladner attack the stereotype of the black matriarch, a figure "invoked as one of the fatal by-products of slavery" by the Moynihan report in 1965, which endeavored to depict the contemporary black family as "a tangle of pathology," devoid of adequate male role models and ruled by emasculating, dominating women.[18] Hazel Carby, meanwhile, attacks the equally pervasive myth of the black slave woman as sexually acquiescent with her white masters, viewing male historians' and sociologists' "reluctance to condemn as an act of rape what is conceived in patriarchal terms to be sexual compliance."[19] Carby puts forward a powerful and elaborate argument that this construction of the slave woman as a promiscuous "breeder" was a necessary counterpart to the white slaveholder's construction of a cult of true womanhood, the "glorified" proper lady of the plantation manor. Still in 1987 Carby is forced to conclude that most current historiography tends to reproduce unquestioningly stereotypes of black female sexuality, "even where other aspects of the institution of slavery have been under radical revision."[20]

Deborah Gray White's study encapsulates these stereotypes in her discussion of the twin myths regarding female slaves, the saintly mammy and the libidinous Jezebel. The figure of the Jezebel became crucially important after 1807 and the abolition of the overseas slave trade, when the slave woman's breeding capacity became the only means to ensure the continual production of slave labor.[21] The image of the mammy, on the other hand, personified the "ideal slave," the all-caring nurturer "in keeping with the maternal or Victorian ideal of womanhood prevalent in nineteenth-century America."[22] Only such a figure, purged of the sexual associations of the Jezebel, could be allowed such close contact with white families and their children. Thus, the two myths, one that "excused miscegenation" and the other, which "helped endorse the service of black women in Southern households,"[23] helped cover over the social and economic contradictions inherent in the institution of slavery.

The notion that black slave women acquired any power either through sexual relations with the master or through the role of mammy, a role to be reconstructed after slavery as matriarch, is a gross distortion of their actual social and economic relations. Angela Davis says, "It is cruel because it ignores the profound traumas the black woman must have experienced when she had to surrender her childbearing to alien and predatory economic interests."[24]

In her 1990 Clark lectures at Cambridge University Morrison addressed what she called a "silence of four hundred years . . . the void of any historical discourse on slave parent/child relations," which she discussed via a deconstructive analysis of Willa Cather's *Sapphira and the Slave Girl.* Morrison's discussion of the novel centered on the silence surrounding the relationship between the slave mother, Till, and her daughter, Nancy, the mulatto girl, whose virtue is under a threat posed by the jealous machinations of her white mistress to whom the slave mother has given a lifetime of devoted service. Till's response to her daughter's eventual escape is recorded only in a single half-murmured question to the mistress's daughter: "Have you heard anything?" Morrison argued that the centuries-old assumption surrounding this silence is that slave women were not mothers to their own children. Till embodies the ideal of the black mammy as she has been represented in much cultural production, literary, historical, and cinematic: as White points out, such representation has been of "a woman completely dedicated to the white family, especially to the children of that family,"[25] the surrogate mother to her white masters and mistresses, fulfilling a role delineated for her which completely effaced the relationship she might have with her own children. It is this latter, hidden story, or, as Morrison puts it, the "fugitive plot," which has escaped the histories and literatures concerning slavery in North America.

In her own novel, I believe, Morrison is providing a space for the recovery of that fugitive plot, of the mother and child under slavery. But she is not just filling in an absence in our knowledge, for the past, especially one that has been either unrecorded or erased, is never fully recoverable, as White's thorough but inevitably limited empirical history testifies. Rather, she employs fiction to redefine the ways in which the history of the African American family may be read, in terms of resistance rather than acquiescence to white supremacist ideology, a project that bears a particular salience in the 1980s and 1990s, given the persistent and undermining critical attention that the black family continues to receive. Her text attacks that pathologizing perspective at its root, by unraveling the myth of the black matriarch. If black women have been historically captured between representations of themselves as lascivious whores and emasculating matriarchs, images that derive directly from the enslaved condition of their maternal ancestors, then Morrison's vision of the stories of mothers and daughters under slavery can be seen as undoing those deadly cultural myths. This she does by confronting certain crucial questions in her text: as the slave woman's role as mother was appropriated as the production of marketable goods for her masters, what then was her relation with the children she produced? In particular, what was her relation to the daughters whose bodies would also be required to fulfill that function? What notions of identity and culture could the mother transmit to the daughter whom she had enslaved by the very fact of giving birth to her? Even after emancipation, what sense of the past or future could the ex-slave mother pass on to her daughter which would not reenslave her within the logic of their history? And, finally, for the late-twentieth-century black American woman, how can she read her own heritage through that grid of stereotypical images? *Beloved*, therefore, confronts two stories of black women's history at once, one the overwritten, heavily mythologized story of the black matriarch and the other the hitherto unwritten story of mother and daughter in the slave family. Out of the unweaving of the former evolves the creation of the latter.

In discussing the important political role that women had in many traditional African societies, Joyce Ladner points to evidence that in some tribal courts the official function of certain groups of women was to "remember what had happened"–that is, in the absence of written records they acted as the tribal memory.[26] It is therefore significant that *Beloved* opens with the female ancestral figure Baby Suggs. Having finally been brought down by the painful return of her past, she gives up her role as communal preacher and guide and retires to bed to die. Baby Suggs, who cannot remember the eight children she gave birth to because they were taken from her, represents the crisis of four hundred years of a history under slavery in which a cultural tradition, dependent for its transmission on oral history, could either not be remembered at all or else the memories had become too painful to transmit.

Morrison's narrative traces this tension between the loss of knowledge of the past, the need to remember and tell, and the desire to forget, in a complex reproduction of the processes of memory and storytelling. One story, one memory, breaks into another in an at first quite bewildering series of shifts in time and place and narrative voice. As the pieced-together story of a group of ex-slaves who have shared a bitter past, it reverberates out into the histories of all North American slaves and becomes, in the telling, a representative attempt to relate that past from the subjective positions of those who lived through it or its effects.

The work of Henry Louis Gates Jr. in the form of literary criticism

and recovery of once lost texts has highlighted the particular significance of orality and literacy, of reading and writing, in African American history. Discussing the nineteenth-century slave narratives,
Gates emphasizes a complex relation between oral and written forms
of narrative, pointing out that many of the slave narratives were
"structured formal revisions of their spoken words organized and promoted by anti-slavery organizations."[27] From the seventeenth to the
late nineteenth centuries the spoken voice of the black subject turned
into written form had become the recognized sign that the "African
would become European, the slave become ex-slave, the brute animal
become the human being," in answer to European assumptions that
the lack of a written discourse meant an absence of humanity.[28] Writing had become the vital means of establishing a black subjectivity,
but, as Gates's work suggests, its inscription was locked within the
terms of the rhetoric of European and Euro-American ideology.

In *Dessa Rose* Sherley Anne Williams revisions this issue by using
the interior monologue of a slave woman to subvert the attempts of a
white man to inscribe her self and her story within the discourse of
white supremacism, to highlight the tension between the orality of
the black subject and the discursive power of white writing. Morrison, however, focuses the issue elsewhere. Her text circulates around
the question of how slaves and ex-slaves might have spoken that past
to one another and, by implication, raises the question for contemporary African Americans of how they might speak and write about that
history now, within their own community. Through *Beloved*'s multiple, dialogic structure, an interaction of voices of both the living and
the dead, Morrison shifts the boundaries imposed by the traditional
tension between orality and writing which marked the early autobiographical slave narratives. The intersubjective voices of her ex-slaves
and their children, piecing together the fragments of their damaged
past, become an attempt to evolve a subjective language with which
to attach different meanings to slavery, outside the ways in which it
has become fixed in historiography and myth. By focusing that inter-
subjectivity on the relations between a slave mother and her children, Morrison both acknowledges her literary foremothers, the female authors of autobiographical slave narratives, and at the same
time extends the discursive possibilities within which the histories of
slave women can be read.

Harriet Jacobs's 1861 slave narrative, *Incidents in the Life of a Slave*

Girl, published over 120 years before *Beloved,* highlights the extent of both that debt and that revision. Hazel Carby argues that the shift from the writing of slave narratives to fiction by black women at the end of the nineteenth century became the woman writer's means of "cultural and political intervention in the struggle for black liberation from oppression."[29] Therefore, the writing of *Beloved* at the end of the twentieth century marks a return across that span of a hundred years to the beginnings of African American women's engagement with their own histories.

Jacobs's *Incidents* is one of the few slave autobiographies written by a woman which is known to scholarship. According to Jean Fagin Yellin, Jacobs's text is the only slave narrative that takes as its subject the sexual exploitation of female slaves and thus addresses directly the interrelation of sexual and racial oppression.[30] Jacobs's story centers around her prolonged resistance to the sexual advances of her white master, culminating in an extraordinary act of self-assertion: she takes a white man as a lover as a form of protection and gives birth to two children by him. Forgoing the opportunity to flee to the North because she refuses to leave her children, she escapes her master's wrath by spending several years hiding in an attic in the house of her grandmother, who is a freed slave and respected member of the local community. Although she is betrayed by her white lover, who fails to honor his promise to buy her children's freedom, she does eventually achieve that freedom through her own efforts.

Fearing condemnation arising from the scandalous nature of her story, Jacobs wrote under the pseudonym Linda Brent and with the encouragement and help of two white abolitionists, Amy Post and Lydia Maria Child. Although well received on publication, Jacobs's work has been subjected to much controversy regarding its authenticity by twentieth-century scholarship. Mary Helen Washington refers to John Blassingame's criticisms, in his *Slave Testimony* (1972), that Jacobs's story was "too melodramatic to be authentic."[31] Hazel Carby argues that this dismissal stems from a refusal to accept a text that deviates "from the conventions of male authored texts."[32] It has only been since the 1980s, through the research of these critics and particularly that of Jean Fagin Yellin, that Jacobs's text has been fully authenticated. Yellin's research into Jacobs's correspondence reveals that, contrary to some critics' assumptions, her editors changed the style and language of the text very little. It also reveals that Jacobs feared publication because of the text's disclosures about her sexual life but that this fear was overridden by a social purpose that motivated the publication, to rouse the sympathy for other poor "slave mothers that are still in bondage" and to "plead for their helpless children."[33]

There are a number of interesting parallels between elements in Jacobs's narrative and the life of Morrison's slave mother, Sethe, which highlight the particular relation between slavery and motherhood. But I will also argue that, by measuring those parallels, the differences between the two texts can show how Morrison, from her historical vantage point and as a writer of fiction, has been able to inscribe that relationship in a way that eluded Jacobs, owing to the discursive constraints imposed on a woman writer at that historical moment.

All the researchers agree that Jacobs's narrative reveals marked differences from male-authored slave narratives. First, Valerie Smith points out that Jacobs's text does not fit the conventional bildungsroman plot of male narratives because such a plot formula fails to account for the mark of her gender. The typical male-authored slave narrative may be seen "as not only the journey from slavery to freedom but also the journey from slavehood to manhood," while Jacobs's is not a story of the triumphant individual will but, rather, of the slave woman in relation to her children and family. Smith adds that, significantly, Jacobs's text does not open with a focus on the solitary "I" but insists, instead, that her desire for freedom is commensurate with the desire to free her children.[34] This focus, maintained consistently throughout the narrative, establishes Jacobs's story as a precursor to that of Morrison's Sethe. Washington makes the telling observation that a male slave narrator did not feel compelled to discuss his sexuality or his children, but for slave women children are inextricable from questions of freedom and bondage.[35] The second way in which Jacobs's story does not fit the conventional formulas of male slave narratives is, according to Washington, that, whereas male slaves' writing enabled them to establish their masculinity, through representations of their independence, resolution, and physical skill, Jacobs's confession revealed that "she did not have the qualities valued in white women," that is, she was not chaste, and she was the mother of illegitimate children. So, while her narrative adhered to contemporary notions of propriety regarding devoted motherhood, it disturbed that ideology with its scandalous revelation of her sexual life. Thus, her very act of defiance provoked disapprobation, not only from the oppressors she escapes but also from her own community. In *Beloved* Morrison replays that link between defiance and communal condemnation but with an appallingly painful twist: Sethe's act of defiance is infanticide, death being the only available route to freedom for her child. If Jacobs's act defied a nineteenth-century ideology regarding chaste femininity, Morrison's protagonist defies conventional assumptions regarding mother love, a defiance that still has the power to shock in the late twentieth century.

Jacobs's story conforms to Hazel Carby's observation that slave narratives by black women tend to foreground slave women's active role as historical agents as opposed to passive subjects and that they document suffering, but also resistance.[36] What is more, they appear to document that crucial link between resistance and motherhood. Although most historians argue that childbearing and caring was the single most predominant restraint on slave women's power to resist and especially to escape, Jacobs's narrative highlights that it was motherhood above all that provoked the desire and necessity to resist the oppressors. Although Jacobs's children were the "fruits of her shame," they are represented in her text as her links to life and the motivating force of an additional determination to be free."[37] It is here that Jacobs's narrative can be seen to subvert the codes of its own discursive form, that is, the codes of sentimental fiction. This was a problematic choice of mode given that it is a style of novel that valorizes the submissive, pious wife and, therefore, implicitly mocks the condition of the slave woman.[38]

Previous critics of *Incidents* argued that its subversive power is undercut by its adherence to the formal mode of sentimental fiction. This form was dictated in part by Jacobs's audience, the white northern abolitionist women to whose sympathies she wished to appeal, and the narrative voice makes persistent pleas for understanding regarding her compromised femininity and violation of decorum. But, as Carby and others argue, Jacobs in fact subverts that mode in several ways: the logic of her actions is that the sentimental fictional code "death, as preferable to loss of purity" is replaced by "death is better than slavery," or, alternatively, it is better to be free even if that means sexual compromise,[39] thus rejecting the mythicization of death in relation to femininity. Furthermore, in being rejected by her lover, she does not represent herself as a "cast-off lovesick mistress, but as an outraged loving mother" because of his failure to emancipate her children.[40] There is an echo here of Morrison's comment about the source for her own narrative. She says that Margaret Garner, on whom Sethe is based, "did not do what Medea did and kill her children because of some guy": "It was for me this classic example for a person determined to be responsible."[41]

Yellin concludes her evaluation of the importance of Jacobs's narrative by arguing that its very conflicted quality, the tension between its conventional form and its unconventional content, between its "heroic-tale" and "confession," neither of which quite fit the style of sentimental fiction, only serves to underscore Jacobs's struggle to find a new mode, a new language even, which could adequately inscribe her perspective of the slave mother resisting that enslavement. "These formal problems suggest that new forms were needed, new language, new structures, new characters, new narrative voices, if literature was to express the fullness of Jacobs' new point of view and her new content."[42] It would seem that it has taken over a hundred years for that particular story of motherhood in slavery to be reformulated so that the subjectivity of the slave mother can be inscribed without the formal or ideological constraints that bound the slave woman writer herself: that reformation can be read in Williams's *Dessa Rose* and most especially in Morrison's *Beloved*.

Finally, at the core of Jacobs's text is another echo of *Beloved*. In a chapter entitled "The Confession" the mother/narrator, Linda Brent, confesses her sexual sins to her daughter and begs her forgiveness. Yellin points out that this confession and the daughter's loving acceptance of it provide a dramatic resolution in the plot but that, nevertheless, the narrative voice continues to be caught in a contradiction between endorsing the sexual conventions of her time and the insistence that slave women cannot be judged by them.[43] At the heart of *Beloved*, also, the mother confesses to the daughter and pleads for her forgiveness and understanding, a plea, however, which cannot be acknowledged. The two dialogues between slave mother and daughter cannot be read exactly as parallels. Nevertheless, they both underscore the way in which the slave woman's roles as both mother and resister to slavery are caught up in a particular contradiction that involves the mother-daughter relationship. That is to say, the gender kinship between mother and daughter provides the mother with a fundamental motive for resistance, that is, to prevent the daughter from being subjected to her own fate, the commodification of her female body, either as a concubine to a slave master or as object of sale, a brood mare purchased to produce human capital. That very act of resistance, however, seems inevitably to involve a sacrifice that may not only sever the bonds between the mother and daughter but which may bind them to the past they were trying to escape. Jacobs's text makes clear that, as writers, slave women were attempting to break through the discursive limits that bound their subjectivity within a white, male, European ideological framework, whether that involved a distaste for slavery or not. It also makes clear that any rupture of those discursive binds would expose the ways in which a confrontation with an ethics of motherhood was woven into the history of slave women's subjectivity.

Morrison's exploration of the interior life of a slave mother breaks down the discursive limits evident in the female slave autobiography through a reencoding of the black maternal body, undoing the violent inscription of that body within the rhetoric of slavery. Her story of maternal love and responsibility, and of its awesome price, is encoded in the milk of the mother's breasts and her baby daughter's blood, both material substance and symbol of the love and violence that bespeak the impossible contradiction of motherhood under slavery, a contradiction exemplified by the figure of the other baby, Denver, who, suckling at her mother's breast, drank in the milk along with her just killed sister's blood. With the stories of these bodily fluids, metonyms for the connection between mother and child which slavery tried to sunder, Morrison creates a subjective language of the experience of enslavement which not only expresses the unspoken of the slave autobiographies but also counters the reductive metonymies of slavery which divided the female body into its productive and reproductive parts, each representative of the means to create the master's surplus capital. Sethe's story of milk and blood writes out the inscription in the slave owner's book–written, with painful irony, in the ink she made with her own hands–which divided her body into its animal and human characteristics. To equate writing with bodily fluids, especially those associated with the maternal body, is to appear to suggest that Morrison is employing a maternal metaphor to symbolize her writing practice along the lines of the French feminists' *écriture feminine*. I am not arguing, however, that Morrison as a woman writer "writes her body" in any Cixousian sense nor that her writing on motherhood comes out of or produces some fetishized metaphor of maternal *jouissance* or plenitude.[44] Rather, her language of the maternal body acknowledges motherhood as both a place of social inscription and also of internal division.

I wish to suggest that the text functions on an axis that is simultaneously metaphoric and metonymic. Recent literary criticism has picked up on the challenges put forward by both Jacques Derrida and Paul de Man to the Western tradition of privileging metaphor over metonymy as the trope "revealing unexpected truth."[45] Domna Stanton, for instance, has critiqued the maternal metaphors in the feminist texts of Julia Kristeva, Hélène Cixous, and Luce Irigaray, suggesting that the totalizing tendency of this metaphorization could be replaced by exploring the maternal via metonymy, which, because of its associations with contiguity, is context bound and therefore exposes specific cultural values, prejudices, and limitations.[46] Homi Bhabha also argues that metonymy is a preferable trope through which to read postcolonial literatures because, unlike metaphor, which tends to universalize and thus to ignore cultural specificity, metonymy can be employed to symptomatize the social, cultural, and political forces that traverse those texts.[47]

I believe, however, that *Beloved* is a text that privileges neither the one nor the other but, rather, reveals an interrelation of both these tropes. Morrison creates a subjective language of enslavement which articulates the metonymic relation between the bodies of mothers and daughters which the institution of slavery would deny. Her text, however, does not simply rest with the reversal of a rhetorical trope, and it does not settle for a privileging of the reconnection of mother and daughter in the history of slavery but, instead, echoes out into the stories of all slaves, male as well as female. By focusing her narrative of slavery on motherhood, she is able to delineate the particular interrelation between maternity and the history of African Americans and to undo the stereotypical mythologizing of black women's identities. At the same time the struggles of her protagonists to find a way to speak about their past, and thus to confront its horror, function metaphorically to suggest the historical dilemma of African Americans of finding a means to write their own history outside the rhetoric and disenabling mythologies of the hegemonic culture.

Beloved is a story that revolves around contradiction: a story of an infanticide motivated by the mother's fierce love, a story that is itself about a preoccupation with storytelling. Moreover, it is not just one story but many, involving the personal histories of the protagonists, which, in the telling, become representative of the history and culture of the tribe, stories that bind the group together but which also have a violent potential to destroy those bonds. These contradictions are textually embodied in the figure of the baby Denver, who takes in her mother's milk along with her sister's blood. An analogy between feeding and storytelling is drawn repeatedly throughout the narrative, suggesting that the culture's history and the myths created out of it are its sustenance, its means of survival, especially since that history is constantly under threat of erasure.

Out of these many stories I want to focus on three that are bound into one. They are all the mother's story, but two of them are also the daughters': there is the story of Sethe's life at Sweet Home, the fragile creation of the small slave community of one woman and five men, and its catastrophic conclusion; then there is the story of the escape, which is also the story of Denver's birth, and Sethe's frantic journey to get her breast milk to the older baby, Beloved; finally, there is the story of Beloved's death and the mystery of her return, the fearful, locked-away story around which the narrative circles and which Paul D's return releases. But this is also ultimately the story of Denver's survival. Each story unfolds in fragments of narration, picked up by different narrative voices, a sign that each is too painful to be delivered whole, as Sethe puts it, "like a tender place in a corner of her mouth that the bit left" (58), but also emblematic of the fractured nature of that past.

The second story, Sethe's escape and Denver's birth, is the first to be spoken of, as Sethe relates it to Paul D while she rolls out dough for bread: "I was pregnant with Denver but I had milk for my baby girl. . . . All I knew was I had to get my milk to my baby girl. Nobody was going to nurse her like me" (16). But it is also Denver's story, the friendly, magical story of her birth, of the white woman, Amy Denver, who helped her fugitive mother in labor and whom she was named after. It is the story her imagination is ever hungry for: "Denver hated the stories her mother told that did not concern herself, which is why Amy was all she ever asked about. The rest was a gleaming, powerful world made more so by Denver's absence from it" (62). The gleaming powerful world consists, in fact, of the other two stories that frame this one, the story that precedes it, the violent ending of Sweet Home life, and the one that followed it, the killing of Beloved, the story that Denver literally turns deaf to when she first hears it.

If the story of escape and birth is the one around which Denver exclusively binds her identity, it is also the story she uses to bind to herself the miraculously returned sister, Beloved: "She swallowed twice to prepare for the telling, to construct out of the strings she had heard all her life a net to hold Beloved" (76). As she responds to Beloved's plea to "tell me how Sethe made you in the boat," the naive metaphor of making the child is echoed in the way the story is molded by Denver's telling and Beloved's listening:

> Denver was seeing it now and feeling it – through Beloved.
> Feeling how it must have felt to her mother. Seeing how it
> must have looked. . . . She anticipated the questions by giving
> blood to the scraps her mother and grandmother had told her –
> and a heartbeat. The monologue became, in fact, a duet as they
> lay down together, Denver nursing Beloved's interest like a
> lover whose pleasure was to overfeed the loved. . . . Denver
> spoke, and Beloved listened, and the two did the best they
> could to create what really happened, how it really was, some-
> thing only Sethe knew because she alone had the mind for it
> and the time afterward to shape it: the quality of Amy's voice,
> her breath like burning wood. (78)

In recreating the story together, the daughters produce a subjective discourse for the mother as pregnant fugitive; the image of giving life-blood and a heartbeat to the story is the trope whereby that subjectivity is actualized, just as the blood and heartbeat of the unborn baby pumps inside the mother's womb and the milk destined for the other baby seeps from her breasts. The storytelling process mimicked here takes on the resonance of mythmaking. It shifts from a monologue to a duet, from the individual to the communal; it is represented as mythic story in the process of becoming, Denver lovingly embellishing its details as she tells it, continuous, never complete, always capable of repetition and expansion. The mythic quality exists in its meaning as well as in its telling, for it is a heroic story of female liberation from slavery: the mother's death-defying flight is a venture not only to ensure her own survival but also that of the daughter inside her and the one who was sent ahead. And it images the absolute identification of the three, mother and two daughters, an identification figured narratively in the plot and figuratively and literally in the mother's body, one baby inside and nipples seeping milk for the other.

Morrison here, I suspect, defies the limits of empirical history. Deborah Gray White points out that some of the reasons why women were underrepresented among fugitive slaves had to do with childbearing. Runaways were mostly between the ages of sixteen and thirty-five, and most slave women of this age were pregnant, nursing, or had children, and few would leave without them.[48] But the very extraordinariness of Morrison's tale is part of its compelling and mythic power; in combining in one event both the woman slave's fierce desire for freedom and the fierce devotion to her children, she figures something that the historiography has largely been unable to represent.

The significance of the story, however, resonates beyond heroic myth. As the only story of the past Denver wants to hear and as the story of her own birthing, it is synonymous with her identity: she is this story. But it is a story about a moment of transition, between the there of slavery and the here of freedom, between the past and the future. Especially, as I have indicated, it exists between one barely speakable moment of violence and another that is utterly unspeakable. Denver and the mythic story of liberation are locked in by two moments of pain which cannot be purged, because to purge them would be to kill off the only precious thing that remains, the trace of what has been lost, the child returned from the dead. Thus, the heroic myth of liberation can ultimately be seen to entrap, a trap both of history and of personal identity. As the narrative unfolds, it becomes clear that the mother and daughters are locked together in a circular narrative from which the heroic myth is not sufficient to liberate them.

When Denver does ask for more of the story of the past—"You never told me what happened. Just they whipped you and you run off, pregnant. With me"—the answer is: "Nothing to tell except schoolteacher," and Sethe provides a glimpse of life turned sour at Sweet Home after Garner dies and Schoolteacher, the brother-in-law, the small, polite man with book learning takes over. "He liked the ink I made. . . . He preferred how I mixed it and it was important to him because at night he sat down to write in his book" (37). This is the book, she is to discover later, in which he records the "animal" and "human" characteristics of his slaves; it contains the lessons in slave "nature" and "behavior" which he passes on to his nephews. It is the sudden realization of what these lessons signify, for which Garner's "soft" treatment had not prepared them, which prompts Sethe to agree to the escape plan, her recognition of what slavery really meant to the slave owners, that is, the absolute appropriation of the slave, body and mind, which renders him or her inert matter on which the master writes his own script.

It is through this, the story of the ink that Sethe made with her own hands and her discovery of its purpose, that Morrison weaves into her text the problematic relation of the slave to the master's tools: reading and writing and the way that learning was used to inscribe its own economy on the body of the slave mother. Barbara Omolade writes that to the master the slave woman was "a fragmented commodity":

> Her head and her heart were separated from her back and her hands and divided from her womb and vagina. Her back and muscle were pressed into field labor where she was forced to work with men and work like men. Her hands were demanded to nurse and nurture the white man and his family. . . . Her vagina, used for his sexual pleasure, was the gateway to the womb, which was his place of capital investment – the capital investment being the sex act and the resulting child the accumulated surplus, worth money on the slave market.
>
> The totalitarian system of slavery extended itself into the very place that was inviolable and sacred to both African and European societies – the sanctity of the woman's body and motherhood within the institution of marriage.[49]

Morrison represents this dissection of the woman's body both in Schoolteacher's "book of learning" and in the punishment his nephews give Sethe after the first attempt to escape: they milk her like a cow, taking away her baby's milk. Then they whip her on the back while her stomach is placed in a pit to protect the fetus. Jacqueline Jones writes that this punishment was commonly used against pregnant and nursing slave mothers and adds, "Slave women's roles as workers and as childbearers came together in these trenches, these graves for the living, in southern cottonfields."[50] After the whipping Sethe bears on her back a scar so deep and elaborate that it looks like a tree, which ensures that the slave owner's inscription of her identity is not only held in her "rebellious brain," which would not let her forget, but is also carved permanently into her flesh.

In this representation of the maternal body carved up (breasts for milk, back for whipping) and carved into, Morrison figures the reductive metonymy through which the institution of slavery signified slave women. Sethe's own definition of motherhood involves a rejection of that metonymic division and the construction of her own metonymic relation located in a conception of maternal responsibility and connection between the maternal body and the child's body: "The best thing she was, was her children. Whites might dirty *her* all right, but not her best thing, her beautiful, magical best thing – the part of her that was clean. . . . And no one, nobody on this earth, would list her daughter's characteristics on the animal side of the paper" (251). Sethe's maternal subjectivity is figured in this defiant claim to her own definition of motherhood, motherhood being not a state she finds herself subjected to for someone else's economic advantage but, rather, the part of herself which exceeded the bounds of slavery, which refused its limits and thus her own means of self-inscription. The narrative makes clear, however, that this definition of a female self within slavery was not entirely a matter of choice, that is to say, that many slave women did not have the choice. Baby Suggs reminds Sethe that she is lucky even to have any children with her at all: "Be thankful, why don't you? I had eight. Every one of them gone away from me. . . . My first-born. All I can remember of her is how she loved the burned bottom of bread. Can you beat that? Eight children and that's all I remember" (5).

In the community of former slaves there is Ella, the root woman, who spent her puberty locked in a house and shared by a father and son, whom she called "the lowest yet." "Ella had been beaten every way but down. . . . She had delivered, but would not nurse, a hairy white thing, fathered by 'the lowest yet'" (258–59). Ella's rejection of enforced motherhood is echoed in Sethe's faint memory of her own mother's life, a woman she hardly knew, the only sign of recognition she could recall being the brand in her flesh – a woman whose story stretches back to her capture in Africa and the horrors of the Middle Passage and who bore children to the crew on the ship and to other white men but "threw them all away," keeping only Sethe, the child she conceived with a black man. So Ella and Sethe's mother did exercise a choice of sorts, one that provokes in Sethe a wave of anger and shame that she cannot quite comprehend. Thus, Sethe's definition of motherhood is a defiant answer to slavery's brutal destruction of

maternal connection. Maternity is, therefore, not a fixed or naturalized category. Sethe's response is one extreme point in a range of possibilities in which mothering or the rejection of it becomes a register
of female resistance to the condition of enslavement and the commodification of the female body. It is also a radical assertion of the bonds
of the slave family and the bond between the slave mother and the
father.

Despite this radical resistance, however, Sethe is haunted by the
smell of the ink she made out of cherry gum and oak bark; it was the
ink made with her hands which was used in Schoolteacher's book to
place her characteristics "on the animal side of the paper." Somehow
the inscription of that ink cannot be erased but is, instead, engraved
in the memory as well as on the page. This is Sethe's secret shame, her
innocent complicity with the violence of Schoolteacher's letter, his
assumption of the power to name and to brutalize with that naming.

If Sethe's double act of flight and infanticide was her way of renaming herself, not animal but mother, for the other survivors – Paul D,
Baby Suggs, and Stamp Paid – the question of identity and self-naming
remains problematic. For Baby the only name she knows is the
endearment her husband gave her, and she never acquired "the map
to discover what she was like." Stamp Paid, the name he gave himself,
carried within it the sacrifice he had made in allowing his wife to
become the mistress of his master's son, without killing either her or
himself. And Paul D is haunted by his title, "one of the Sweet Home
men," so named by Garner but unnamed and unmanned by Schoolteacher with the bit he put in his mouth: "Was that it? Is that where
the manhood lay? In the naming done by a whiteman who was supposed to know? . . . It was schoolteacher who taught them otherwise.
A truth that waved like a scarecrow in rye: they were only Sweet
Home men at Sweet Home" (125).

But embedded in the stories of two who did not survive Schoolteacher's brutality, Sixo and Halle, there exist alternative responses to
the violence of the slave owner's power to name. Sixo, the wild man,
the Indian, "Indigo with a flame-red tongue," who danced alone at
night among the trees "to keep his bloodlines open," the spiritual connection with his people, is in many respects a male counterpart to
Sethe. Like her, he radically refuses the white man's definitions and
rejects the master's tools; as the man most acutely aware of the white
man's power to brutalize them, he stops speaking English and refuses

to learn the master's numbers because "it would change his mind." But he is also a nurturing man who helps Sethe with her children, cooks potatoes for the other slaves, travels thirty miles overnight to see his woman, and is the one who provides the others with the knowledge of an escape route. Halle embodies a different response, as the one who learns to write and to count. However, he puts the master's knowledge to his own use: he buys his mother's freedom, and his knowledge of the land ensures that his wife and children can escape.

In Halle's acceptance of the learning Garner offers him Morrison's text touches on the debate in literary criticism and historiography concerning the slave community's response to reading and writing. Hazel Carby points out that most contemporary literary critics regard the slave's acquisition of literacy, especially as it is figured in the autobiographical slave narratives "as a means of asserting humanity." But she argues that historians of the WPA interview material suggest a different response to literacy among the slaves. In particular, she cites Arna Bontemps, who edited a collection of these interviews and wrote a historical novel about slavery, *Black Thunder,* in which it is clear that literacy was the slave's path to resistance and revolution and was regarded as such by many.[51] Sixo and Halle represent two possible revolutionary responses to enslavement on the part of the slave man; neither can be read as an assertion of their humanity, as that was never in question. Sixo's resistance is an assertion of his cultural difference and a selfhood marked as cultural (communal) connection; Halle's resistance is a means to find a way out of enslavement. And both, in their different ways, assert the possibility of a future for the enslaved beyond slavery.

The issue for Morrison's survivors is somewhat different. It is not so much whether or how the master's tools can be stolen from him in order to read and write one's way to freedom and self-inscription; rather, it is a question of how to live with a past too terrible to remember, let alone to tell or record. The question that haunts the narrative is, how did the individual and the community of slaves deal with their own history? How, for instance, could they speak of their history without being forced to relive its horror and its indignities (in the case of Paul D), or how was it possible for those who refused that horror to persuade the others to accept the enormous price exacted by that refusal (in Sethe's case)? Paul D's story of the prison farm in Georgia is locked away in the little rusty tin that contains his lost heart; Sethe's story of infanticide, although comprehensible to herself, is locked away in her mind because it is unbearable for everyone else. The danger involved even in telling each other is suggested in Paul D's response when Sethe finally tells him her story; his response threatens to return them to the brutality they had escaped: "'What you did was wrong, Sethe. . . . You got two feet, Sethe, not four,' he said, and right then a forest sprang up between them; trackless and quiet. . . . How fast he had moved from his shame to hers" (165).

The difficulties of approaching Sethe's story of infanticide are replicated textually in Morrison's narration. Although hints of the story are woven through the narrative, it is not fully told until midway into the text, and what is more, it is first approached from the perspective of the slave catchers, Schoolteacher and his nephews, the only moment in the text which is focused from their viewpoint. Thus, the first picture the reader receives of Sethe in the woodshed with the slaughtered baby is presented through the discourse of the slavers. The effect is one of shock, profound disturbance, but it enables the reader to register the distance between their perspective and that of the mother herself. But before Sethe tells the story herself it is filtered through the perspectives of the other witnesses, first Baby Suggs then Stamp Paid, emphasizing again and again the pain involved in its telling. When it is finally told by Sethe she too finds it difficult to express, because she cannot be sure that it will be understood:

> Sethe knew that the circle she was making around the room, him, the subject, would remain one. That she could never close in, pin it down for anybody who had to ask. If they didn't get it right off – she could never explain. Because the truth was simple. . . . Little hummingbirds struck their needle beaks right through her headcloth into her hair and beat their wings. And if she thought anything it was No. No. Nono. Nonono. Simple. She just flew. Collected every bit of life she had made, all the parts of her that were precious and fine and beautiful, and carried, pushed, dragged them through the veil, out, away, over there where no one could hurt them. (163)

Why did Morrison choose this story of infanticide on which to base her novel, one might ask, particularly since the research of historians such as Eugene Genovese and Deborah Gray White seems to show that it was not an especially prevalent phenomenon in slave life? Perhaps that is the point. As the Harriet Jacobs story testifies – that is, both her narrative and the story of its publication – it is the scandalous nature of the slave mother's resistance, its transgression of conventional moralities, which provides the measure of the intolerable contradictions of her position. How could Morrison hope to reproduce in her late-twentieth-century readers that experience of scandal, of shock? But what issue could have more emotional and political resonance in the contemporary United States than a representation of infanticide at a moment when a vociferous debate is raging regarding abortion and the rights of the fetus over those of the mother? In focusing her story of a mother killing her own child, an event still with the power to shock an audience blunted by pervasive representations of violence, Morrison is able to capture the horrific contradiction of the slave mother, a contradiction signified in her maternal body, caught between the image of brood mare (which the nephew's act of milking her and their protection of her unborn baby emphasized) and that of the mother desperately trying to get her milk to her hungry baby. This intolerable contradiction finds its logical consequence in Sethe's appalling act.

It is the return of that story in the ghostly form of Beloved which finally brings all the horror to the surface again and causes it to be spoken of so that it can be confronted. Who or what Beloved signifies, whether she is just the ghost of the dead daughter or represents something more is a question that dwells on the minds of the other protagonists as well as the reader. Discussions of the psychoanalytic implications of the narrative tend to regard the figure of Beloved as the return of Sethe's repressed, which she "must 'conjure up' . . . and confront . . . as an antagonist."[52] Beloved is clearly a cathartic force, a "materialization" of Sethe's memory.[53] However, I would like to offer a variant reading of the text's psychoanalytic implications, since, in my view, to read Beloved as primarily the return of Sethe's repressed somewhat elides the full political significance of Morrison's text and her evocation of the history of black women in general.

To speak of repression is to speak of what is unconscious or unacknowledged, a trace of the past which remains in the present in disguised form. But Sethe has not forgotten either her daughter or the fact that she killed her. Nor are any of the other ex-slaves surprised by Beloved's reappearance, since, as Baby Suggs says, "not a house in the country ain't packed to its rafter with some dead Negro's grief. We lucky this ghost is a baby" (5), suggesting that remembering or acknowledgment is not the problem but, rather, how to forget, how to lay the past to rest, is. Sethe is trapped in the past and cannot go forward. She is locked into what she remembers, not a process of disavowal or unconscious repetition of what she has forgotten. Beloved is not a "detour-return."[54] The bind that entraps Sethe is the contradiction that slavery imposed on a woman who acted out her sense of maternal responsibility to its logical conclusion and who, in the face of slavery's destruction of the mother-child relationship, insisted upon its indissolubility. The daughter's return constitutes the fulfillment of the mother's desire for that unbreachable bond and the re-membering of the maternal body. What separates Sethe from the other ex-slaves and isolates her from them is that she had the mind to commit an act that encompassed the enormity of slavery's contradiction and to take responsibility for it.

The climactic realization of this desire in the text is the epiphanic moment when the three women are skating on a frozen creek: "Holding hands, bracing each other, they swirled over the ice." It is a magical moment of fulfilled desire; the refrain that punctuates the scene, "Nobody saw them falling," suggests the absolute identification of the three, not split into subject or object, gazer or gazed upon, an idealized moment of absolute unity, as fragile as the ice they skate upon.

In the three women's interior monologues that follow Morrison creates a subjective discourse of motherhood, daughterhood, and sisterhood, a discourse that the institution of slavery would ignore or deny. Sethe's monologue is a reverie on the day of her flight and the day of Beloved's death, on the milk her daughter was being deprived of and of Beloved's blood, which she shed. The boundaries between life (milk) and death (blood) are broken down, as are the boundaries between the mother's identity and the daughter's. This fluidity of identity is expressed in Sethe's memory of the baby's face being blotted out by the sun, but it is still a face she recognizes: "When I tell you you mine, I also mean I'm yours. I wouldn't draw breath without my children." Her reverie also constitutes a rebellious rewriting of her own experience as a daughter born into slavery who had hardly tasted her mother's milk and who wouldn't recognize her mother's face.

Denver's monologue expresses not identity with her mother but, rather, with the lost sister returned, who embodies all the losses she has suffered, of the father she never knew and the brothers and grand-mother who left her. In Denver the mother's milk and the daughter's blood come together: "Beloved is my sister. I swallowed her blood right along with my mother's milk." But her monologue also heralds a break in that magic circle of identification. She fears the mother love that can kill and identifies with the father for whom she has waited all her life.

Beloved's monologue reasserts the indivisibility of the mother-child bond from the daughter's perspective: "I am not separate from her there is no place where I stop   her face is my own and I want to be there in the place where her face is" (210). It is a surreal mixture of densely packed allusions, providing a sense of the child in purgatory trying to reach the mother's face, but also there are references that resonate beyond the tragedy of Sethe and Beloved, an amalgam of the experiences of all other slaves who died, stretching back in time to the Middle Passage. The figure of Beloved, therefore, is not only the lost daughter, but she is also all the dead victims of slavery, reaching out to the living, demanding to be remembered. The voices of all those dead gather around the house, "voices that ringed 124 like a noose," merging with those of the three women and providing an ominous warning of the battle to come.

The verbal battle between Sethe and Beloved which follows, a bat-tle for survival, marks the cost of Sethe's radical assertion of her own subjectivity in terms of the absolute identification between mother and daughter. I want to suggest that this battle can be read from a double perspective, simultaneously historical and psychological, which is figured on that metaphoric-metonymic axis I have previously men-tioned. Once Sethe has acknowledged Beloved as the returned daugh-ter, she becomes locked in a cycle of impossible atonement and expia-tion. She embarks on an orgy of giving food, clothes, and games. As Beloved's demands grow with the gifts, the mood of their exchange shifts from pleasure to resentment, and Sethe is caught in an unend-ing bind in which she attempts to explain and justify the killing: "Any-thing she wanted she got, and when Sethe ran out of things to give her, Beloved invented desire." This process of giving and taking is materialized in the women's bodies: the mother begins to starve her-self in order to feed the daughter, so that her body withers, while the daughter "was getting bigger, plumper by the day." Thus, the story that began with the mother's impassioned loving gift of her body to her daughter turns into a story of the daughter voraciously devouring that body; the mother and daughter's desire for the other has grown monstrous, like an incubus feeding on itself.

This situation can be read on a psychoanalytical level, the two locked into an unfinished story, the child's process of separation having been untimely cut off by her death, before she has discovered that, "if it completely devours or controls the other, it can no longer get what it originally wanted."[55] This is a stage in the child's development when she cannot recognize the possibility of the mother's subjectivity independent of itself: "Beloved accused her of leaving her behind. . . . She said they were the same, had the same face, how could she have left her?" (241). Sethe's act has meant the relinquishing of any possible subjectivity outside of that prescribed by the mother-daughter bond. The killing of Beloved was the only means left to her to resist the deathly metonymy inscribed with Schoolteacher's ink, whereby her own and her daughter's bodies existed as merely sites of the production of capital which ensured the survival of slavery. Sethe rewrote that metonymic connection, based on maternal love and connection in the milk she finally got to the daughter and the blood that placed that daughter beyond the slave owner's reach. But in defining those connections as indissoluble – mother/daughter, milk/blood, life/death – the mother and daughter became locked in another kind of bondage, a psychological trap that sets in motion an eternal repetition of the past, an endless reassertion of the necessity of that loving murder.

Sethe's act is also a radical assertion of the inseparability of the personal and the political, emphasizing, I believe, how crucial the parent-child bond is to any reading of slavery, historical or literary. As Morrison suggested in her analysis of Willa Cather's literary evocation of slavery, it is a story that could not be acknowledged so long as Euro-America continues to interpret that past in terms of the slave's subjective dependence on the masters. It seems to me that, in focusing on the mother-daughter relation in particular, Morrison's text focuses on a crucial area of resistance to that inscription of the female body. This is figured in Baby Suggs's words to Denver: "Slaves not supposed to have pleasurable feelings on their own; their bodies not supposed to be like that, but they have to have as many children as they can to please whoever owned them. . . . She said for me not to listen to all that. That I should always listen to my body and love it" (209).

Yet the bondage that Sethe and Beloved become locked into signifies a rejection of any idealization of motherhood.[56] It is a site of
resistance and of subjective expression for the slave woman, but it exposed her to the threat of another form of bondage. The mother cannot speak to the daughter, cannot get her to understand, because the
daughter cannot hear. Beloved is a figure from the past, locked in the
past: "Beloved wasn't interested. She said when she cried there was
no one. That dead men lay on top of her. That she had nothing to eat.
Ghosts without skin stuck their fingers in her and said beloved in the
dark and bitch in the light" (241). Therefore, even in the verbal battle
with Sethe there are echoes in Beloved's curses of other histories,
other torments, beyond those of the dead baby girl. The "ghosts without skin" are presumably white men who fingered her lovingly at
night but with hatred in the day; this is suggestive of the experience
of many slave women, as Barbara Omolade describes it, a split between their daytime and nighttime lives. Of the white slave owner
Omolade writes: "He would never tell how he built a society with the
aid of dark-skinned women, while telling the world he did it alone.
. . . History would become all that men did during the day, but nothing
of what they did during the night."[57]

Denver later acknowledges to Paul D these echoes that reverberate
in the figure of Beloved after she has disappeared:

> "You think she sure 'nough your sister? . . ."
> "At times. At times I think she was—more." (266)

Thus, the battle between mother and daughter figures, metonymically, the complexities of gender identity within slavery and, metaphorically, the difficulties for African Americans both in telling the
story of their past and in releasing themselves from it. If Beloved represents all the dead of the past, then she also represents the threat of
being engulfed by that past. Morrison has created a fiction out of a
fragment of recorded history. In so doing she has also created a myth,
in the sense that it is not just a fiction that attempts to bear witness
to historical event but also a story that embodies a particular historical contradiction, that is to say, the desire and necessity to remember
and honor the past and the dangers of becoming locked in it. The
stories of the two daughters represent a double movement: the story

of Beloved, a pulling back into the past; the story of Denver, a pulling forward into the future.

Michele Wallace has criticized Morrison for "attempting to reverse the terms of interpretation, so that 'myth' or the 'oral tradition' reads 'History,'" which Wallace regards as a mystification of the "grossly unequal" relation between the two. She argues that "the Afro-American literary tradition acquires its present character as the writing down, or the translation, of a predominantly oral or mythic tradition previously sealed off from mainstream white American culture," and suggests that this focus serves to encourage a view of black culture as inadequate compared to a more "scholarly," or historical, Euro-American tradition. This tendency she sees as dangerously underwritten by a current postmodernist criticism, which privileges "myth" in a suspicion of "history" as linear and ideological.[58]

The reading I have offered has attempted to highlight the ways in which *Beloved* resists any such closure within one category or the other. In imaginatively exploring the subjective possibilities of the slave mother, Morrison is telling a story that "history" has been unable to tell. Nevertheless, Morrison has acknowledged her debt to historiography, saying that she was able to write this story only because of the greater information about slavery which has become available through scholarship over the last fifty years. She does not claim that her text provides a privileged discourse on slavery, pointing out that it can be read alongside other kinds of literature on slavery.[59] At the same time, although I have argued that her story assumes the power of myth, it pursues neither a Utopian nor universalizing trajectory, the conventional *telos* of the mythological. On the contrary, it is a tale that speaks of the dangerous power of myth to rigidify meanings and fix identities. If readers of *Beloved* were invited to regard the text as a historical document, albeit in fictional guise, then there would be some justification for Wallace's criticism. Although the temptation to do so may be strong, given the text's rhetorical power, I believe that a careful reading of Morrison's narrative strategy reveals that she is not attempting to reproduce history but, rather, to explore the problems involved in recovering and dealing with history itself. *Beloved*, in other words, is not a reconstruction of historical event so much as a reflection on history itself. Equally, it is about the mythmaking processes always at work in our attempts to recover and reconstruct the past.

It could be argued that the cycle of mother-daughter bonding which threatened its own annihilation was broken by the arrival of the man, Paul D – a patriarchal solution to an excessive female identification. But Morrison's figurations are never so simple. Certainly, it is the father-identified daughter, Denver, who makes the necessary break –"Her father's daughter after all, Denver decided to do the necessary"– but it is her grandmother's words that ring in her ears as she steps outside the yard for the first time in twelve years and sets in motion the process that finally releases them all from Beloved's insatiable demands:

> But you said there was no defense.
> "There ain't."
> Then what do I do?
> "Know it, and go on out the yard. Go on." (244)

In Denver the three stories that I have focused on come together, the stories of the milk, the ink, and the blood. In taking the mother's milk along with the sister's blood as a baby, she consumed both the life-giving nourishment and the act of violence which was the condition for her future as a free woman. She also picks up the story of the ink where her father had left off. In beginning again to learn to read and write, she reasserts her father's dictum: "If you can't count they can cheat you. If you can't read they can beat you." But, further than this, these tools may provide the means for the daughter to deal with the past as well as providing the possibility of a future. Thus, the dilemma surrounding that traditional distinction between orality and literacy in African American writing, for which Wallace's myth-history opposition may be taken as a paradigm, is played out in Morrison's text, not in binary terms but, instead, through a kind of dialogic engagement, the one with the other.

Nevertheless, the violence of the master's word threatens finally to crush Sethe as it did Baby Suggs, her mind unable to erase the ink: "I made the ink, Paul D. He couldn't have done it if I hadn't made the ink." The man who shares the horror of her past, however, promises to put the fragmented parts of her body together, not the maternal body, which is no longer needed, but the body of the woman, Sethe. He offers to bathe her just as Baby Suggs did after the terrible flight and birth of Denver: "Will he do it in sections? First her face, then her hands, her thighs, her feet, her back? Ending with her exhausted breasts? And if he bathes her in sections, will the parts hold?" (272). There is an echo here of the epiphanic moment in *Song of Solomon* when Milkman bathes the woman, Sweet, an image of a healing process for the man. Here in *Beloved* it images a process of healing for both the man and the woman. Putting the fragmented pieces of her body together expresses his acceptance of her history and her "rough solution," her refusal of slavery's inscription. "He wants to put his story next to hers," her story no longer subsumed within his. So it is both the bodies and the stories that are placed together, the man's and the woman's, an acknowledgment of their shared struggle to free themselves from bondage and to write their own stories of the past and the future.

Morrison's mythic story of the slave mother Sethe and her two daughters acknowledges the contradictions inherent in mythmaking itself. The emblematic instance of this in the text is the skating scene, when the mother and two daughters have finally come together in mutual recognition. It is a moment of Utopian unity, of mythic resolution. It can be read as paradigmatic not only of the reassertion of the relation between slave mother and child but also of black political consciousness itself, paradigmatic of the power of myth and cultural identification to mobilize and vitalize political and cultural consciousness. But that moment of idealized unity cannot remain locked in stasis, or in the endless repetition of one story, and will inevitably dissolve into new formations, new histories.

Morrison's evocation of the necessity of recreating and coming to terms with a past both painful and hidden is rendered with searing clarity, yet so too is an understanding that myths of heroism and of suffering ultimately have to be relinquished in order to realize new possibilities. Morrison has created a fiction that holds that opposition between myth and history in delicate tension.

NOTES

I would like to thank Elaine Jordan, Richard Gray, Peter Hulme, Jerry Phillips, and Jonathan White for their help in discussion, comments and criticisms at various stages in the production of this paper.

1. See Chandra Talpade Mohanty's introduction to *Third World Women and the Politics of Feminism*, ed. C. T. Mohanty, A. Russo, and L. Torres (Bloomington: Indiana Univ. Press, 1991), for a lucid discussion of the necessary inclusion of

"minority peoples or people of color in the U.S.A." in definitions of the Third World.

2. Paul Gilroy, "Living Memory: Toni Morrison Talks to Paul Gilroy," in *City Limits* (31 March–7 April 1988): 10.

3. In interview with Margaret Busby, Bandung File, 25 July 1989, TV channel 4.

4. I borrow this term from Gayatri Spivak, who uses it to refer to the way "metropolitan countries discriminate against disenfranchised groups in their midst" in order to distinguish the histories of these groups from other histories of postcoloniality (Gayatri Chakravorty Spivak, "Who Claims Alterity?" in *Remaking History*, ed. Barbara Kruger and Phil Mariani, DIA Art Foundation Discussions in Contemporary Culture no. 4 [Seattle: Bay Press, 1989], 274). Michele Wallace has applied Spivak's term to African American culture, which, she says, as a "product of 'internal colonization,' constitutes an important variation on postcolonial discourse" (*Invisibility Blues: From Pop to Theory* [London: Verso, 1990], 2).

5. See Jerry Phillips's essay "Educating the Savages: Melville, Bloom and the Rhetoric of Imperialist Instruction," in the present volume, for a discussion of this issue.

6. Bill Ashcroft, Gareth Griffiths, and Helen Tiffin, *The Empire Writes Back: Theory and Practice in Post-Colonial Literatures* (London: Routledge, 1989), 175.

7. Sherley Anne Williams, *Dessa Rose* (London: Macmillan, 1987), 5.

8. Information about the case of Margaret Garner, on whom the figure of Sethe is based, is recorded in Gerda Lerner's *Black Women in White America: A Documentary History* (New York: Pantheon Books, 1972), 60–63.

9. Hazel V. Carby, "Ideologies of Black Folk: The Historical Novel of Slavery," in *Slavery and the Literary Imagination*, ed. D. E. McDowell and A. Rampersad (Baltimore: Johns Hopkins Univ. Press, 1987), 143.

10. Ibid., 139.

11. I am indebted here to Peter Hulme's discussion of George Lamming's exploration of this problem in his essay "The Profit of Language: George Lamming and the Postcolonial Novel," in this volume.

12. The historian Eric Foner, who specializes in the history of the Reconstruction period, takes a critical distance from Morrison's representation of the lives of recently emancipated slaves. He writes: "Nothing that Morrison relates is 'untrue,' but she offers the reader no hint of the remarkable achievements of blacks in the *public* world in these years, of how the former slaves' quest for individual and community autonomy and for equal rights as citizens of the American republic helped to shape the nation's political agenda, and helped them leave behind the legacy, although not the memory, of slavery" ("The Canon and American History," *Michigan Quarterly Review* 28, no. 1 [1989]: 48–49). Conceding that *Beloved* is set in Cincinnati, close to Kentucky, where the situation for ex-slaves was particularly bad and Klan violence rampant, Foner claims this was not typical of the South. He argues also that Morrison's depiction of the legacy of slavery, dwelling "more on disruption and degradation than resiliency and creativity," stems from her fear that the horror at slavery has become blunted in the wake of recent historical research which has

endeavored to refute Stanley Elkins's thesis of the total subjection of slaves to their condition of servitude. The distinction Foner makes between "legacy" and "memory" in the quotation above, however, is more significant with regard to Morrison's text than he allows. I read *Beloved* less as a reconstruction of history than as a symbolic evocation of the burden of memory, of how to deal with the past on a subjective level that is both individual and communal. In not attending to that distinction in his argument Foner fails to "read" the modes of resistance, resiliency, *and* creativity which Morrison delineates, that is, in terms of psychological reconstruction. *Beloved* suggests how the psychological effects of the past may live on long after the actual conditions of oppression have passed. Foner's comments about the text fail to acknowledge any distinction between history and fiction.

13. In particular, the work of the historians Deborah Gray White and Jacqueline Jones and of the cultural and literary critics bell hooks, Hazel V. Carby, Mary Helen Washington, Jean Fagin Yellin, and Valerie Smith.

14. Deborah Gray White, *Ar'n't I a Woman?: Female Slaves in the Plantation South* (New York: W. W. Norton, 1985), 22.

15. Ibid., 23.

16. Ibid., 22.

17. Angela Davis, "Reflections on the Black Woman's Role in the Community of Slaves," in *Black Scholar* (December 1971): 4; Hazel Carby, *Reconstructing Womanhood: The Emergence of the Afro-American Woman Novelist* (Oxford: Oxford Univ. Press, 1987), 20.

18. Davis, "Reflections," 4. That such views have maintained currency twenty years on was highlighted by the 1986 CBS documentary by Bill Moyers, "The Vanishing Black Family: Crisis in Black America," which reiterated Moynihan's scapegoating of the black family by regarding the crisis in black communities in metropolitan centers in the United States as the result of an apparent disintegration of black family life, a failure on the part of African American men and women to be adequate parents to their children. In the words of one contributor to an issue of the *Nation* devoted to this question, the emphasis of Moyer's report seemed to be that "racism is no longer the problem, self-destructiveness is" (J. H. Gresham, *Nation*, 249, no. 4 [1989]: 118-19).

19. Carby, *Reconstructing Womanhood*, 22.

20. Ibid.

21. White, *Ar'n't I a Woman?* 68.

22. Ibid., 56.

23. Ibid., 61.

24. Davis, "Reflections," 5.

25. White, *Ar'n't I a Woman?* 49.

26. Joyce Ladner, "Racism and Tradition: Black Womanhood in Historical Perspective," in *The Black Woman Cross-Culturally*, ed. F. C. Steady (Cambridge, Mass.: Schenkman, 1981), 273.

27. Charles T. Davis and Henry Louis Gates, Jr., eds., *The Slave's Narrative* (Oxford: Oxford Univ. Press, 1985), xvi.

28. Ibid., xxvii.

29. Carby, *Reconstructing Womanhood,* 61.

30. Jean Fagin Yellin, "Text and Contexts of Harriet Jacobs' *Incidents in the Life of a Slave Girl: Written by Herself,"* in Davis and Gates, *Slave's Narrative,* 263.

31. Mary Helen Washington, ed., *Invented Lives: Narratives of Black Women, 1860–1960* (London: Virago, 1989), 7.

32. Carby, quoted in ibid.

33. Jacobs, quoted in Yellin, "Text and Contexts," 269.

34. Valerie Smith, *Self-Discovery and Authority in Afro-American Narrative* (Cambridge: Harvard Univ. Press, 1987), 34.

35. Washington, *Invented Lives,* 4.

36. Carby, *Reconstructing Womanhood,* 36.

37. Ibid., 59.

38. Washington, *Invented Lives,* 5.

39. Smith, *Self-Discovery and Authority,* 43; Carby, *Reconstructing Womanhood,* 59.

40. Yellin, "Text and Contexts," 274.

41. Gilroy, "Toni Morrison Talks to Paul Gilroy," 11.

42. Yellin, "Text and Contexts," 277.

43. Ibid., 272.

44. Although the following discussion of the inscription and counterinscription of the body of the slave mother bears some echoes of the use of maternal metaphors to describe women's writing in the work of Hélène Cixous and Luce Irigaray, it would be misleading, I believe, to assume any equivalence between that particular theory and Morrison's textual practice. While acknowledging the enabling potential of such metaphorization for women, I read Morrison's text as resisting any totalizing or universalizing model of the maternal. See my response below to Mae G. Henderson's claim that within the text the maternal as metaphor becomes "a primary metaphor of history and culture."

45. Ashcroft, Griffiths, and Tiffin, *Empire Writes Back,* 51.

46. Domna C. Stanton, "Difference on Trial: A Critique of the Maternal Metaphor in Cixous, Irigaray, and Kristeva," in *The Poetics of Gender,* ed. Nancy K. Miller (New York: Columbia Univ. Press, 1986), 175.

47. Bhabha, summarized in Ashcroft, Griffiths and Tiffin, *Empire Writes Back,* 52.

48. White, *Ar'n't I a Woman?* 70.

49. Barbara Omolade, "Hearts of Darkness," in *Desire: the Politics of Sexuality,* ed. A. Snitow, C. Stansell, and S. Thompson (London: Virago, 1984), 365.

50. Jacqueline Jones, *Labor of Love, Labor of Sorrow: Black Women, Work, and the Family from Slavery to the Present* (New York: Basic Books, 1985), 20.

51. Carby, "Ideologies of Black Folk," 137–38.

52. Mae G. Henderson, "Toni Morrison's *Beloved:* Re-membering the Body as Historical Text," in *Comparative American Identities: Race, Sex and Nationality in the Modern Text,* ed. Hortense J. Spillers (New York: Routledge, 1991), 74.

53. Ibid., 73.

54. Ibid., 74.

55. Jessica Benjamin, "Master and Slave: The Fantasy of Erotic Domination," in Snitow, Stansell, and Thompson, *Desire,* 296. Benjamin's argument is made within the context of object relations psychoanalytic theory. Her point that a

very young child has no conception of the mother as an autonomous being with needs of her own is redolent of the relationship between Sethe and Beloved.

56. Mae Henderson argues that Morrison's representation of "maternal delivery . . . becomes a means of 'deliverance' from the dominant conception of history as a white/paternal metaphor" ("Toni Morrison's *Beloved,*" 76). While I would not disagree with this, it seems to me that Morrison's text does not conclude with this maternal metaphor "as a primary metaphor of history and human culture." Rather, I regard the text's closing scenes as provoking questions about the dangers of such all-embracing metaphors; Morrison implicitly challenges the very process of remythologizing which she has engaged in.

57. Omolade, "Hearts of Darkness," 374–75.

58. Wallace, *Invisibility Blues,* 243–44.

59. Bandung File (see n. 3).

3   V. S. Naipaul and the
Postcolonial Order

Reading *In a Free State*

Dennis Walder

In September 1960 V. S. Naipaul returned to his home country, Trinidad, after ten years in England. He was on a visit funded by the Trinidadian government. While he was there, the premier, Eric Williams, a historian, proposed that he should write a nonfiction book about the Caribbean. The twenty-eight-year-old novelist was already widely known as an author, with two novels and a collection of short stories behind him. He had just completed what was to become a "classic," and his most popular work, *A House for Mr Biswas* (1961), a richly humorous, semiautobiographical account of the impact of change upon an enclosed, traditional Indian family from rural Trinidad – his own background. For all the enjoyment of its subject, however, and the accuracy of its account of this particular Caribbean subculture, *Biswas* revealed a level of irony and disillusion which might have warned its Caribbean audience, at least, of what was to come. But *The Middle Passage* (1962), Naipaul's "impressions" of five colonial countries in the West Indies and South America, shocked and dismayed West Indians at home and abroad for its acid dismissal of Caribbean culture, history, and society. Even more upsetting was the enthusiastic reception it received from English and American critics, who praised its critical detachment and descriptive power.

This highlights the main problem involved in approaching Naipaul's writing. He is unquestionably the best-known and most prolific

Anglophone writer of the Caribbean, with some twenty books, innumerable articles, and most of the major English literary awards (and a knighthood) behind him. Far from making him a cultural hero, however, the nature and impact of his work have been such as to make him among the most problematic, if not actually disliked, of Caribbean authors. A. Sivanandan says: "I never liked Naipaul. I could never read him without a sense of self-betrayal, I could not enter into his stories without being turned off from myself. . . . I was just beginning to come out of the self-hate that colonialism had implanted in me when I first encountered Naipaul – a fellow colonial who knew my condition better than I did, described it with a fine and acute understanding, and then delivered me up to my subjugation in the pursuit of his own deliverance."[1]

It is more than just a question of Naipaul's criticism of postindependence Caribbean society, of a Third World writer attacking his own home. Chinua Achebe has become increasingly critical of postindependence Nigeria, for example, in *Anthills of the Savannah* (1987); so, too, has Wole Soyinka, whose work since *Madmen and Specialists* (1971) has spared nobody in its attack upon his self-seeking, warmongering compatriots. Yet their writings also express a powerful and intimate sense of belonging to specific, living cultures, as their use of traditional Igbo and Yoruba ritual, legend, and myth suggests. And their voices are recognized, listened to, as such. Is it that the Caribbean writer has lost even these surviving, alternative traditions, to oppose or transform the colonial inheritance? As the Trinidadian historian, the late C. L. R. James, pointed out: "The West Indies has never been a traditional colonial territory with clearly distinguished economic and political relations between two different cultures. Native culture there was none. The Aboriginal Amerindian civilization had been destroyed. Every succeeding year, therefore, saw, the labouring population, slave or free, incorporating into itself more and more of the language, customs, aims and outlook of its masters."[2] Transplanted, enslaved, or indentured, those brought in to replace the massacred original inhabitants of the West Indies have lost their customs and languages, their cultures, and so they cannot be expected to express more than the inevitable alienation and despair consequent upon that loss – or so the argument might run. But, as anyone can see from the writings of Derek Walcott or Grace Nichols, it is perfectly possible for Caribbean voices to establish, even celebrate, their own past and multitudinous traditions, and this is as true for writers based in the West Indies as it is for those who have gone abroad. How, then, to approach a Caribbean voice that sums up the history of the Caribbean thus: "Nothing was created in the West Indies" (*Middle Passage,* 29)?

Criticism of Naipaul is apparent from the beginning of his career. Thirty years before Sivanandan, George Lamming observed in *The Pleasures of Exile:* "His books can't move beyond castrated satire; and although satire may be a useful element in fiction, no important work . . . can rest safely on satire alone. When such a writer is a colonial, ashamed of his cultural background and striving like mad to prove himself through promotion to the peaks of a 'superior' culture whose values are gravely in doubt, then satire is for me nothing more than a refuge. And it is too small a refuge for a writer who wishes to be taken seriously."[3] Lamming, himself from Barbados, places "superior" in scare quotes to emphasize that this borrowed superiority comes from a culture whose values are "gravely in doubt." His is clearly a postcolonial perspective. And it continues to frame the predominant response to Naipaul's work, right up to the present, from those who perceive themselves to be outside the Anglo-American, metropolitan centers of power.

Our own responses will depend upon our own contexts, by which I mean that our own situation, history, and ideology must inevitably come into play here. Arguably, this is always the case. But Naipaul's writings push us toward becoming *more* aware of our contexts; they push us sharply and disturbingly toward an acknowledgment of our position as readers caught up in one way or another, according to different orders of perception, by the networks of power in the postcolonial dispensation. And, I want to argue, that is the most important reason why we should attend to his voice.

Lamming's remarks were made in response to Naipaul's first two novels, *The Mystic Masseur* (1957) and *The Suffrage of Elvira* (1958). Both works took a comic but jaundiced look at the operation of British-style democratic processes in the Caribbean, a view that coincided with nationalist fervor and rising expectations in the West Indies and among West Indians (such as Lamming) abroad. The focus of these first two novels was upon the rural Indian community, their aim to show up the squalid corruption and trickery of postwar politics in Trinidad, or Elvira, as it is called. "Democracy had come to Elvira four years before, in 1946," the narrator coolly observes, "but it had taken nearly everybody by surprise and it wasn't until 1950, a few months before the second general election under universal adult franchise, that people began to see the possibilities" (*Suffrage*, 12). These "possibilities" turn out to be the making of money and power.

When Naipaul returned to the Caribbean and wrote *The Middle Passage* the interests and themes of his preceding fiction were picked up and sharpened – this was to become a characteristic procedure – even, as John Thieme has pointed out,[4] to the extent of repeating some of the same phrases: "Nationalism was impossible in Trinidad. In the colonial society every man had to be for himself; every man had to grasp whatever dignity and power he was allowed; he owed no loyalty to the island and scarcely any to his group. To understand this is to understand the squalor of the politics that came to Trinidad in 1946 when, after no popular agitation, universal adult suffrage was declared. The privilege took the population by surprise. Old attitudes persisted" (*Middle Passage*, 78). This characteristically generalizing, cynical, and sarcastic note is what most offended those who, like Lamming, felt part of the rising nationalist movement of the postwar period and whose own writings contributed to it. It is as if Naipaul was stuck within what Frantz Fanon called the first stage of interaction between the metropolitan and colonial cultures: successfully assimilating European modes of expression but not going on to assert an identity, much less becoming Fanon's revolutionary "awakener of the people."[5]

Things are not quite so simple, however. If we count Derek Walcott as a major voice from the Caribbean, that means admitting the legitimacy of satire, since one of the many accents of that voice is satire – a kind of satire which characteristically fuses the learned, literary, high-cultural European tradition and the popular, oral forms of the Caribbean. One of the best examples of this is "The Spoiler's Return" (1981), in which Walcott uses the persona of a famous Trinidadian calypsonian from the 1940s and 1950s, Theophilus Phillip, or the "Mighty Spoiler," for a witty exploration of how the Caribbean might appear if the Spoiler were to return. What he finds to begin with is that "nothing ain't change but color and attire," and the old round of exploitation seems to be continuing as before. So, he muses:

> I see these islands and I feel to bawl,
> "area of darkness" with V. S. Nightfall.[6]

An Area of Darkness (1964) is the title of a book Naipaul went on to write about his first visit to his grandfather's homeland, India, an "area of darkness" to him as a child growing up in rural Trinidad and later the focus of his often bitter criticism. The phrase is adapted by Walcott to suggest the dark and gloomy, not to say apocalyptic, pronouncements on Caribbean society and culture for which Naipaul soon became so well known at home and abroad. But for Walcott (in the Spoiler's words), "this ain't the Dark Age, is just Trinidad."

In the end Walcott celebrates his place, his complex inheritance. His satire is critical, subversive, but it allows for something positive too: for acceptance. And so he distances himself from Naipaul. Whatever Caribbean writers may think of Naipaul, however, his is a voice they cannot ignore. This is why, for example, the Caribbean critic Selwyn Cudjoe—who has no doubts about Naipaul's limitations, his prejudices, arrogance, reactionary politics, and so on—nevertheless insists that, "like it or not, Naipaul's work represents an important postcolonial impulse/response that begs to be understood and interpreted." Indeed, it does. According to Cudjoe, Naipaul's position, or "problematic," has remained the same: "Who or what am I in this colonial world?" And yet, argues Cudjoe, the meaning of his work is never "given"; it must be "progressively discovered."[7] The point is that, while Naipaul's specific Trinidadian origins have indelibly marked his work, Trinidad has been overtaken by India, Africa, South America, Iran, Pakistan—and England and North America. That is to say, by a larger, international context: the context of the *postcolonial* world. This context is proposed by one of Naipaul's books above all, the book I wish to consider in some detail here: *In a Free State*.

Edward Said suggests that earlier writers such as Yeats, Fanon, and Achebe, whose work marks the "first moment of resistance to imperialism," a moment culminating in the birth of new states throughout the world, did not engage with the achievement of "moral hegemony" by the "new political order" that comes *after* decolonization and which leaves us with at least "part of the difficulty we live with today in Ireland, Asia, Africa, the Caribbean, Latin America and the Middle East."[8] But Naipaul's *In a Free State,* ranging worldwide in its account of decolonization, retrieving the varied pasts of empire as it anticipates the future, does engage with the new order of our times. Who or what am I in this *postcolonial* world? That is its central concern. The result may not make anyone feel very cheerful—although *In a*

Free State is not without a mordant, ironic humor. But it does provide a resonant, challenging perspective upon the fundamental issues of postcolonial writing: identity, history, cultural conflict and assimilation, exile, language.

In a Free State is postcolonial because the book takes as its starting-point the end of empire and raises the question of what kind of freedom the departure of the colonizer has left, a question with implications for the First World as well as the Third, the past as well as the present. What is Naipaul's answer to this question? It isn't easy to say, even after you have read the book. Before you begin there are the ambiguities of the title, in which *state* may refer to a political entity or a psychological condition, or both. And this is only one of a series of puzzling ambiguities that confront the reader.

The moment you open the first few pages of *In a Free State* it becomes clear that here is a kind of "new writing," a voice, which is different. This is particularly clear if you recall the opening of such classic, originating texts of the new writings as *Things Fall Apart,* in which we were brought into an immediate, intimate relationship with a traditional, precolonial African clan, by means of Achebe's authoritative and yet sympathetic, unpatronizing narratorial voice. Even before the opening words of *In a Free State* something unexpected occurs: in place of the usual chapter number or title, or even simple blank above the prose, what we have is *"Prologue, from a Journal,"* followed by a title. And, if the reader turns the page back, she or he finds that the contents list is also unusual, with, instead of chapter, several headings, the first and last of which, the prologue and epilogue, are distinguished from the rest by being italicized. So the prologue and epilogue provide some sort of frame for the three headings between them: a frame that, it is implied, is different in quality or importance from the intermediate material and yet part of it. We might well expect *journal* to signify a factual personal account of someone's travels, common enough in colonial discourse. But what do we then get? A title: "The Tramp at Piraeus," followed by fourteen pages of narrative.

A moment's reflection on "The Tramp at Piraeus" reveals that this is a journal only in the attenuated sense of having a first-person narrator recounting an incident witnessed during his travels. The tramp in question is an eccentric, frail, and elderly Englishman traveling alone on a crowded steamer during a two-day journey from Piraeus to

Alexandria. He arouses the fascination but also the anger of several of the other passengers. Some unspecified overnight misdemeanor leads the three men sharing his cabin to gang up on, tease, and provoke him, until "the game" and the trip come to an end. All this is observed by one of the other passengers, a fascinated yet detached observer. The originating voice is first person, from within the narrative, but the perspective is authoritative, unparticipatory, almost but not quite omniscient. The basic story, the *histoire*, is familiar within Western cultural parameters, from Sebastian Brandt's fifteenth-century satire *Narrenschiff* to Katherine Ann Porter's *Ship of Fools* (1962): it is about the temporary relationships between people thrown together – from different parts of the world or belonging to different cultures and races – while on board ship, and, like them, it exposes the corruption of power. Taking a cue from the book's title leads us a step further: all the characters are in some sense "free": free of their countries, their roots, even simply their usual securities.

Although we might well have expected a prologue to address us directly, and although the journal-narrator uses the first-person pronoun, what we have is an event witnessed and a major theme established: what it means to be free, in different but related senses of the word. Free to return to a place, like the refugees, free to travel, like the businessmen and tourists, free to speak your mind and to behave eccentrically, like the Englishman – except that he isn't really free, since he ends up locking himself in his cabin to avoid his three persecutors. This prompts the question: are the freedoms of the characters compromised in some way? If so, is this compromise a matter of individual states of mind or history or politics? Or all of these? There are specific verbal echoes of the book's title running through the prologue. These help alert us to its function of introducing the book's themes. The fourth paragraph is the most explicit. The bulk of the passengers on the overcrowded little steamer "were Egyptian Greeks. They were travelling to Egypt, but Egypt was no longer their home. They had been expelled; they were refugees. The invaders had left Egypt; after many humiliations Egypt was free; and these Greeks, the poor ones, who by simple skills had made themselves only just less poor than Egyptians, were the casualties of that freedom" (7-8).

Who are, or rather were, "the invaders"? The British, of course: this was published less than two decades after the Suez crisis (a clearer signal of the end of direct imperial power than the independence of

India in 1947). We quickly realize that it is typical of the narrator's economic, elliptical, and indirect manner to adopt for the moment the term that those he is talking about would have used; this is part of what gives the narration its omniscient feel, although it is in the first person. To the Egyptians the British colonizers were the invaders, who humiliated them – doubly so, by going on to try and control the country after having granted it formal independence. Using the generalized term *invaders* has a further resonance: it serves to remind us that this is a country that like others in the region (such as Iraq), has seen other invaders, other empires: the French before the British and the Turks before them. Hence, "many humiliations."

And yet in the decolonized, free Egypt not everyone has become free. Certainly not the Greek workers, who were forced to flee, "the casualties of that freedom," and who are now returning – with what hope? The phrase describing them as the casualties of that freedom is crucial because of the clear implication that freedom has its losers as well as its winners and because it highlights the fact that the whole of the opening narrative has to do with the losses rather than the gains of freedom. This is even the case for the former rulers. British power as it is represented here, in the form of the tramp, is not just on the wane; it is in pathetic tatters. It is striking, and anticipates the structure and method of the entire book, that the different casualties of freedom are in different subject positions and are represented in different ways. Nor are we drawn into the same level or quality of sympathy for them. The tramp is individualized as a character, which helps gain more sympathetic attention for him, whereas the refugees below deck are quite another matter. We return to them as they are about to reenter Egypt. They are described coming up from the lower deck, with the "slack bodies and bad skins of people who ate too many carbohydrates. Their blotched faces were immobile, distant, but full of a fierce, foolish cunning. They were watching" (19). The description is hardly sympathetic; on the contrary, it stereotypes the refugees as an anonymous, barely human, and frightening "other." Yet – and we will come back to his strategy again later, when considering Naipaul's "racism"– the little detail about their diet makes for at least an ambiguous response, since we aren't allowed simply to dislike them but are made to realize simultaneously that there is a reason why they may appear repellent to an observer on the upper deck. This observer has described himself as being unwilling, even fearful, of "being involved" with what he sees going on around him (12), which undermines his position a little too. Is he, then, also some kind of casualty?

What I'm trying to suggest is twofold: that the reader's response toward and understanding of what's going on here relies upon discovering some quite subtle detail in the narration; and that, since this is all within the prologue, it must anticipate what is to follow, in the main body of the book. Further, if we recall that, according to the contents list, there is an epilogue, also *"from a Journal,"* we would expect the concluding part of the book to have some kind of relationship with this part. As it happens, the epilogue also concerns the narrator arriving in Egypt (although from Italy, not Greece). In both instances, therefore, he is traveling from what used to be a peak of European culture (he notices the liner *Leonardo da Vinci* as their ship leaves Piraeus) to the source of a far older civilization. And Egypt is in a sense the center point of the cultures of the world: Europe to the north, the Orient to the east, Africa to the south, and last, but by no means least, America to the west. All these other places, the origins of ancient and modern empires, are touched on in the book, as are many other times, other histories. Another telling little detail in the opening sequence hints at which empire now prevails, which now empowers its people: the entire ship is held up at the start of its journey because "some of the American schoolchildren had gone ashore to buy food" (8). These children are shown to be quite indifferent to what happens to the other passengers, gazing out to sea as the little drama concerning the English tramp takes place.

So this is a book about empires and about what happens as one empire comes to an end and another begins. It is also about what happens to individuals caught up in these large movements of history, their struggles (generally futile) to be free. The focus of the prologue section is upon a member of the most recent empire to decline, the British. In this context it is a particularly rich irony that the tramp should say, after a brief account of his travels around the world (all to former British colonies): "What's nationality these days? I myself, I think of myself as a citizen of the world" (9). One of several layers of irony in this boast in the postimperial period is that it alludes to a time when British culture and society were growing in power and respect around the world and "English gentlemen" traveled abroad, secure in the knowledge of their country's superiority. This is clear even if we do not immediately recognize the origins of the phrase "citizen of the world," which alludes to Oliver Goldsmith's eighteenth-century satire upon the English, in which a sophisticated Chinese man provided a nicely critical outsider's view of his host's customs and peculiarities. (Goldsmith got his title from Sir Francis Bacon, who remarked in one of his famous essays that, "if a man be gracious and courteous to strangers, it shows he is a citizen of the world.")

A further irony is that it is Naipaul himself, the Asian cosmopolite diarist-writer, who is claiming the authority to comment upon the customs and peculiarities of others in the prologue and, by implication, throughout the book. Only in the epilogue, however, does he come before us in person; elsewhere he is behind, above, or beyond his narrators, paring his nails. I will return to the function of the epilogue. What should be clear is the function of the prologue. It is not to "set the scene" in a conventional sense: scene, character, and narration change immediately afterward, in a way that (if you aren't expecting it from the contents list) is astounding; and this change is followed by another, and another. Instead, the prologue introduces certain themes, most obviously that of the struggles of displaced individuals in the postcolonial world. "Struggles" may be an understatement, if we think of the easy cruelty toward the Englishman of those other, more powerful citizens of the world, the Lebanese furniture maker, the Egyptian student, and Hans, the "well-developed" young Austrian. As the narrator remarks: "It was to be like a tiger-hunt, where bait is laid out and the hunter and spectators watch from the security of a platform. The bait here was the tramp's own rucksack" (15).

And, so, a final twist: he is to be tormented in a way reminiscent of an old imperial pastime of the British, hunting tigers in India on the backs of elephants. What the reader has been encouraged to expect here, then, is an allusive, ironic, indirect — in short, modernist — narrative, which deals with the contemporary postcolonial world and characters from a multitude of backgrounds, the whole resonating with large historical movements, the rise and fall of empires. We hardly need recall the Gulf war to recognize its complex and continuing drawing in of postcolonial contexts.

The way in which we read the so-called new writings depends on the production and status of the author just as much as (if not more than) it does when we read the writings of the more familiar "canon." The new writings are not so new anymore, and their themes have been identified and packaged to a surprising extent already. This puts peculiar pressures upon authors who are institutionalized in this way. Reviewing a collection of academic papers on Commonwealth literature over twenty years ago, Naipaul ruefully noted the appearance of "occasional references to myself" and continued:

> Things move so fast nowadays, even in the Literature Schools. Commonwealth writing as we understand it is so new, and it is already being picked to pieces . . . it all seems to have been codified already. . . . Then there is the West Indian with his search for identity. Here is a phrase that has gone deep. Students, already – how disquieting! – preparing theses, write or even telephone to say that they get the impression from my books that I am engaged in a search for identity. How is it going? At times like this I am glad to be only a name.[9]

Yet the question of identity is unavoidable in any discussion of Caribbean writing, and Naipaul's work, including *In a Free State*, is no exception. As Gareth Griffiths has pointed out, "the force with which the educational and social myths of borrowed identity have split the West Indian from his own reality . . . is not the invention of tortured intellectuals but an overwhelming and continuous pressure experienced by all classes and groups within West Indian society."[10]

There are, however, radically different ways of responding to this split, including attempts to accept one's fractured inheritance, to return and rediscover one's society, one's place – even to look ahead, as Derek Walcott does, to a fusion of the fragments into a heterogeneous local culture of the future. Naipaul's writings display a different response, being pervaded by an overwhelming sense of personal dislocation, apparently defeating any potential reconstruction of the personality, the self, in some future Caribbean culture. Each of Naipaul's narratives – whether autobiography, documentary, or fiction – seems to represent another attempt to discover or establish the sense of self which eludes him and which, he insists, eludes the colonial subject from the Caribbean, if not all colonial peoples. "Living in a borrowed culture, the West Indian, more than most, needs writers to tell him who he is and where he stands," he observed in *The Middle Passage* (73). Writing itself takes on a peculiar, quasiredemptive authority.

Naipaul's first persuasive attempt to show this was embodied in *A House for Mr Biswas* (completed just before he wrote those words), in which the central character (based on his journalist father) aspires toward the secure identity that he feels a house of his own would give him, but the novel ends with his dying in a jerry-built wreck that, despite the "romantic aspect" provided by his laburnum tree, destroys him through debt and despair. Mr Biswas's failure, underlined by Naipaul's use (for the first time) of a framing prologue and epilogue, leaves the inescapable conclusion that all such attempts at redefinition in the colonial context are illusory. The reasons for this view are not hard to find. Again and again Naipaul describes the societies of the Caribbean in terms of lack. The Trinidad of his childhood, "too unimportant" and peripheral to have a history and with a society based upon slavery, exploitation, and crass materialism, left

> everyone [as] an individual, fighting for his place in the community. Yet there was no community. We were of various races, religions, sets and cliques; and we had somehow found ourselves on the same small island. Nothing bound us together except this common residence. There was no nationalist feeling; there could be none. There was no profound anti-imperialist feeling; indeed, it was only our Britishness, our belonging to the British Empire, which gave us any identity. (*Middle Passage,* 45)

The position is paradoxical: Naipaul himself goes on to try to uncover the supposedly nonexistent history of his place, his culture. In *The Loss of El Dorado* (1969) he records "two moments when Trinidad was touched by 'history,'" the two "forgotten stories," of Raleigh's failed search for El Dorado which began with his raid on Trinidad in 1595 and, nearly two hundred years later, the British occupation of the island as a springboard for that nation's own slave-based trade in South America. The author's reliance upon public documents in London for these rewritten, reclaimed histories of colonization does not preclude an imaginative understanding of the New World perspective he appears to deny. And in *The Middle Passage* we find that, while Naipaul insists that the West Indies "are so completely a creation of Empire that the withdrawal of Empire is almost without meaning," he also admits that in such a situation "nationalism is the only revitalizing force." But that is in British Guyana – to which troops were dispatched to destroy the radical nationalism of the early 1950s – just as in Notting Hill, London, when assertion turned to riot, "the energy which, already gathered, ought to have gone towards an ordered and overdue social revolution was dissipated in racial rivalry, factional strife and simple fear" (*Middle Passage*, 153).

And so we end up where we were before. The futility of communal, *political* action, no matter how necessary, is a constant, and Naipaul simply cannot conceive of an individual gaining a sense of identity from the common history, the common cause. We are always left with the isolated individual, without a community, circling back upon himself.

But what about Naipaul's own "race, religion, clique," the rural Hindu community? Vidiadhar Surajprasad Naipaul was, in fact, born (17 August 1932) in Chaguanas, a small market town in the heart of the sugarcane area of Trinidad, and was grandson of indentured laborers of Brahmin descent. As a young man, he could understand, but not speak, Hindi, developing a Brahmin delicacy about cooking and personal habits while resisting Hindu belief and ritual. He belonged from the start, then, to a particular subculture within the multicultural, multiracial, multilayered society of his island colony, a subculture permeated with a sense of difference. At first this sounds as though it offers a refuge:

> Everything which made the Indian alien in the society gave
> him strength. His alienness insulated him from the black-white
> struggle. He was taboo-ridden as no other person on the island:
> he had complicated rules about food and about what was un-
> clean. His religion gave him values which were not the white
> values of the rest of the community, and preserved him from
> self-contempt; he never lost pride in his origins. More impor-
> tant than religion was his family organization, an enclosing
> self-sufficient world absorbed with its quarrels and jealousies,
> as difficult for the outsider to penetrate as for one of its mem-
> bers to escape. It protected and imprisoned, a static world,
> awaiting decay. (*Middle Passage*, 88)

By its religion, its alternative system of values, this community is protected from succumbing wholesale to the dominant, colonial, white values and, hence, from the "self-contempt" of those who have, according to Naipaul, had such alternatives erased by the historic experience of the Middle Passage.

But, if his community protects, it also imprisons, and Naipaul admits his own overwhelming urge to escape it. On the other hand, members of the community retain an identity: "He never lost pride in his origins." If Indian and African alike have been left in a void by the processes of history, the Indian can at least grasp the root of an earlier, identifiable culture. Naipaul escapes Trinidad (the first time at eighteen, on an "island scholarship" to Oxford); he returns on visits (the first time at twenty-four, after graduation, marriage, and a job at the BBC), but he also goes to India for a year, to the very village in Uttar Pradesh from which his grandfather migrated to Trinidad – and he returns, again and again, to India. What does he seek? His identity. What does he find? The titles of the books he has written about the country and its attitudes suggest what he thinks he finds: *An Area of Darkness* (1964), *India: A Wounded Civilization* (1977), and *India: A Million Mutinies Now* (1990). As he confesses early in the first account, "even now, though time has widened, though space has contracted and I have travelled lucidly over that area which was to me [as a child] the area of darkness, something of darkness remains, in those attitudes, those ways of thinking and seeing, which are no longer mine" (30). It is a darkness he continues to explore: "but increasingly I understand that my Indian memories, the memories of that India which lived on into my childhood in Trinidad, are like trapdoors into a bottomless past" (*India: A Wounded Civilization,* 10).

The identity is unreachable, in other words. Even when, in the third Indian book, *India: A Million Mutinies Now*, he sets out to introduce "people who have ideas now about who they are and what they owe themselves" (517), he cannot relate to them; he withdraws. His failure to settle in India brought with it from the start the realization that what he finds – instead of a land of achievement based on a whole, living, and longstanding traditional culture – is another fractured, or at least wounded, culture, lost in a "double fantasy," a mixture of mimicry of the West and "oriental" resignation (*Area of Darkness,* 216-17). He compares his search for an identity with a piece of patterned cloth unwoven to trace the figures, which ends up a heap of tangled threads (266). The image is doubly suggestive: of personal frustration at the inevitable outcome of his search for a common identity and of the tangle of differing narrative forms, ways of writing, in which he represents that frustration, that search. In *In a Free State* that tangle becomes part of the very texture of the book, in which Trinidad and India figure as points of contact, and of questioning, rather than as either home or destination.

The search for identity is evident in the first story after the prologue of *In a Free State*, "One out of Many," which takes us from Bombay to Washington. The title suggests multiple ironies: it is a play on the motto of the United States of America, *E pluribus unum*, and the familiar American notion that everyone can become an American; it also reminds us of U.S. hegemony in the world, hinted at in the prologue; and it anticipates the ironic contrast between Western individualism and Hindu communalism which runs through the story. If we are tempted to think that the I with which it begins is the same as that of the narrator of the journal, we are quickly made aware that this cannot be so. In any case, comparing the opening sentences with the opening of the book reveals a quite distinct tone and syntax: in place of that earlier sophisticated, detached, and ironic tone and complex syntax, we have here a simpler, confessional mode.

"I am now an American citizen and I live in Washington, capital of the world. Many people, both here and in India, will feel that I have done well. But" (21). That *But* alerts us to the potential for undermining, ironic reversal which typifies what follows. We are at the heart of the new empire, aspired to by many, and, significantly, in light of what we now know about Naipaul's own struggle to come to terms with his Indian identity, the Indian central character's predicament is a provocative yet sympathetic reversal of his own: instead of the Westernized and insecure former colonial from the New World coming to ancient India, here is an Indian of India, secure in his own culture and beliefs, part of the crowd on a Bombay street, coming to the New World. What happens to him? What does he see?

To answer these questions involves coming to grips with the new mode of narrative adopted here. I've called it confessional, but there's more to it than that. It is a variant upon the prologue, since it is another kind of journal: first person, direct discourse. But, instead of the I as witness, hardly participating in his account, this is the I as teller of his own tale. Indeed, everything is viewed from his perspective, and it seems very much the point that we realize this is a limited perspective, unlike the neo-omniscient prologue. Furthermore, it is satire. As with all the other segments of narrative in the book, it involves a journey, but this is the journey of an innocent abroad, a traditional satirical subject within Western literary discourse (again), from *Candide* to *Huckleberry Finn*.

The narrator's attempts to apply the simple values of his Hindu background on the Air India flight go farcically wrong, as he swallows the betel juice he isn't allowed to spit, unknowingly sips champagne and ends up vomiting over his bundles. He is that familiar satirical figure, the simpleton who fails to come to grips with reality and suffers accordingly, but whose adventures show up his moral, if not spiritual, superiority to those he encounters. Naipaul expressed disgust at the ubiquitous evidence of casual excretion he found in India. Here it is the hysterical air hostess, who is made to look absurd when she is disgusted by her compatriot's physical habits, not the frightened man who cannot control himself in the "tiny hissing room" at the back of the aircraft. The humor is light and delivered at the expense of the "civilized," whether Indian or American:

> "He's a cook" my employer said.
> "Does he always carry his condiments?" (26)

This exchange becomes analeptically even more amusing when we realize, later, that the U.S. customs have missed what else Santosh has carried in: "The poor country weed I smoked" (34). His simplicity helps him to survive, but at what cost? Formerly free to stroll on the Bombay streets, enjoying the "respect and security" shed upon him by the importance of his employer (for all his dependence upon the man), he now finds himself in a place where a "wild race" roams the streets "so freely," while he is "like a prisoner" under the "imitation sky" in the corridor of his master's apartment block (26–27).

As we proceed with Santosh's account of his journey of self-discovery, the irony of his position becomes more complex, if bleaker. His development toward the freedom he desires – leaving domestic employment, finding more independent work, marrying to legalize himself as a U.S. citizen – is marked by a series of telling little moments, sometimes comic, sometimes pathetic, but all tending to the conclusion that his freedom (the word itself is kept in play throughout) is an illusion. But it is an illusion of which he is aware, unlike those he meets. The added irony develops as we are brought to realize that this is 1960s America – the time of hippies, black urban riots, and a popular youth culture of the Orient, with different groups aspiring toward their ideas of freedom, all set in the critical perspective implied by Santosh's condition as a colonial immigrant.

To begin with this means that it is others who are shown to be living an illusion. The hippies and their specious Orientalism make him wonder if "perhaps once upon a time they had been like me . . . brought here among the *hubshi* as captives a long time ago and . . . become a lost people, like our own wandering gipsy folk and . . . forgotten who they were" (30).

This wonderfully ironic fantasy makes them seem, with their bad Sanskrit and odd dancing, "something that should be kin but turns out not to be, turns out to be degraded, like a deformed man, or like a leper, who from a distance looks whole" (30). (In Achebe's *Things Fall Apart* the clanspeople first think of the invading whites as lepers without toes.) Their lack of identity is like a disease to Santosh because of his own insecurity. The entire white American world outside seems unreal—"Americans have remained to me, as people not quite real, as people temporarily absent from television"—while the black American world of the streets seems all too real, so that when the *hubshi*, as he calls them, try to burn down Washington he wants his own block to burn, "even myself" to be destroyed and consumed (40).

It has been suggested by Selwyn Cudjoe that this is "an intensely racist story," in that Santosh's "liberation" is sketched against a background of stereotyped black people, whose activities are indicted as "lost" and "make-believe."[11] And yet, when he wanders around the smoking ruins of the city, "they smiled at me and I found I was smiling back. Happiness was on the faces of the *hubshi*. They were like people amazed they could do so much, that so much lay in their power. They were like people on holiday. I shared their exhilaration" (41). This feeling of exhilaration, of power, is what enables Santosh to escape from his employer. It's of course true that black power has been expressed destructively. But I myself don't quite see Naipaul's attitude as racist. Not only does the narrator's response acknowledge a kinship (unlike his response to white Americans), which can be interpreted as acknowledging the oppression of black Americans, a colonial people within the metropolitan state and, like him, struggling to achieve a sense of identity. But it is through the interest shown by a black American woman, and not by other Indian expatriates, that he achieves even the dubious status that allows him to stay where he is.

It is arguable that the presentation of the black servant he marries to obtain citizenship is racist—and sexist. Her otherness is stressed, and the narrator's attempt to naturalize it only demeans her further: she is large and threatening, the incarnation of Kali, the black Hindu goddess of destruction (38, 53); furthermore, "it is written in our books, both holy and not so holy, that it is indecent and wrong for a man of our blood to embrace the *hubshi* woman. To be dishonoured in this life, to be born a cat or a monkey or a *hubshi* in the next!" (34–35). But Kali's other aspect is of creation, and there is more than a hint of ironic humor in the presentation of Santosh's Hindu fastidiousness, as he succumbs to the *hubshi*'s vitality and her difference from himself. She has also, after all, been the first to teach him English ("Me black and beautiful" and "He pig" [34]) and helps create the self-awareness that enables him to break out of his servitude. Yet that freedom leaves him, consistent with the rest of the book, a "casualty." Does this thematic, structuring pressure rob the story of conviction? It depends, I think, on what the reader makes of the concluding paragraph. Santosh was once "part of the flow"; all that his freedom has brought him "is the knowledge that I have a face and a body, that I must feed this body and clothe this body for a certain number of years. Then it will be over" (58). The last word echoes the last word of the prologue: "That passion was over" (20). A certain Hindu submissiveness, it seems, is all that remains.

From an author who claims to have left Hinduism behind in childhood and finds its manifestation in India dubious and constricting, this engagement with its discourse comes as something of a surprise. Elsewhere, Naipaul argues that Western attempts to enter "Hindu equilibrium" may be possible for scholars, at the level of "intellectual comprehension," but to try to enter it as a reality is another matter. "The hippies of Western Europe and the United States" give the illusion of having done so, but "they break just at that point where the Hindu begins: the knowledge of the abyss, the acceptance of distress as the condition of men" (*India: A Wounded Civilization,* 27). Is this the knowledge toward which *In a Free State* is tending?

In a Free State explores the shifting and ambiguous relationship between the developed West and the Third World. As we read on through the sequence of seemingly disconnected narratives, it becomes increasingly apparent that they involve a progressive narrative exploration of this fundamental, this paradigmatic, "story," and its implications for the predicament of individuals caught up in the network of forces – social, political, historical, and economic – that story reveals. In particular, we see the painful illusion of freedom which continues to grip them. A full exploration demands that we experience the perspective of the colonial, or rather ex-colonial, masters themselves, and in the title story, also the longest narrative, the earlier perspective upon immigration and exile is reversed, as two members of the dominant metropolitan culture and former empire journey through an independent African state.

But, as Naipaul went on to admit in *The Enigma of Arrival* (1987), his most autobiographical "novel" so far, when writing *In a Free State* the Africa of his imagination "was not only the source countries—Kenya, Uganda, the Congo, Rwanda; it was also Trinidad, to which I had gone back with a vision of romance and had seen black men with threatening hair" (156). If a certain impossible dream of his Indian roots is perceptible in the second sequence of the book, another vision, this time a nightmare from his Trinidadian home, emerges in the third, as if it has to be confronted explicitly before it becomes part of the African title story. The book *In a Free State* is like a palimpsest, a series of layers through which the reader can perceive from time to time, as we peel them off, what lies beneath. It may be that in the end this makes it more, rather than less, representative of the history and culture of Naipaul's origins: multilayered, multifarious, and impossible to reduce to the experience of one nation, place, or people.

In "Tell Me Who to Kill," the third sequence of *In a Free State*, we have, as in the second, the predicament of the colonial who has journeyed to the metropolitan center, seeking freedom but finding the imprisonment of exile. A step ahead of Santosh, the moment he embarks upon his journey he feels like a prisoner; he "will never be a free man again" (79). His story is told entirely in his voice and from his perspective, but this time he is West Indian and so, according to Naipaul's view, *already* deracinated. And, whereas Santosh mildly accepts what he understands as fate handing out to him a condition of homelessness and isolation, the anonymous narrator here responds to what happens to him (and, another difference, to his brothers) out of an inner potential for disorder and violence. His brother Dayo's marriage to a white girl is analogous to Santosh's marriage—but the wedding is like a funeral, and the narrator feels he is already "the dead man" (102).

This destructive potential is evident from the moment we first encounter the fractured, obsessive, and frightening narrative consciousness. It is hard to know how far, or in what sense, we can rely on this man's account of what is going on around him. His paranoia is signaled, for example, by the contradictory accounts of Frank as a friend and comforter, on the one hand, and as someone who exposes him to pain, even challenges him to become violent, on the other. In contrast to Santosh's home life, his early experiences in the colony (Trinidad is implied, not named) have practically severed his sense of belonging to any viable culture. Occasional hints of a Hindu background ("No turban, no procession, no drums" at the wedding [99]) serve only to increase the feeling that he has been robbed of self-worth, of identity. He has been aware, since before he left, of "how ordinary the world was for me, with nothing good in it, nothing to see except sugarcane and the pitch road, and how from small I know I had no life" (64). His understanding of himself and the world is rendered in a distinctive Caribbean Creole voice, which, far from allowing us to celebrate its vital and popular origins, is used to signal further the humiliating in-adequacy that prompts his anger.

The Trinidadian narrator's lack of authentic selfhood is further sug-gested by the fragments of 1940s American film culture, imperfectly recollected, which dominate his consciousness and which Naipaul has elsewhere registered as characteristic of the city life of his child-hood. Earlier in his career Naipaul exploited the richness and humor of Trinidadian popular culture and everyday speech, even while he be-wailed its limitations, its secondhandness. There are some contradic-tions in this position. The sentence that, according to his own account (*Finding the Centre,* 16), initiated his writing career included the dialect utterance "What happening there, Bogart?" This "Port of Spain mem-ory" developed as the central, poignant thread running through his first book (but third to be published), *Miguel Street* (1959). In part a cel-ebration of his Port of Spain experiences (the Naipauls moved there when he was six), the stories collected in *Miguel Street* also drama-tized the frustrating meanness of small-town colonial life. Its cast of characters, from B. Wordsworth (B for "Black. White Wordsworth was my brother. We share one heart" [46]) to Bogart the bigamist (named after the wildly popular Hollywood "tough guy"), were depicted with increasing detachment by the young narrator whose consciousness links the stories and who determines to leave the limited world of colonial Trinidad at the end, observing only "my shadow before me, a dancing dwarf on the tarmac" (172).

And so only mimicry or parody remains for the departed colonial, doubly deceived in that he imitates an imitation of an imitation, Hollywood in the tropics. In Naipaul's fifth novel, *The Mimic Men* (1967), the exiled politician Ralph Singh (born Ranjit Kripalsingh) sits in London writing his memoirs, trying to create order out of the disorder of decolonization. But his writing is like his life; it can only issue in failure, for it is based upon the self-deception of former colonial subjects, "abandoned and forgotten" on their "unknown" island (a thinly disguised Trinidad), where they can only pretend "to be real, to be learning, to be preparing [themselves] for life"; "we mimic men of the New World" (146). Wherever they find themselves they are in a state of exile, because they are exiled from reality. For the writer this means feeling at a loss for an adequate discourse. When Singh's wife leaves him at the island airport for Miami the only way he can find to describe the moment is in terms of "the cinematic symbol: Bogart in *Casablanca*, macintoshed, alone on the tarmac, the Dakota taking off into the night" (183).

Many other West Indian writers have dealt with the alienating predicament of the immigrant in London in terms of the unfriendly natives, the unfriendly climate. Naipaul's "Tell Me Who to Kill" shows all this and also white racism, but the central image is a threatening fantasy/dream image from Hitchcock's *Rope* (1948), of the body in the chest (62), to which the narrator returns in his last words (102). The reader is left unclear about whether or not there has been a killing but certain that there will be. *Rope* was set in the United States and was based on the Leopold and Loeb murders: in the film version two homosexual boys murder another student for "kicks" and serve his relatives a meal from a chest containing the body. There are hints of a suppressed, disturbed sexuality in the relationship between the narrator and Frank (59–60, 64), suggesting that the narrator may be a sexual casualty of freedom as well. This anticipates the characterization of Bobby in the succeeding narrative, whose reasons for living in the newly independent African state are at least partly bound up with a struggle to find sexual freedom.

But the precise reason for the breakdown of the narrator in "Tell Me Who to Kill" is not made quite clear. Or, rather, the main point seems to lie elsewhere, in the arbitrariness of the assault at its center and the conscious and unconscious collusion of all those involved. What Naipaul is suggesting here (perhaps not wholly successfully, though) is that the colonized subject becomes a seething mass of unfocused anger: who, indeed, to kill, when your condition has been brought about by such large, incomprehensible forces? No wonder, then, that so much of the hatred is directed inward, or to those nearest–his own people–since there are no *individuals* to blame. The colonizers have in any case departed. There is little enough to be gained by threatening the English "louts" who provoke him in the roti shop; indeed, it is this momentary surge of power which leaves him feeling "dead." In place of the colonizers there are now the "neocolonials," like Bobby and Linda in the long title story. The hatred and violence they witness is also directed mainly by the colonized toward one another. But there is more to it than that.

The title story, or novella, is set in a recently independent, or "free," African state during a period of civil unrest. It follows the journey of two white English expatriates–the homosexual civil servant Bobby and the adulterous colonial wife Linda–as they travel by car from the capital through a changing landscape and set of experiences to the shelter of a government compound. We first see Bobby, the main character, humiliated when he makes an advance toward a black South African exile. Then, finally, he is beaten up when he tries to pacify an African soldier. Linda has to face both the rejection of a suitor who is following them and Bobby's antagonism. Their escape to the compound only confirms the inadequacy of both Bobby's liberal, pro-African stance and Linda's pragmatic colonialism. The narrative concludes with Bobby taking on the role of the white master. As for the way it is told ("In this country in Africa there was a president and there was also a king. They belonged to different tribes. The enmity of the tribes was old . . ."), the opening resembles nothing so much as a traditional, or folk, tale. And yet, very quickly, that voice modulates to the more familiar (in Western fictional traditions) authoritative, third-person narrator. As the focus narrows during "this week of crisis," with Bobby in the capital attending a seminar on development while civil war grows, so too does the irony develop. In the capital, with its half-acre gardens "in what was still an English suburb," "there was no sign of war or crisis." That is to be found in the "wilderness," beyond even the "bush villages" that tourists visit for souvenirs (103).

It is clear from the first page that yet another new terrain is being mapped out here: a former colonial capital much as it was, the embodiment of a certain genteel, imported conception of order, of Englishness, and the growing, anarchic forces at large in the recently decolonized country. As in any narrative, we are evidently being invited to develop a set of meanings from this opening, but what is unexpected, even after the variety of narrative styles the reader has met in the sequence, is the starting point in an almost mythic, symbolic realm. Why is it like that? And why shift into the more "classic realist" mode as well? Are we being alerted to earlier forms of narrative, especially earlier forms of narrating the colonial encounter? It would appear so. As critics have pointed out, Conrad's *Heart of Darkness* (1899) is especially close here, and there is an important sense in which "In a Free State" is a comment on, and rewriting of, that classic colonial text.

"In a Free State" suggests a much closer and more specific connection, however, than is usually allowed for. Indeed, at one point Bobby tells Linda, "You've been reading too much Conrad. I hate that book, don't you?" (161). This is after Linda has observed of a group of Africans in brightly colored gowns walking past them in the rain: "I feel that sort of forest life has been going on forever." Her observation is one of a series of references to the existence of some kind of primeval Africa, predating colonialism and going back to earlier empires. The question is: how are we to respond to them?

On one level what Linda says appears simply as a typical colonial-expatriate reflex, that "Kenya settler" exoticization of the "pre-man side of Africa" which Bobby sneers at in her (119) and which anyone familiar with, say, Karen Blixen's *Out of Africa* (1937) (one of the best of the genre), would easily recognize. Emphasizing the "primitive" and "timeless" in Africa appeals to Europeans made insecure by the larger changes in their world, such as the loss of empire, and enables them to patronize the African people even when they have gained their independence ("Poor little king," Linda remarks elsewhere [135]).

But to understand the specific allusion, and to see the point of the Conradian echoes that reverberate through the story, we need to recall "that book," *Heart of Darkness* itself, for a moment. *Heart of Darkness* is an account of a journey into the "heart" of an unnamed African country, told from the perspective of the colonizers. Marlow, the teller of the tale to an anonymous narrator, is himself skeptical of the colonial enterprise. Marlow's search for Mr. Kurtz, the company agent whose commercial dealings with the "natives" have taken him beyond the bounds of "civilized," if not human, behavior, is described in terms simultaneously suggestive of an exotic adventure, a critique of imperialism, and a semi-allegorical or parabolic exploration of the psyche. Although based upon the author's personal experience and knowledge of the Belgian exploitation of the Congo in the early 1890s, Conrad's narrative is made geographically and historically unspecific: replacing Matadi, Kinshasa, and Stanley Falls on the Congo with the Company Station, the Central Station and the Inner Station and avoiding proper names by referring to pilgrims, savages, the Manager, and so on.

It soon becomes clear that the element of moral fable implicit in the opening of "In a Free State" is only the first of a series of Conradian echoes and parallels. Naipaul, too, involves his colonial characters in an emblematic journey away from the Europeanized world toward an increasingly challenging "primitive" Africa: from the unnamed capital through rainforest, mountain, plain, and savannah, stopping along the way at rundown colonial outposts such as the Hunting Lodge or the colonel's hotel until, finally, in the Southern Collectorate, they get to the ruined palace of the murdered king. The further south Bobby and Linda go, the more they reveal the illusions and self-deceptions of the white expatriates they represent—although, unlike Conrad's Marlow, neither of them gains any self-knowledge as a result. Instead, their own prejudices and inadequacies emerge more and more clearly until, in the heat of the moment, they become hostile, even vicious, toward each other and so, inevitably, toward the Africans upon whom they project their own inner disorder.

Order and disorder, power and powerlessness, freedom and its lack, then, continue to occupy the book's narrative development. Bobby's angry response to Linda's account of her confused and frightened arrival in the country is: "You came for the freedom, though." This, in turn, drives her to exclaim: "You should either stay away, or you should go among them with a whip in your hand" (218). This exchange takes place after their relationship has gone through various stages, from irritation to affection, from compassion to hatred. But at this point Linda's statement alerts us to, and brings back into range, Conrad's vision of colonialism as something that can push those who participate in it toward violent extremes. In *Heart of Darkness* the idealist Kurtz ends up exclaiming: "Exterminate all the brutes" (51). Violence, or the threat of it, accompany Bobby and Linda throughout, just as in Conrad's novella the possibility of sudden death lurks around every bend in the river. Here, whether it is the *yak-yak-yak* of the helicopter overhead or the overweight soldiers jogging under an Israeli instructor, the colonel waiting to be murdered by his staff, the wild dogs roaming the streets, or just the sudden sharp changes in the road or the weather, there is a pervasive sense of threat, to the extent that it feels like a condition of life. In other words, as in *Heart of Darkness,* the pressure of a symbolic, or representative, level of narrative discourse seems unavoidable.

And so, if like Conrad's Congo, Naipaul's free state is based upon known places and events, it also seeks a certain symbolic autonomy. It has been suggested that the politics of Naipaul's story are those of Uganda in May 1966, when the Kabaka of Buganda, or King Freddie (as he was known overseas and to the expatriate community), was overthrown by the prime minister, Milton Obote, who controlled the army; and that the allusions to oath taking refer to Kenya and the Mau Mau guerrillas, while the disappearance of the president during the mutiny is derived from the experience of Dr. Nyerere in Tanzania.[12] Bobby and Linda's journey southward, based in part on a daylong drive Naipaul made between Nairobi, Kenya, and Kampala, Uganda, is similarly derived from different East African landscapes, and no place names are offered. As a journey, it is literally impossible, as is common in fiction – but this helps confirm its symbolic resonance. Few of the characters are named, and insofar as Africans are identified, they are named after places: Sammy Kisenyi (Bobby's "minister") after a town in Ruanda, John Mubende-Mbarara (the painter Linda feels has lost his primitive purity) after two towns in Uganda.[13]

Such parallels with Conrad's earlier narrative are striking. More important, however, is the way in which, while suggesting a closeness of interest, they also indicate the irretrievably postcolonial perspective of Naipaul's text, as it implicitly locates itself in relation to what one might call the Western narrative paradigm of Africa, established in its fullness by *Heart of Darkness.* A good example of this is provided by the account of the army prisoners Bobby and Linda discover toward the end of their journey, in the deposed king's territory:

> They were sitting on the ground; some were prostrate; most were naked. It was their nakedness that had camouflaged them in the sun-and-shade about the shrubs, small trees and lorries. Bright eyes were alive in black flesh; but there was little movement among the prisoners. They were the slender, small-boned, very black people of the king's tribe, a clothed people, builders of roads. But such dignity as they had possessed in freedom

had already gone; they were only forest people now, in the hands of their enemies. Some were roped up in the traditional forest way, neck to neck, in groups of three or four, as though for delivery to the slave-merchant. All showed the liver-coloured marks of blood and beatings. One or two looked dead. (228)

Now this is what Conrad's Marlow finds as he reaches the Company Station, where blasting is in progress:

A slight clinking behind me made me turn my head. Six black men advanced in a file toiling up the path. They walked erect and slow, balancing small baskets full of earth on their heads, and the clink kept time with their footsteps. . . . Each had an iron collar on his neck and all were connected together with a chain. . . . At last I got under the trees. . . . Black shapes crouched, lay, sat between the trees, leaning against the trunks, clinging to the earth, half coming out, half effaced within the dim light, in all the attitudes of pain, abandonment, and despair. Another mine on the cliff went off followed by a slight shudder of the soil under my feet. The work was going on. The work! And this was the place where some of the helpers had withdrawn to die. . . . These moribund shapes were free as air – and nearly as thin. I began to distinguish the gleam of the eyes under the trees. (19–20)

In both these groves of death we are drawn in to witness the anonymous suffering of African people, treated like slaves, swept aside by those more powerful than they or simply abandoned. Both passages offer chilling reminders of the human cost of the larger movements of history. But different histories are invoked: Conrad's workers have been discarded by the great civilizing, road-building, overseas mission of imperialism and left to die; Naipaul's prisoners have been captured by the new African government of their country and are being forced to submit to the postimperial order. Both narrators draw an ironic resonance from the idea of freedom: for Conrad the exploited "were free as air – and nearly as thin"; for Naipaul, "such dignity as they had possessed in freedom had already gone." The imperialists claimed to be freeing their subjects from enslavement to pagan brutality, but they brought their own cruel enslavement; the independence fighters helped to free their people from the yoke of imperialism, but they also opened the way for new enslavement.

Put like this, it seems as if "In a Free State" suggests an inevitable cycle of corruption, arising out of the darkness within humanity. The forest dwellers were "a clothed people, builders of roads" (elsewhere compared to Roman roads [226]), yet they have been slaves before and are becoming so again. Conrad's narrative, we are reminded from time to time, is being related to a group of men in a boat on the Thames, itself once "one of the dark places of the earth," as when the Romans came to civilize the Britons (9). Both narratives are pervaded by this sense of lengthy historical perspective, of empires rising, falling and rising again, although it is the corruption and decay of empire through the exploitation of difference which receives most emphasis. Despite the fact that Conrad's text is mainly in the first person, the perspective is authoritative, neo-omniscient, here; while Naipaul has chosen to narrate this section of the book in the third person, the comments about the king's people sound almost personal, as if they are being made by an individualized narrative voice.

The question of narrative voice is difficult and subtle here, more so than elsewhere in Naipaul's book. Conrad's account of his "manner of telling" catches Naipaul's well: it was, he once wrote, "perfectly devoid of familiarity as between author and reader," yet it "aimed essentially at the intimacy of a personal communication," and the difficulty we might have with it was because of its "fluid" and shifting perspective.[14] Naipaul himself has testified that Conrad was "the first modern writer I was introduced to" (by his father, an aspiring writer). Conrad's books, especially those set abroad such as *Heart of Darkness* and *Nostromo,* came to provide "a vision of the world's half-made societies" which answered "something of the political panic" Naipaul felt as he turned toward those societies for his subject. He said: "Conrad . . . had been everywhere before me. . . . .[He had] meditated on my world, a world I recognize today. I feel this about no other writer of the century. His achievement derives from the honesty which is part of his difficulty, that 'scrupulous fidelity to the truth of my own sensations.'"[15]

This honesty, this fidelity to his own sensations, is something Naipaul aims at too. How does it manifest itself in his post-Conradian, post-colonial narrative? In the first place, in his drive to undermine the stock response, to show up the hypocrisy that glamorizes or sentimentalizes the situation of people in the newly free states of the world. Nadine Gordimer, another postcolonial anatomist, praised Naipaul's "In a Free State" when it first appeared precisely for the accuracy of its exploration of the ways in which "two rather seedy members of the master race" see themselves and their surroundings. In particular, she noted their contempt for the very society that grants them the freedoms they seek—a contempt that, in Bobby's case, is complicated by his so-called liberal views, his conscious struggle to criticize Linda's cruder judgments.[16] But in the second place, I'd suggest, the individualist and ahistorical assumptions built into the Conradian position continue to exert a determining force upon Naipaul's narrative, to the extent that, although it creates a sense of histories past (as in the above extract), that is effectively undermined or contradicted by the presentation of Africa as an arena for the futile struggles of the decolonized mimic men (forest dwellers with "English" hairstyles) set against a backdrop of irrational, timeless grandeur. This latter point touches on the question of Naipaul's racism, which I will be coming to in a moment.

But, first, it's important to show how—to bring out both points—the detailed texture of the narrative asks for close attention. Only by doing this, for example, can we see how scrupulously Bobby's position, and not just Linda's more obviously questionable viewpoint, is undermined by the honesty or evenhandedness of the author. This is a matter as much of small shifts of sympathy and perspective from line to line as it is of the larger, set-piece scenes such as the exchange between Bobby and the Africans at the roadside filling station, when he loses both his temper and his liberalism at once because his windscreen gets scratched (144–49). Consider, for example, the following little exchange between the two travelers during an evening walk after dining at the colonel's hotel. The lakeside boulevard is apparently deserted, a shabby reminder of colonial glories.

> "It's funny," Linda whispered, "how you can forget the houses and feel that the lake hasn't even been discovered."
>
> "I don't know what you mean by discovered," Bobby said, not whispering. "The people here knew about it all the time."
>
> "I've heard that one. I just wish they'd managed to let the rest of us know." (187)

Linda's response indicates that Bobby's eagerness to display his critical ear for expatriate cliché is itself a stock response. Her whispered comment is innocent in intent, presumably supposed to communicate a sense of awe at the silence, the emptiness, of the place, its decayed grandeur – although it is also an example of how expatriate discourse takes over such responses. Bobby's criticism is undermined as he makes it, by that little narratorial insert "not whispering," which implies that *he* has no need to hide what he says or thinks about his surroundings. Linda turns this neatly into a joke. And yet is it a joke we can simply accept? The ideology of imperialism continues to provide the parameters for her humor, doesn't it? The pronouns alone imply as much, the use of "they" and "us." Who are "they," and who are "us"? As soon as the reader thinks about the prior history that made this colonizers' discourse available, he or she begins to ask, how could they have informed us of their world? And why should they have?

In short, Bobby is shown to be equally imprisoned within the postcolonial discourse he tries to distance himself from. Furthermore, he needs the black people of this free state to bolster his view of himself as a friend and supporter of their cause, which he serves to the point of betraying white colonial loyalties – for example, when he informs the new government (itself corrupt) of the South African Denis Marshall's corruption. This is also a personal betrayal, we realize, since it was Marshall who helped his old Oxford chum Bobby to escape persecution and breakdown at home by getting him his present job in Africa. Naipaul's narrative strategy allows none of his characters to escape condemnation, usually in the implication of their own remarks, only very occasionally aided by narratorial comment.

But where, then, is the narrator? Is he so very detached as not to be implicated within his own set of discourses? This question is all the more important when we consider how Naipaul himself gets attacked for his racism in this story and elsewhere. "In a Free State" has drawn particular criticism on this score, for example, by Adewale Maja-Pearce, whose extended attack on Naipaul (and his writer-brother Shiva) was prompted by *In a Free State* – or, rather, "In a Free State": he doesn't mention the other stories in the book, presumably because they don't deal with Africa. I give his attack at some length because of its importance as a postcolonial response.

Nothing is more calculated to infuriate Africans than the arrogance with which foreigners take it upon themselves to pass judgement on them and their continent. . . . The Naipaul brothers are merely the latest in the long line of such people. They despise Africans with a passion and they make no secret of it. Take V. S. Naipaul's *In a Free State*. . . . Africans appear in only very minor roles (not necessarily a criticism) but he leaves us in no doubt of the physical distaste they arouse in him: "The African opened the door himself. He filled the car with his smell"; "The boy was big and he moved briskly, creating little turbulences of stink"; "The tall boy came to clear away Bobby and Linda's plates and left a little of his stink behind" [136, 175, 178]. And not only Africans but Africa itself has a bad smell; in the words of one of the main characters:

> I got it this time, when we came back from leave. It lasts about half an hour or so, no more. It is a smell of rotting vegetation and Africans. One is very much like the other [139].

Academics have attempted to excuse this by pointing out that it isn't only Africans who smell bad:

> There is little point in objecting to his emphasis on physical unpleasantness; words like "fat" and "smell" enter the story as part of Linda's vocabulary and are adopted as Naipaul's from the Hunting Lodge incident onwards; but the same points are made about the Colonel.

This is true, but it misses the point: The Colonel is the only European who smells, and he is portrayed as a figure of pity, as a man who, trapped by Africa and his own weakness, has become contaminated.

Maja-Pearce goes on to bring in Naipaul's later novel *A Bend in the River* (1979), which expands and develops some of the material in "In a Free State" at a lower level of intensity, including its Conradian echoes (it is set on the Congo). Maja-Pearce singles out the moment in this later novel at which the narrator-hero, Salim, reflects on his unease at the clamor for independence in his African state: "I feared the lies – black men assuming the lies of white men" (22). Once again Maja-Pearce refuses to concede that this is the insecure narrator's view, rather than the author's. Why?

Reading through the works of the Naipauls on Africa nothing
strikes the reader so forcibly as the suspicion that their constant quips have become automatic reflexes over which they
have lost all control. . . . Everything is reduced to farce. . . .

But no-one is denying that Africa is in a state of tremendous
upheaval; no-one is denying that many of the perversions of
modern Africa are absurd. . . . But our laughter [at its tyrants]
is tempered by the knowledge of the suffering they cause, suffering which affects real people who feel real pain. The laughter of the Naipaul brothers isn't tempered by this knowledge
because, to them, Africans can't be taken seriously: in an insidious way they don't exist for them as real people. This is what
offends. And the key to their attitude lies in their worship of
the West and the Western tradition. . . . Ironically, as West Indians, they are themselves products of a society struggling to find
itself after the bloody legacy of defeat and enslavement at the
hands of the very tradition they extol.[17]

This is effectively a development of the criticism of Naipaul by Lamming and Sivanandan referred to earlier, although more sharply focused upon racism in the African context. They, too, locate the source
of their unease with Naipaul's satiric vision in what they perceive as a
"wholesale" adoption of the Western tradition. But Maja-Pearce – in an
echo of Achebe's well-known attack on "colonialist critics" in Uganda
in 1974[18] – goes a step further, rebutting the academics who defend Naipaul. In my view the argument is to some extent unanswerable. Naipaul does make many of his African characters distasteful in precisely
the offensive, physical manner Maja-Pearce enumerates, while excluding the whites, unless they are, and this is significant, crippled in some
way, such as the Colonel or (as Maja-Pearce might have added, but
doesn't) *women:* Linda's smell and her pathetic attempt to deodorize it
lead to Bobby's appalling outburst, in which he accuses her of being
"nothing but a rotting cunt," along with "millions more" colonial wives
(219). It is arguable that this outburst reveals no more than Bobby's
obvious and predictable misogyny and is the product of his sexual dis-
appointment and fear. So, too, you could argue, Linda's remarks about
the rotten smell of Africa and Africans are placed by their context: a
glance at page 139 shows she is reacting against the ridiculous Mar-
shalls and their exoticizing talk about their beloved "smell of Africa,"

even as they decide to clear out and head back to their South African homeland; she is also repeating (while claiming it makes her ashamed to do so) her dubious husband's, Martin's, views.

But what about Maja-Pearce's point that it is Naipaul who makes the specific comments? I think you will find on close analysis that in each of his examples there is at least a question about who is speaking at that moment in the narrative. Naipaul's frequent and subtle use of free indirect speech suggests that we are inhabiting the expatriate consciousness, and not the narrator's, much less the author's. Does this undermine the overall argument? Not quite, since there is still the question of how adequately the author has distanced himself from the racism of his characters. Further, there are other, sometimes more extended examples of narratorial commentary which can be used to support the general argument, if not the specific one, about the text's emphasis upon distasteful physical detail.

Readers might notice, for example, the way in which the African servants at the Colonel's hotel are characterized. Peter, Timothy, and Carolus (whom Bobby tries to seduce) are individualized to an extent, but for the rest we only hear, in the repeated phrase, their "squealing" and "high-pitched chatter," as if they were not fully human. Indeed, they are "like the birds," says the Colonel; they are "fresh from the bush" (184). And, if this is defended as part of the story's emphasis upon the marginalization of the king's people – the forest people, who are, as we've seen, enslaved by the new president's army – there remains the problem of what we make of a people we only see from the outside and who are depicted as somehow part of nature, exoticized afresh by Naipaul's imagination, which, to that extent, seems to share, at least as much as it criticizes, the settler vision exemplified by the Colonel.

This is where Naipaul's narrative appears, on close inspection, to inhabit the same questionable area of discourse as Conrad's, that discourse in which, for example, Conrad makes Marlow talk of the necessity of having to "put up with sights, with sounds, with smells too, by Jove! – breathe dead hippo so to speak and not be contaminated" (*Heart of Darkness,* 50): in short, to contemplate unflinchingly the barbaric practices ("unspeakable rites," he calls them [50]) revealed by penetration into Africa. It is the abiding aura of mystery, the incomprehensibility, of the forest people as depicted by Naipaul which renders them similarly other. Their chatter is, we're told at the start of the hotel episode, the "language of the forest"–hence, its incomprehensibility (169). Similarly incomprehensible, but more mysterious and suggestive of the unspeakable, are those running men painted white, who emerge from the bush/forest (210–11) and who, in the 1987 Penguin edition, are displayed on the cover, presumably as an invitation to contemplate their exotic nakedness. Naipaul is not responsible for the cover of his book, and the moment of their mysterious emergence is framed by his two expatriate protagonists, so that the way they are described can be understood as a continuation of the expatriate viewpoint. But is it?

It seems to me the narrator and his characters are inseparable in their perception of these men, involved as they are in some ritual known only to themselves and as much part of nature ("white as the knotted scaly lower half of the tall cactus plants," for example) as alien, or other, as any colonial imagining of the primitive. This isn't to deny the powerful resonance of the moment and the inadequacy of Bobby and Linda's perceptions which it suggests. The aim, rather, is to show how Naipaul's imaginative perspective too readily accommodates the familiar, dehumanizing, dehistoricizing stereotyping in Western, if not racist, ideology.

This is the more obvious if you consider for a moment how such a scene would appear in *Things Fall Apart,* a classic of the colonial encounter which seems to have passed Naipaul by. Naipaul's narrative isn't as patronizingly limited as the district commissioner's at the conclusion of that novel, although the viewpoint expressed by Maja-Pearce would presumably see them as similar. On the other hand, the scene is a long way from inviting our sympathetic understanding for a people whose world has been destroyed, as the forest people's has been. Or are we being unfair to Naipaul? The narrative tone of "In a Free State" is remarkably neutral, uncommitted, and to that extent is subject to different interpretations. Exploring its covert encounter with *Heart of Darkness* highlights one way in which Naipaul's book may be said to reinforce the colonialism that he seems to be attacking. But it also suggests the possibility of subverting the residual colonial discourse present in the postcolonial era. And there remains the fact that "In a Free State" is one, though a very important, part of the whole sequence of narratives, the last of which we haven't yet considered.

The ambiguities and contradictions that my scrutiny of Naipaul's title story has begun to produce are not resolved by the epilogue, in contrast to what that label might lead us to expect. But they are taken to a new level of interpretative possibilities. As I've been suggesting, the book as a whole seems to ask to be read as a layered series of narratives, framed by the prologue and epilogue, although that framing itself is thematically inflected. That is to say, both prologue and epilogue appear to articulate conscious responses to the *theme* of freedom in the postcolonial era, rather than proposing some final or closed reading. In this way they push the reader to a further awareness of our contexts, "metropolitan" or "colonial," in the postcolonial order.

How, then, to read "The Circus at Luxor"? Dickens's circus people in *Hard Times* (1854) may be said to offer an alternative set of possibilities for a mid-Victorian Britain stubbornly determined upon a path of continuing exploitation and hardheaded profiteering; in the context of a postimperial world what are we to make of the circus people in the concluding section of Naipaul's book? We cannot ignore the fact that it *is* concluding, the deliberately placed last piece of narrative, nor that it obviously echoes the themes and situation of the prologue. Recording a second visit to Egypt, this time from Italy, the journal writer of the prologue finds himself once again surrounded by people of various nationalities, contemplating the remains of empire: the country and its people are still nominally free, and, again, the Greeks and Lebanese are discussing how to make money (out of illegal Rhodesian tobacco, ironically enough), while the peasant poor are disregarded, as before. Once again an act of gratuitous violence takes place, and various responses to it are depicted. Exploiter and exploited are involved in an unpleasant "game," once again focusing on the main themes: freedom, power, order and their absence in the postcolonial dispensation.

But there are differences, too, between prologue and epilogue. The most obvious difference is that this time far from just observing what happens when the Italians toss food at the beggar boys to film them being beaten away by the man with the camel whip—as would have been consistent with the careful, reluctant neutrality of the prologue narrator—the journal writer, whom we cannot but help take as the author, intervenes. He takes away the whip and threatens to "report this to Cairo" (243). It is as if Linda's urge to use a whip has found its analogy, just as the forest people have become the desert boys, who spring up "like sand-animals" around the institutions of the decolonized state. Naipaul's resistance toward sentimentality or hypocrisy continues in the narrator's awareness that, nevertheless, nothing is achieved by his action; he feels "exposed, futile" (243). But this time it is the narrator, not one of his characters, who thus expresses himself.

Even more notable, however, is the presence of the Chinese, who present medals, postcards, and peonies to all the ragged Egyptian waiters.

> Peonies, China! So many empires had come here. Not far from where we were was the colossus on whose shin the Emperor Hadrian had caused to be carved verses in praise of himself, to commemorate his visit. On the other bank, not far from the Winter Palace, was a stone with a rougher Roman inscription marking the southern limit of the Empire, defining an area of retreat. Now another, more remote empire was announcing itself. A medal, a postcard; and all that was asked in return was anger and a sense of injustice. (245–46)

If U.S. power in the world was alluded to in the prologue, here it is the potential world power of the Chinese which is being proposed as taking over the cycle of empires from the distant past. But, unlike the Americans, or any other of the people depicted in the book (or elsewhere in Naipaul's work), the Chinese are presented as a finely made, relaxed, gentle, and self-contained people – above all, as a community, and, what is more, a community of artists.

So, do we take it that the narrator's display of "anger and a sense of injustice" is what is being asked of us, in the context of the new order in the making? And that his decision to act, which this produced, is to be understood as positive, despite his own immediate reaction to it himself? Or does his feeling of exposure and futility represent more truly the impulse behind this scene and the book as a whole? For Peggy Nightingale: "Naipaul thus suggests that the world's peoples are no more than a cosmic circus responding to the crack of fate's whip. Those who imagine themselves to be in a free state are in reality the prisoners of the colonial experience; each is a citizen of a world that offers neither security nor fulfilment."[19] This is the more accepted view, and, although Nightingale writes from a persuasively nonmetropolitan perspective, her position is perhaps too easily accommodated to the urbane, modernist reading of Naipaul as a cynical stylist. John Thieme, on the other hand, has argued that, in dropping his earlier masks of irony and anonymity and coming forward to protest and stop the whipping, "the act of humanitarian concern has been performed. Though in one sense it is futile (the children jostling for crumbs at the tables of the rich are willing whipping-boys), the gesture of protest nevertheless shows the extent of Naipaul's movement beyond the karma-like detachment of the colonial/determinist mentality."[20] But, he went on, Naipaul soon confirmed the pessimistic view of his work with his succeeding novels, *Guerillas* (1975) and *A Bend in the River* (1979). Every reader is, of course, subject to the appearance of later works when dealing with a living and active writer. But Thieme seems to have gone back on what he found in the epilogue, although surely his is an arguable position.

If, for Naipaul, the histories, the cultures, of new and old worlds alike are insufficient – offering no escape, much less a fruitful redefinition of our place in the world – there remains the condition of exile. This is more than merely a matter of Naipaul situating himself within a familiar modernist tradition, a tradition of formal inventiveness and fragmentation, of concentration upon the power of language, which has sprung from an earlier European experience of dislocation and rootlessness; it is a matter of him struggling to create a tradition of his own, a kind of order in the postmodern disorder, while resisting the blandishments of postmodernist discourse, of *nothing* but style.

What strikes me most in rereading the book now is the penultimate paragraph and the note of almost despairing nostalgia it sounds: looking back to "the only pure time, at the beginning, when the ancient artist, knowing no other land, had learned to look at his own and had seen it as complete." The longings of the exile in a time of universal upheaval seem to touch Naipaul most. Is this no more than the result of reading into it his most recent fictional narrative, *The Enigma of Arrival,* in which the *acceptance* of his incomplete, impure state (a Hindu-Brahmin notion?) provides creative renewal? Perhaps.

But what, then, of the *very* last lines, anticipating another cycle of war and defeat, which leaves the Egyptian peasant soldiers "lost, trying to walk back home, casting long shadows on the sand"? The shadow of the incinerated victims of a new world order overtakes this, even as we recognize in it Naipaul's own first journey from the concluding words of his first narrative, *Miguel Street:* "my shadow before me, a dancing dwarf on the tarmac."

NOTES

V. S. Naipaul is to date (1992) the author of nine novels; seven works of travel/ reflection; two collections of short stories; one "history"; a collection of articles, *The Overcrowded Barracoon* (London: André Deutsch, 1972) and *Finding the Centre* (London: André Deutsch, 1984), which contains two personal narrative pieces "about the process of writing." I have referred to most of these works, all of which are in print, although my main focus has been *In a Free State*, published first in Britain by André Deutsch in 1971, then by Alfred Knopf in the United States in 1973. For all references to his works I have used these currently available paperback editions:

FICTION

The Suffrage of Elvira, 1958 (Harmondsworth: Penguin, 1969)
Miguel Street, 1959 (Harmondsworth: Penguin, 1971)
A House for Mr Biswas, 1961 (Harmondsworth: Penguin, 1969)
The Mimic Men, 1967 (Harmondsworth: Penguin, 1969)
In a Free State, 1971 (Harmondsworth: Penguin, 1973)
A Bend in the River, 1979 (Harmondsworth: Penguin, 1980)
The Enigma of Arrival, 1987 (Harmondsworth: Penguin, 1987)

NONFICTION

The Middle Passage, 1962 (Harmondsworth: Penguin, 1969)
An Area of Darkness, 1964 (Harmondsworth: Penguin, 1969)
The Loss of El Dorado, 1969 (Harmondsworth: Penguin, 1973)
India: A Wounded Civilization, 1977 (Harmondsworth: Penguin, 1979)
India: A Million Mutinies Now, 1990 (London: Minerva, 1990)

References to Conrad's *Heart of Darkness* (first pub. 1899) are to the Norton Critical Edition, ed. Robert Kimbrough, 3rd ed. (New York: W. W. Norton, 1988).

Apart from the critical works referred to below (Thieme, White, Hamner, Cudjoe, Griffiths, and Nightingale), I would recommend the V. S. Naipaul Special Number of *Modern Fiction Studies* 30, no. 3 (1984), which also contains a useful select bibliography. Kenneth Ramchand's *The West Indian Novel and Its Background*, 2d rev. ed. (London: Heinemann, 1983), provides important information about the Caribbean literary context. A brief introductory study (up to *The Enigma of Arrival*) from a postmodernist perspective may be found in Peter Hughes, *V. S. Naipaul*, Routledge Contemporary Writers (London: Routledge, 1988).

I should also like to acknowledge a general debt to Edward Said's work and in particular to *Nationalism, Colonialism and Literature*, Field Day Pamphlet no. 15, Field Day Theatre Company Ltd., Derry, 1988, 5–22.

1. A. Sivanandan, "The Enigma of the Colonised," *Race and Class* 32, no. 1 (1990): 33.
2. C. L. R. James, *The Black Jacobins*, 2d rev. ed. (New York: Vintage, 1963), 405.
3. George Lamming, *The Pleasures of Exile* (London: Michael Joseph, 1960), 225.
4. John Thieme, *The Web of Tradition: Uses of Allusion in V. S. Naipaul's Fiction* (Mandelstrup, Denmark: Dangaroo Press, 1987), 35.
5. See Frantz Fanon, *The Wretched of the Earth*, trans. C. Farrington (Harmondsworth: Penguin, 1967), 178–79.
6. Derek Walcott, "The Spoiler's Return," *Collected Poems* (London: Faber, 1989), 433.
7. Selwyn R. Cudjoe, *V. S. Naipaul: A Materialist Reading* (Amherst: Univ. of Massachusetts Press, 1988), xiv, 5.
8. Edward Said, from *Nationalism, Colonialism and Literature* (Derry: Field Day Theatre Company, 1988); reprinted in *Literature in the Modern World*, ed. Dennis Walder (Oxford: Oxford Univ. Press, 1990), 39–41.
9. V. S. Naipaul, "Images," *New Statesman* (24 September 1965), 452–53; reprinted in *Critical Perspectives on V. S. Naipaul*, ed. Robert D. Hamner (London: Heinemann, 1979), 26–27.
10. Gareth Griffiths, *A Double Exile: African and West Indian Writing between Two Cultures* (London: Boyars, 1978), 106.
11. Cudjoe, *V. S. Naipaul*, 146.
12. Landeg White, *V. S. Naipaul: A Critical Introduction* (London: Macmillan, 1975), 195.
13. Ibid.
14. Letter, 14 July 1923; reprinted in the Norton Critical Edition of *Heart of Darkness*, ed. Robert Kimbrough, 3rd ed. (New York: W. W. Norton, 1988), 233–34.
15. V. S. Naipaul, "Conrad's Darkness," *New York Review of Books* (17 October 1974), 16–21; reprinted in Hamner, *Critical Perspectives*, 54–65.
16. Nadine Gordimer, "White Expatriates and Black Mimics: *In a Free State*," *New York Times Book Review* (17 October 1971): 5.
17. Adewale Maja-Pearce, "The Naipauls on Africa: An African View," *Journal of Commonwealth Literature* 20, no. 1 (1985): 111–12, 114–15. The specific academic quoted by Maja-Pearce is Landeg White, *Naipaul*, 200.
18. See Chinua Achebe, "Colonialist Criticism" (Paper read at Makerere University, Uganda, January 1974); reprinted in *Hopes and Impediments: Selected Essays, 1965–1987* (London: Heinemann, 1988), 46–60.
19. Peggy Nightingale, *Journey through Darkness: The Writing of V. S. Naipaul* (St. Lucia: Univ. of Queensland Press, 1987), 171.
20. Thieme, *Webb of Tradition*, 161.

4   The Profit of Language

George Lamming and
the Postcolonial Novel

Peter Hulme

The colonial situation is a matter of historical record. What
I'm saying is that the colonial experience is a *live* experience
in the *consciousness* of these people. And just because the
so-called colonial situation and its institutions may have been
transferred into something else, it is a fallacy to think that the
human-lived contents of those situations are automatically
transferred into something else, too. The experience is a continuing *psychic* experience that has to be dealt with and will
have to be dealt with long after the actual colonial situation
formally "ends." – George Lamming, in conversation

For political history the event that separates the colonial and
the postcolonial is called "independence." In that sense the United
States has been a postcolonial society since the late eighteenth century, Haiti and most of the South American countries since the early
nineteenth, and Cuba since 1898. Many of the British West Indian
islands finally became postcolonial in the 1970s. Meanwhile, Marti-
nique and Guadeloupe remain "colonial," although formally they are
not colonies but simply parts of France. Puerto Rico cannot be postcolonial since it is not independent: it is a colony, according to many
Puerto Ricans, but to the United States it is an associated commonwealth. These rather crude divisions may not bear much analysis, but

neither are they entirely dispensable. Like other ex-colonies, the United States went on to become a colonial power but one marked by its own prior status – as Melville's writing so clearly shows. And in the Caribbean, the focus of this essay, the very different patterns that colonial power has taken on different islands are always worth recalling.

Finally, though, the term *postcolonial* reverberates most within cultural history: it names something less tangible than the dates of a political independence ritually celebrated every year. Politically, most of the ex-British islands assert an independence that puts them on equal footing with, say, other member countries of the United Nations. Culturally, the term *postcolonial* carries the assertion of the end of an era and the name of that era, memory of which still marks its supersession. As George Lamming implies, the psychic experience of colonialism is as present in postcolonial culture as the word *colonialism* is in the term *postcolonialism.*

Almost all intellectuals and writers educated in colonial countries before independence were introduced to metropolitan values through reading the classics of European literature and have then spent most of their subsequent careers negotiating a relationship to this inheritance. In the English-speaking colonies Shakespeare was the embodiment of such "civilization," and, as is now widely acknowledged, *The Tempest* was seen by many colonial and postcolonial writers as the key play in the canon, the one that came closest to articulating at least some of the questions about colonialism which were at the forefront of intellectual debate in the 1950s and 1960s. Four writers made pioneering contributions to the rereading of *The Tempest* from a colonial perspective. In 1950 Octave Mannoni, a French colonial official sensitized by the violent repression of the 1947 Madagascan uprising and about to begin analysis with Jacques Lacan, published a psychological reading of the colonial situation which named its "complexes" after the characters of Prospero and Caliban. Mannoni's efforts were soon severely criticized in two of the seminal books of anticolonialism, Frantz Fanon's *Black Skin, White Masks* and Aimé Césaire's *Discourse on Colonialism*, and were not paid serious attention in studies of Shakespeare until quite recently. Nevertheless, his analysis of the character of Prospero remains a landmark in the study of the colonial situation.

The other three writers are from the Caribbean, and all wrote to

some extent under the influence of Frantz Fanon. In 1969 the Martiniquan playwright Aimé Césaire published his version of the play as
Une Tempête, with Prospero as a much clearer exemplar of colonial
oppression and Caliban as a devotee of African gods. Then in the
early 1970s the Cuban writer Roberto Fernández Retamar wrote a
series of essays that extended the use of Caliban as a cultural figure,
drawing on the work of Fanon and Césaire but connecting it to a
broader Caribbean tradition in which the figure of the Cuban radical
José Martí plays a key role.[1]

In a recent essay Retamar regrets not paying more attention to
George Lamming's 1960 essay "A Monster, A Child, A Slave," published in his collection *The Pleasures of Exile.*[2] Here Lamming reads
the play from the position of Caliban, overturning the usual identification of the critical reader with the position occupied in the play by
Prospero. But for Lamming the parallel is only secondarily a piece of
literary criticism. What *The Tempest* offers Lamming is a model for
thinking about his relationship as a writer to the past: in that sense
the figure of Caliban permeates all the essays in *The Pleasures of Exile,*
not just the reading of *The Tempest.* The past is on trial, and Lamming's
language is openly inquisitorial. And yet the roles are not as simple as
the model might initially imply. Lamming sees himself as both pros-
ecutor and witness for the prosecution, defense attorney and judge.
He is also guilty himself, since "this trial embraces only the living"
and only the eternally dead are innocent. He speaks of himself, as
one might expect, as a direct descendant of Caliban, but he also regards himself as in some way a descendant of Prospero (*PE,* 11). So
Lamming, according to his own analysis, has more than one part to
play in the rewriting of *The Tempest.* And, of course, even the part of
Caliban is itself by no means uncomplicated.[3]

There is one special complication that Lamming confronts in these
opening pages of *The Pleasures of Exile.* He recalls Hakluyt's narrative
of John Hawkins's first slaving trip in 1562. Hawkins, like Prospero,
had a difficult voyage but was succored by "Almightie God, who never
suffreth his elect to perish" and brought safely to the island of Dominica, "an Island of the Canybals":

> The Canybals of that Island, and also others adjacent are the
> most desperate warriers that are in the Indies, by the Span-
> iardes report, who are never able to conquer them, and they

are molested by them not a little, when they are driven to water there in any of those Islands: of very late, not two moneths past, in the said Island, a Caravel being driven to water, was in the night sette upon by the inhabitants, who cutte their cable in the halser, whereby they were driven ashore, and so taken by them, and eaten. (*PE*, 13, quoting from Hakluyt)

Part of the importance of *The Tempest* for West Indian history is the early date of the play (1611), after first English contacts with the island, as Hakluyt suggests, but before the first colonies were established. The Prospero-Caliban relationship has something of the pristine encounter between European and native. The complication though, for modern writers like Lamming who want to use Shakespeare's story is that Caliban is clearly related to Hakluyt's "Canybals," the Carib Indians who lived on islands such as Dominica during England's early attempts at colonization. To identify with the figure of Caliban is inevitably, for a modern black writer, a move fraught with difficulties: the Caribs have disappeared from almost all the Caribbean islands, but the strong memories of them which survive, not least in the islands' toponymies, make it clear that there are three historical actors on this sixteenth- and seventeenth-century stage – a native population as well as the Europeans and Africans from across the Atlantic.

The story of the native inhabitants is told in allegorical form by Lamming in several places in his work. In the first chapter of *The Pleasures of Exile*, called "In the Beginning," three young boys, Bob, Singh, and Lee, tell a Lady about the history of the Tribe Boys, their underground resistance to the arrival of the Bandit Kings, and their eventual heroic suicide from the top of Mount Misery (*PE*, 18–22), a story that also acts as an important rallying point for the resistance movement in Lamming's novel *Of Age and Innocence* and which returns again, in a different but particularly intense form, in *Natives of My Person*.

The founding genocide of colonial history is given its place in Lamming's work, with the figure of Caliban then extended to include the other victims, equally reviled, equally decultured by Prospero's discourse, and sharing equally the spirit of revolt which Prospero is determined to conquer (*PE*, 13).

Given the small size of the Caribbean islands and the relatively modest level of cultural life on most of them, the Caribbean novel has achieved an impressive reputation. *The Lost Steps, A House for Mr Biswas, Paradise, Wide Sargasso Sea, The Ripening, In the Castle of My Skin, Macho Camacho's Beat*–all have achieved the status of classics, widely read outside the region in which they were written. And yet the novel is a comparatively young form on the islands: of the major figures only Alejo Carpentier has a completed novelistic career. Others now dead, like Jacques Roumain and Jean Rhys, had larger careers of which novel writing was only one part, or they lived most of their lives out of contact with the islands.

From the English-speaking Caribbean a set of careers is now drawing to a close belonging to that generation of writers who left the islands in the years after World War Two and whose writings have bridged the independence of their countries: V. S. Naipaul, Sam Selvon, George Lamming. Naipaul's career is paradigmatic of a certain idea of the postcolonial: cynical traveler, at home nowhere, anatomist of the idiocies of the Third World. Lamming, like Edouard Glissant, the Martiniquan contemporary with whom he has much in common, has kept his writing more local, more concerned with the West Indies and West Indians. Lamming's first four novels were published between 1953 and 1960, and all are rooted in the experience of growing up and coming to terms with the political and cultural processes of West Indian life in the 1950s: education, emigration, prejudice, organization, and struggle. The mode is seemingly "realist," the concerns seemingly "political," in the sense of dealing with the changing topography of the years before and after independence. And yet, although conventionally seen as occupying the opposite political pole to Naipaul, Lamming's novels chart the complexities and difficulties inherent in those processes: there is no celebration and little obvious optimism about the future. Finally (to date), after a ten-year gap two novels appeared within a few months of each other in 1971 and 1972, *Natives of My Person* and *Water with Berries,* each of which offers a fraught meditation on *The Tempest,* the first a historical novel (or allegory) about the sixteenth-century Atlantic, the second a contemporary narrative that takes place mainly in suburban London. The settings are those established in Lamming's earlier novels–San Cristobal, a representative Caribbean island, and England–but the novels differ markedly from their predecessors. In the terms previously introduced it could be said that in these two books Lamming broke with the political sense of the postcolonial and set out to examine in quite radically different terms the psychic residue of colonialism's long history.[4]

Natives of My Person, although a deeply unconventional novel in many respects, is at least conventionally historical in its sixteenth-century setting. Some of the terms of its allegory are also familiar, those that allow us to identify Lime Stone as Britain, Antarctica as Spain, and the now familiar San Cristobal as an amalgam of various Caribbean islands. The principal characters, too, follow conventional lines, often named for their tasks and therefore representative of the kinds of Europeans who colonized the Caribbean islands.

The Commandant in *Natives of My Person* is in some ways a Prospero-like figure, although the relationship of the novel to *The Tempest* is by no means as close as in the case of *Water with Berries.* For my purposes here the most intriguing figure in the novel is the Lady of the House, daughter of Master Cecil, ex-mistress of the Commandant, and wife of the powerful Lord Treasurer, Gabriel Tate de Lysle. Her story emerges gradually from the pages of the novel, as the different "natives" coalesce as versions of the one "person." She begins as Cecil's daughter, taken out to the Demon Coast of San Cristobal, where she observes the practices of colonial mining firsthand. The official story, related by the fisherman Marcel, is that she "went mad what with living so near the blasphemies of the savage Tribes under her father's command" (38), but it is, in fact, the sight of the butchery of the indigenous population which stays with her. The Commandant remembers bringing her back a necklace made from pearls and rubies left behind by the Tribes at Sans Souci when they fled underground; as they talked, his voice drove "every cry of the mines from her memory" (65). But not for long.

When the Commandant breaks his promise to her and accepts charge of another voyage, she remembers well enough what she saw with her father and knows just what it is he means by his "work":

> "Work, you call it. You will sail again, I know. So tell me,
> answer me now. What will you kill when all the mines are
> empty, when every offspring of the Tribes is dead and buried?
> Tell me. You will sail, I know. So answer me now. Whose
> women will you murder next? Tell me, answer me, before you

> sail. Whose children will you strangle next? . . . Go feed on
> your humans. That's your work. Like the vultures over the
> Demon Coast, you feed on humans. . . . Name any monster,"
> she cried, "and he is no match for you. He never will be. A
> human-eater is what you are." (*NP,* 78–79)

The accusation of cannibalism made against the natives of the islands – remember Hakluyt's "Island of the Canybals"– is here turned
back in devastating fashion against the European colonizers, purvey-
ors of death and destruction to the island Tribes. That Lamming
should introduce a woman as a central character into a tradition of
writing which from *The Tempest* to *Robinson Crusoe* to *Treasure Island*
had been so resolutely masculine is a sign of his awareness of the connections between sexual and colonial politics. It is the Lady who sees
through the duplicities of colonial ideology and the Lady who demands
that the Commandant's new start should be a new start between sexual equals. She and the other women themselves sail to the Caribbean
to await their menfolk, but the burden of the past proves just too
heavy. The final chapter has the women sheltering in a cave, talking
to each other about the men, gradually coming to terms with the fact
that they are not going to arrive. The Lady speaks the last lines of the
book: "We are a future they must learn" (351).

If *Natives of My Person* is a reworking of *The Tempest*'s themes in its
original sixteenth-century setting, *Water with Berries* is in some sense
a continuation of the story of *The Tempest,* though with surprising
twists. As in Shakespeare's play, although the action, when it comes,
is intense, much of the earlier part of the novel moves slowly, with
any "action" coming through exposition of what has happened before
the present time of the fiction. In *The Tempest* Prospero tells Miranda
with great deliberation and even greater anxiety the story of their
exile from Milan and their arrival on the island. Later we also hear
the slightly different versions given by Ariel and Caliban.[5] In *Water
with Berries* the story of the past takes even longer to arrive. The first
part is given over halfway through the novel in one of its key scenes,
Teeton's meeting with Myra, a woman so degraded that she gives herself to any passing man on the heath, "an empty port for anyone's pleasure" (*WWB,* 151). Teeton has just learned about his wife's, Randa's,
suicide. He walks onto the heath, and his weariness pulls him down

to the ground. Prospero had commanded Miranda's attention to tell her the story of her origins. Myra starts her story hesitantly, aided by Teeton's questions: "'I was hardly three when we arrived on that island,' she said. 'Five thousand miles from home, and not a face that resembled our own. No native of intelligence to keep him company. Just the two of us. We lived alone until the day he died. The night the storm struck him down. We found his body in the lake next morning'" (145).

Teeton's urge to interrupt and ask her name is obliterated by her "astonishing burst of eloquence":

> "He taught me everything," she went on. "Nature was familiar
> as my own hands. The island had become my only home. I
> could name every plant, every flower. Not a single bird or
> beast could escape Father's curiosity. The rarest creature, the
> moment he saw it, would soon be subject to his learning.
> Never showed any interest in personal fortune. No taste at all
> for possession. He must have been a saint. The estate would
> have gone to ruin if it had not been for the care his servant
> lavished on him. He was the only school I had ever known.
> Until the day he died." (*WWB*, 145)

The parallels with *The Tempest* are close enough for us to recognize the story and to register the changes that Lamming is making to it. The storm, the island, the intense relationship between father and daughter, the absence of the mother, the hated servant, the arrival of a stranger called Fernando – the details gradually accumulate. But, as the parallels become undeniable, so Lamming subtly alters the story. For one thing it becomes contemporary: a sugar estate is inherited in compensation for a robbery borne gracefully by Myra's father (never named as 'Prospero').[6] The father dies on the night of the storm, his body found in the lake, his death perhaps organized – so Myra suggests – by the malevolent servant. And Myra herself (clearly 'Miranda') tells of her rape by the servant and his men and by the dogs:

> They found every crack in my body: operated through every
> opening in my body. I couldn't tell how many they were. But
> they seemed a whole army. Naked as wind they were. Not a
> rag to their skin. How many I don't know, nor how long. It
> seemed like eternity. They would rest and return, giving the

> interval over to the animals: Father's two hounds. It's as though
> they had trained the animals for this moment, put them
> through daily practice in this form of intercourse. They gave
> the animals the same privilege. Until I couldn't tell which body
> was the man's and which belonged to the beasts. (150)

Fernando was tied up and made to watch: "They made him their witness. . . . I believe it drove him mad" (151).

Then, almost at the end of the novel, comes a second and even
more startling set of revelations. The pilot who has taken Teeton and
his landlady, the Old Dowager, over to his tiny and remote Orcadian
island reveals to Teeton that he is Fernando, brother to 'Prospero,' that
the Old Dowager was 'Prospero's' wife, that Myra was her daughter
with Fernando, that 'Prospero' had abducted Myra, that Fernando had
murdered his brother, that Fernando had told the Old Dowager that
Myra had disappeared during the storm, and that the servants' rape of
Myra repeated the actions they had learned from watching 'Prospero'
unleash his dogs on their women. This second set of revelations reverberates backward through the novel, altering everything. It also works,
like Césaire's play, as a "transgressive appropriation" of *The Tempest*, a
deliberately "blasphemous" reworking of the "sacred" Shakespearean
text.[7]

Revisionist readings of *The Tempest* are usually characterized as having placed Caliban center stage, thereby shifting the audience's perception of the relationship between Prospero and Caliban and giving
greater weight to Caliban's own story, especially with respect to the
title to the island. This is not wrong. But Mannoni and Lamming, independently it would seem, have also placed great pressure on those
parts of the Shakespearean text which seem to suggest a deep sexual
anxiety. Some of these could be regarded as aspects of Prospero's
"character"; others are structural to the play itself—for example, the
establishment of an intense father-daughter relationship from which
the mother is totally absent. These undertones in the play are mag-
nified and worked upon in *Water with Berries*. Miranda's question to
Prospero, "Sir, are you not my father?" which provokes her father's
anxious reply, "Thy mother was a piece of virtue, and / She said thou
wast my daughter" (1.2.55–57), licenses the move in which Fernando
(as 'Antonio' from the play) is the lover of 'Prospero's' wife and father
of her daughter. In the novel 'Prospero' is as impotent sexually as he

is in stately affairs, taking his pleasure through dressing his wife in a transparent black nightgown and watching her lie in a coffin. Miranda's judgment on Antonio ("Good wombs have borne bad sons" [1.2.120]) is in the novel turned by Fernando against his brother: "Sprung from the same loins as myself, it's true. But a monster" (*WWB*, 227). If Caliban was the monster in *The Tempest*, in *Water with Berries* that role is clearly played by the Prospero figure.[8]

In his essay on *The Tempest* in *The Pleasures of Exile* Lamming had openly discussed the possible sexual relationships that could result as Miranda reaches puberty, deliberately provocative sentences in which he speculated about how the outcome of Miranda's pregnancy would allow us to tell whether it had been Prospero or Caliban who had penetrated her ("for it is most unlikely that Prospero and his daughter could produce a brown skin baby" [*PE*, 102]). That hint of incest, a theme also seen as present in the play by other critics, recurs in a different way in *Water with Berries*. Fernando arrives on the island and is introduced by 'Prospero' as his partner, his status as father to Myra and brother to 'Prospero' denied to him. He speaks to Teeton in the tones of an outraged father, his daughter estranged from him by 'Prospero's' training and then raped by 'Prospero's' servants. But Fernando does not know that Teeton has spoken to Myra and that she, unaware that Fernando is her father, has spoken of him in terms appropriate to that named role in *The Tempest*, preordained lover of Miranda: "And then the stranger from home arrived. And she learnt, for the first time, what was the origin of these fevers which had started to roast her body in sleep. Her father seemed kind as daylight to the man he introduced as his partner. He had come to help in the management of the estate. And she discovered what could happen when you were a woman. And she was happy" (*WWB*, 146).

As the parallels mount, the obvious question concerns the part of Caliban in this continuation of *The Tempest*. Several answers are possible, indeed probably several are necessary in order to avoid too simplistic an identification of Teeton, the black West Indian, with Caliban. That connection is certainly present. When Myra parries questions about her mother, Teeton is said not to be surprised, "for he had endured a childhood's silence to questions about the absence of a father from his life" (*WWB*, 147), as if Lamming were going out of his way to reestablish the asymmetrical parallels between the half-families of Miranda and Prospero, Caliban and Sycorax. When Myra tells her horrifying story of gang and animal rape Teeton is tortured *by guilt* for what he hears: "For a moment he felt as though he had been the agent of these barbarities" (151). And the Secret Gathering to which Teeton belongs, plotting a political coup on San Cristobal, is a more serious, if ultimately no more successful, version of Caliban's conspiracy. The historical resonance of their plans is strengthened by their deadline of 12 October, presumably – though Lamming does not mention this – the national holiday of an island bearing the same name as Christopher Columbus.

Lamming's own comments on the novel open up two kinds of complications to this seeming identification. Teeton's friends, Roger and Derek, musician and actor, also represent "aspects of Caliban," he says, and, in addition, they are all on a return journey "to Prospero's ancestral home – a journey which was, at the beginning, a logical kind of development because of the relation to Prospero's language. They then discovered the reality of Prospero's home – not from a distance, not filtered through Prospero's explanation or record of his home, but through their own immediate and direct experience."[9] In other words Teeton and Roger and Derek are in a sense Caliban, but Caliban several centuries later, the same but different, aware of the precedent but also aware of their difference from that precedent.[10] One of the differences produced by that lapse of time is that "that power – that imperial power, that spirit of adventure, that extraordinary obsession with turning the earth into one's private garden – is now gone." Prospero is long dead; the empire is represented by Mrs. Gore-Brittain, the Old Dowager, with her memories of the past: "Teeton lives as a *tenant* in her house, which is only another way of describing how he and people like him live in that country."[11] The imperial power has no "magic" with which to enforce the subservience of its subaltern peoples. Nonetheless, Teeton finds it extremely difficult to break the relationship that they have established, however necessary such a break might be to the success of his plans. Prospero's absent wife makes her appearance in *Water with Berries* as "mother" to the exiled West Indian, landlady rather than slavemaster, but, nonetheless, somebody with whom a relationship of interdependence is established – a postcolonial relationship but one that carries some of the psychic weight of the colonial within it.

The abiding problem of trying to read "Third World" literature from the metropolis is how to avoid the twin dangers of assimilation and exoticism. Critical reception of Caribbean novels such as those referred to at the beginning of this essay has gone through a number of stages, with regional variations that would connect some of the novelists to Latin America, others to the States, and others to a more generalized notion of the Third World. A broad historical survey would probably reveal that such novels were first appreciated for their "regional" qualities (local color), were then assimilated to metropolitan models and norms (realism), and have most recently been read in accordance with the supposedly "universal" category of postmodernism. In the different cases, of course, different novels have been valued – then devalued.

One of the few attempts to break away from the hegemony of these openly metropolitan standards is Fredric Jameson's development of the notion of "national allegory" as a way of arguing a different kind of relationship between the public and private spheres in Third World novels: "Third-world texts, even those which are seemingly private and invested with a properly libidinal dynamic – necessarily project a political dimension in the form of national allegory: *the story of the private individual destiny is always an allegory of the embattled situation of the public third-world culture and society.*"¹² This article of Jameson's has come in for heavy criticism, much of it justified.¹³ Yet one of its main points, that we (in the West) might look again at some of the early postcolonial novels seemingly overshadowed in recent years by their more spectacular postmodernist brethren and find in these texts rather more than the derivative realism we once perceived, is far from unhelpful when rereading Lamming, who has described his own task as "the shaping of national consciousness."¹⁴ To European literary critics that phrase might have the pseudoheroic ring of socialist realism, but there are no heroes in *Water with Berries*. If national consciousness is "shaped," then it is through an imaginative reassessment of the relationship between metropolis and ex-colony. And central to that reassessment is precisely the issue of public and private spheres highlighted by Jameson. Indeed, Teeton is caught between the two: trapped by the essentially privatized nature of artistic life in contemporary England yet unable to return to what he clearly sees as his "proper" public role in San Cristobal.

Allegory, or something like it, is also a necessary critical term –

until a more appropriate terminology has been developed – to discuss the mode in which the novel operates. The use of the word *allegory* at least suggests that the development of the novel takes place in accordance with imperatives that are not those of the "realism" to which its opening chapters seem to adhere. To spell this out: the establishment of Teeton and the Old Dowager as the central "characters" takes place within that mode of writing so deeply familiar as to be practically invisible. They seem to be "consolidating" as characters, to use Wilson Harris's helpful term.[15] Yet the plot, when it comes, is complicated by "coincidences" that could have no "realistic" explanation – and which would seriously weaken the novel if it were read according to the criteria of realism: that Teeton should come from the island Mrs. Gore Brittain's husband and daughter had gone to; that Myra should meet Teeton on the heath. Similarly, the "characters" established seemingly in accordance with a recognizable "psychology," begin to "act" in ways considerably in excess of any explanation that psychology might offer.

This is not to suggest that Lamming has some other perfectly formed set of narrative principles along which his book operates; it is difficult to imagine a reading of *Water with Berries* that would not run up against its inconsistencies and awkwardnesses of tone. My point is that the awkwardness is not a sign of a failure to adhere to a norm but, rather, a symptom of a breaking away from that norm toward a new way of writing (and reading) which has yet to be fully formulated, at least in the case of the Caribbean.[16] Lamming himself has offered one model for a writer's relationship to history and, by extension, to writing, which can provide a template on which to set the structure of *Water with Berries*. At the beginning of *The Pleasures of Exile* Lamming recalls having witnessed a "ceremony of the Souls" in the suburbs of Port-au-Prince, the capital of Haiti. The celebrants are relatives of the deceased. On this momentous night the Dead return to offer a full and honest report on their past relations with the living. The Dead have to speak honestly in order to be freed into the eternity that will be their destiny. The living are looking for knowledge of the past and guidance for their future. The ceremony is sometimes disrupted by the arrival of the Law, in which case the rites are performed in the street. Where two or three are gathered together and lines are made in dust, the gods are present. If the police arrive, to get up to greet them is sufficient to erase the lines. The ceremony stands, then, for "religion" in the sense of African ways that are sometimes forbidden by Western Law but which survive, unseen if necessary. Lamming immediately relates the conflict of religion and Law to *The Tempest*. Prospero's magic is clearly the operation of an official Law, upholding his (self-appointed) authority on the island. Caliban has his own religious practices, but they have to be performed out of Prospero's sight.

Throughout *Water with Berries* the presence of the dead presses upon the living. Early in the book the Old Dowager tells Teeton that her husband had spoken to her twelve years after his death (*WWB*, 30). The scene prefigures much of what happens later in the novel, but its significance escapes the first-time reader because we do not yet know that this remembered figure is 'Prospero,' and, in any case, we are at this stage likely to read through the conventions of realism by putting the communication down to an old woman's imagination. Her husband's death-centered fetishism is also described: Fernando later says "He always trafficked with the dead" (228) – as Prospero famously admits toward the end of *The Tempest* (5.1.48–50).

The central scene in *Water with Berries*, in which Teeton meets Myra on the heath, is preceded by Teeton recalling, in what seems part-dream and part-memory, the Ceremony of the Souls from his childhood: "these mourners who by native custom had come to settle their final account with the dead," presumably here assimilated to the Christian holy day of All Souls'. One year he had met Randa at this ceremony, and he tries to recall that meeting, but the face of Jeremy intervenes, "hovering like doom over the pond" (*WWB*, 107). The custom is here remembered by the character and thus becomes part of the fiction, motivated by Teeton's understandable concern with the death of his wife, just revealed to him by Jeremy. But it is after he has "opened his eyes," after, in other words, the fiction seems to have resumed its course in the narrative present, that the ceremony of the Dead truly commences as the ghosts of the colonial past come to haunt Teeton. They come, in a sense, under the cover of realism, but they are governed from outside realist conventions, allegorical figures to the extent that they signify through their relationship to *The Tempest*, however much Lamming alters the detail of their stories: "The world in which one lives is not just inhabited by the living. It is a world which is also the creation of the dead. And any architecture of the future cannot really take place without that continuing dialogue between the living and the dead."[17]

The last chapter of *Water with Berries* consists of four sentences:

> The publican of the Mona died two days after the remains of
> the Old Dowager's body were found.
> Derek alone escaped the charge of murder.
> But the Gathering defied the nation with their furious
> arguing that Teeton was innocent.
> They were all waiting for the trials to begin. (*WWB*, 249)

This may in some sense parody the final chapter of the realist novel,
but it offers none of the satisfactions of postmodernist fiction: there is
no irony, no humor, no excess, no play with conventions, no dramatic
refusal of the "ending." Instead, there is a situated ignorance. We are
placed at the end of the story but before the trials; we end before the
conclusion.

These last sentences of *Water with Berries* imply a text that is never
quoted: the newspaper accounts of the book's events – murder, arson,
indecent assault. Lamming is hardly writing a sociological novel;
there is no sense of these events being explained to an uncomprehending public. The book has no moral stance and offers no judgments.
What is felt is the weight of the past, history as a nightmare that is
still, secretly, writing the script whose lines we are speaking.

The hallmark of *Natives of My Person* and *Water with Berries* is the
extraordinary way in which present and past are combined. Lamming
himself notes that the House of Trade in *Natives of My Person* is as
much a modern multinational corporation as it is a sixteenth-century
institution. *Water with Berries* is a dense meditation on *The Tempest*
and its significance for the postcolonial era, but it is a book deeply
marked by the circumstances of its writing, as racism became a major
component of English social and political life: 1971, when *Water with
Berries* was published, is also the date of the most infamous of the
Immigration Acts that discriminated against West Indians, among other
groups from the so-called New Commonwealth.

From this perspective *Water with Berries* marks a transition in Lamming's work, even if, as yet, it is not clear what lies on this side of the
transition, at least for Lamming himself. The conspiracy in which Teeton is involved fails, and there is no return to San Cristobal. The three
West Indians will have to make their way here, on Prospero's island, for
better or worse. The "exile" has become permanent. "What they will
have to deal with now is the new reality in the experience – that is, the
world – the increasing world of Blacks in England, rather than what

they propose to do about the world on the island. The transformations of their 'homes' would have passed onto another generation."[18]

If the work of the postcolonial writer involves, as Lamming suggests earlier in his interview with George Kent in 1974, a "shaping of the national consciousness," then, perhaps surprisingly, this "nation" turns out to be Britain. No true ceremony of the souls takes place within the book, yet Teeton comes closer than anyone else to acting as a conduit between the living and the dead: he hears the stories, pieces together the past, and listens to its victims, even if, finally, as victim himself, he is hardly in a position to act.

Water with Berries certainly offers no prescriptions. Inasmuch as it can be thought of as a ceremony of the Souls itself, though, it serves as a reminder, if any such is necessary, that Britain too is a postcolonial country and that the heritage of colonialism is not renounced quite so easily as Prospero's example at the end of *The Tempest* might suggest. The souls of the colonial dead are not yet at peace.

NOTES

George Lamming, who was born in Barbados in 1927, has published six novels: *In the Castle of My Skin* (1953), *The Emigrants* (1954), *Of Age and Innocence* (1958), *Season of Adventure* (1960), *Water with Berries* (1971), and *Natives of My Person* (1972); and one book of essays, *The Pleasures of Exile* (1960). References to the last three books mentioned are to *Water with Berries* (London: Longman, 1973), *Natives of My Person* (London: Picador, 1974), and *The Pleasures of Exile*, 2d ed. (London: Allison & Busby, 1984); in these three cases quotations are identified by the abbreviations *WWB, NP, PE*. There is a good general account of Lamming's work in Sandra Pouchet Paquet, *The Novels of George Lamming* (London: Heinemann, 1982). On the last two novels, see also Helen Tiffin, "The Tyranny of History: George Lamming's *Natives of My Person* and *Water with Berries*," *Ariel* 10 (1979): 37–52; Avis G. McDonald, "'Within the Orbit of Power': Reading Allegory in George Lamming's *Natives of My Person*," *Journal of Commonwealth Literature* 22 (1987): 73–86; and Patrick Taylor, *The Narrative of Liberation: Perspectives on Afro-Caribbean Literature, Popular Culture, and Politics* (Ithaca: Cornell Univ. Press, 1989), 183–230.

For helpful comments on a draft of this essay I'd like to thank Dave Ellis, Sally Keenan, Jerry Phillips, Alden Vaughan, Dennis Walder, and Jonathan White.

Epigraph: In George E. Kent, "Caribbean Novelist: A Conversation with George Lamming," *Black World* 22, no. 5 (1973): 92.

1. See Octave Mannoni, *Prospero and Caliban; The Psychology of Colonization* (1950), trans. Pamela Powesland, 2d ed. (New York: Frederick A. Praeger, 1964); Frantz Fanon, *Black Skin, White Masks* (1952), trans. Charles Lam Markmann (London: Pluto, 1986); Aimé Césaire, *Une Tempête: D'après "la Tempête" de Shakespeare—Adaptation pour un théâtre nègre* (Paris: Seuil, 1969); and *Discourse*

on *Colonialism* (1955; reprint, New York: Monthly Review Press, 1972); and Roberto Fernández Retamar, *Caliban and Other Essays,* trans. Edward Baker (Minneapolis: Univ. of Minnesota Press, 1989). On this whole body of writing, see Rob Nixon, "Caribbean and African Appropriations of *The Tempest,*" *Critical Inquiry* 13 (1987): 557–78; Alden T. Vaughan, "Caliban in the 'Third World': Shakespeare's Savage as Sociopolitical Symbol," *Massachusetts Review* 29 (1988): 289–313; and Peter Hulme, "Rewriting the Caribbean Past: Cultural History in the Colonial Context," in *Interpretation and Cultural History,* ed. Joan H. Pittock and Andrew Wear (London: Macmillan, 1991), 175–97.

2. Retamar, "Caliban Revisited," *Caliban and Other Essays,* 119 n. 17.

3. For one thing language ties Prospero and Caliban together: see Lowell Fiet, "Reassessing Caliban's Exile," *Sargasso* 3 (1986): 78–84; and George Lamming and Gordon K. Lewis, "Intersections and Divergences" (interview), *Sargasso* 3 (1986): 3–30.

4. Lamming himself, on the other hand, emphasizes the internal logic of his novelistic career (in Kent, "Caribbean Novelist," 96).

5. See Peter Hulme, *Colonial Encounters: Europe and the Native Caribbean, 1492–1797* (London: Methuen, 1986), 126–27.

6. I have used single quotation marks around names to designate the equivalent characters in *The Tempest* who do not carry a name in *Water with Berries.*

7. For the term *transgressive appropriation,* see Nixon, "Caribbean and African Appropriations," 558. Lamming himself discusses the "blasphemy" of his reading of *The Tempest* (*PE,* 9).

8. On "Prospero's wife" in Shakespearean criticism, see Stephen Orgel, "Prospero's Wife," *Representations* 8 (1984): 1–13.

9. Lamming, in Kent, "Caribbean Novelist," 89.

10. On the three West Indian characters, see the good discussion in Sandra Pouchet Paquet, *The Novels of George Lamming* (London: Heinemann, 1982), 87.

11. Lamming, in Kent, "Caribbean Novelist," 91.

12. Fredric Jameson, "Third-World Literature in the Era of Multinational Capitalism," *Social Text* 15 (1986): 69.

13. See Aijza Ahmad, "Jameson's Rhetoric of Otherness and the 'National Allegory,'" *Social Text* 17 (1987): 3–25. On *allegory* as a useful term for analyzing postcolonial literature, see also Stephen Slemon, "Monuments of Empire: Allegory/Counter-Discourse/Post-Colonial Writing," *Kunapipi* 9, no. 3 (1987): 1–16.

14. Lamming, in Kent, "Caribbean Novelist," 90.

15. See Wilson Harris, "Tradition and the West Indian Novel," in *Tradition, the Writer and Society* (London: New Beacon Books, 1967), 28–47.

16. If there is a model for this kind of writing within the European tradition, it would probably be something as anomalous as Conrad's *Under Western Eyes,* with its intricately wrought dialogues, matched here by the set piece between Teeton and Jeremy. There are some parallels also between Lamming's practice and the theory outlined in Wilson Harris's 1967 essay (ibid.), although their novels are quite different.

17. Lamming, in Kent, "Caribbean Novelist," 94.

18. Ibid., 95.

5 "Unsystematic Fingers at the Conditions of the Times"

"Afropop" and the
Paradoxes of Imperialism

Neil Lazarus

I would like to begin by referring to a scene from *The Healers,* a novel by the Ghanaian writer Ayi Kwei Armah. Published in 1978, *The Healers* offers a perspective on the collapse of Ashanti power and the formal institution of British colonial rule in Ghana in the 1870s. The novel's final scene describes an official ceremony, as the ranks of the British forces against the Ashanti, composed overwhelmingly of African conscripts drawn from the entire region of West Africa, are marshaled to attend the departure for England of the victorious British general Wolseley. Here is how the novel ends:

> West Indian soldiers had come with [Wolseley] to the bay, with their guns and musical instruments. . . . [They] played solemn music to send the white general off. But once the ship had disappeared, their playing changed. The stiff, straight, graceless beats of white music vanished. Instead, there was a new, skilful, strangely happy interweaving of rhythms, and instead of marching back through the streets the soldiers danced. Others joined them. . . . All the groups gathered by the whites to come and fight for them were there and they all danced. . . . A grotesque, variegated crowd they made, snaking its way through the town. . . .
>
> "It's the new dance," Ajoa said, shaking her head. She spoke

> sadly, and her sadness was merely a reflection of the sadness
> of [the other healers] . . . as they watched.
>   But beside them they heard a long, low chuckle of infinite
> amusement. It came from Ama Nkroma. . . . "It's a new dance
> all right," she said, "and it's grotesque. But look at all the black
> people the whites have brought here. Here we healers have
> been wondering about ways to bring our people together again.
> And the whites want ways to drive us farther apart. Does it
> not amuse you, that in their wish to drive us apart the whites
> are actually bringing us work for the future? Look!"
>   Together with Ama Nkroma's laughter, tears came to her
> eyes.[1]

In two respects this scene is exemplary of the line of argument I
want to follow in this chapter. First, there is the recognition, familiar
in its structure to any reader of Marx or Fanon or C. L. R. James, that
colonialism creates the conditions of possibility of its own overthrow,
since it brings the colonized into existence as a collectivity whose
objective interests are not only diametrically opposed to those of the
colonial state but also incapable of realization on the terrain of colonialism. Second, there is the identification of a latently resistive
dynamic of cultural indigenization. The West Indian guard is spoken
of as having appropriated "the white men's instruments." Instruments
whose normative usage in this context is imperial and militaristic are
domesticated and made over, refunctioned to bear the imprint of a
different — and, indeed, opposing — cultural logic.

In what follows I would like to speculate further on this subject of
indigenization, taking as my primary example the case of popular
dance music from contemporary Zimbabwe. Before turning to this
music, however, it is necessary to give some preliminary consideration to the concept of indigenization itself and to some of the theoretical and ideological implications of using it in cultural analysis.

Many ethnomusicologists and scholars of African culture would
reject in principle the idea of taking as one's object of analysis a compound form such as African pop music. Their argument would be that
the putative "Africanity" of this music has been wholly overdetermined
and compromised by Western compositional grammars and styles of
performance. As Deborah James has recently pointed out, the work of
ethnomusicologists of this persuasion "is most often associated with an

interest in 'pure' traditional music, and a scorn for hybrid styles or those which have evolved out of the experience of proletarianized communities."[2] James refers especially to Hugh Tracey and his assumptions that "urban African music lacks the formal integrity of its 'traditional' forebears, and that it has been bastardized by its assimilation of Western forms."[3] But similar assumptions are shared by other prominent scholars of African music: the Cameroonian musicologist Francis Bebey, for instance, opens his classic study *African Music: A People's Art* with the pointed definition of "authentic African music" as "the traditional music of the black peoples of Africa."[4] In terms of such a definition, obviously, the popular music of Africa today would be characterized as nontraditional and dismissed as inauthentic.

Several rejoinders to this kind of argument are possible. One can demonstrate, for instance, as David Coplan in the case of South Africa and John Storm Roberts and others in the general case of sub-Saharan Africa have done, that the so-called Western forms by which urban African music has allegedly been compromised are themselves strongly marked by the African forms on which they, in turn, were substantially predicated.[5] The extensive influence of Cuban and Brazilian music on playing styles in West Africa, Angola, and the Congo, for instance, is patently neither coincidental nor the result of any merely contingent factor. Rather, as Roberts notes, it is a function of the direct historical link between these cultures.[6]

Similarly, one can put pressure on the essentialist notion of tradition which ethnomusicologists such as Hugh Tracey and Bebey typically assume. Tracey's son, Andrew, who shares his father's general disapproval of popular and urban styles of African music, has lamented that "in traditional African music these days, you almost never hear the original harmony. There's always someone putting in that third note and you have this sickly-sounding Western harmony all the time."[7] The point here is that the Traceys' idea of a pure traditional African music is resolutely unhistorical. Like all cultural forms everywhere at all times, African music has been ceaselessly in the process of transformation, as it has moved to assimilate, and to accommodate itself to, new sounds, new instruments, new tongues, and new social imperatives. "The 'purity' of third world music" therefore, as Andrew Goodwin and Joe Gore have recently suggested, "must always be questioned not only for dangerous (we would say *racist*) ideological assumptions about the 'authenticity' of non-western cultures, but also for empirical flaws in the argument."[8] To listen – even as an "insider," which I am not – to a Mande song, sung in traditional style with *kora* accompaniment, is not and has never been to encounter unchanging tradition. Rather, it is to grapple, necessarily, with culture as a historical palimpsest: here the phrasing and intonation will be clearly Islamic; here the *kora's* lyrical range will have been influenced by flamenco guitar, or, in the case of a contemporary musician such as Toumani Diabate, by jazz and blues; here the references will be to a specific historical event in the days of the empire of Mali; and so on.

It is instructive, in this context, to listen to the most recent of Salif Keita's albums, *Soro* (Mango, 1987), *Ko-Yan* (Mango, 1989), and *Amen* (Mango, 1991). Keita is a Malian, born into the dynastic Keita family in 1949. Because of his royal birth, his road to musicianship was difficult. As he put it in 1985, in an interview with Chris Stapleton: "I come from a noble family. We are not supposed to become singers. If a noble had anything to say, he had to say it through a griot."[9] Keita's decision to leave school in the late 1960s to become a musician caused an uproar both in his family and in the wider Malian society. Yet, if he was setting his back against a caste system that had been upheld in Mali and elsewhere in West Africa for hundreds of years, he was emphatically not abandoning his cultural roots. The object of his antagonism was not the Mande cultural tradition but, instead, the rigid and uncritical positing of this tradition as a timeless social code: "At home, we are traditionalists. It's an attitude I disapprove of. It's we who make the history, and if we refer only to what has passed, there will be no history. I belong to a century that has little in common with the time of my ancestors. I want society to move."[10]

Keita's lyrics are addressed prescriptively to the arena of contemporary social existence, but they remain scrupulously attentive to Mande history. And the same nuanced and meditative reworking of traditional forms is evident in his musical arrangements, both with the band Les Ambassadeurs and, since 1985, as a solo artist. Built around his astonishingly expressive voice, in which the rhythms of the Bambara language are infused with Islamic and Arabic registers, Salif Keita's music is "powered by horns, keyboards and electric guitars which carry the inflections of kora and balafon music."[11] The total effect, as Nii Yamotei has written, is to provide a "powerful, seamless, and highly sensitive melting pot of influences; transplanting the traditional music of the griots into the present. He has blended in other

West African influences from Guinea and Senegal, and influences from Cuba, Spain and Portugal, fusing his traditional vocal themes with modern instruments and style."[12] The album *Soro* was recorded at Studio Harry Son in Paris, on a 48-track digital machine. The title track, "Soro (Afriki)" is operatic in conception and features West African musicians on percussion (trap set drums, congas, *djembes*), guitars and vocals, and French session musicians on saxophone, trumpet, trombone, and keyboards. The call-and-response Bambara lyrics encourage Africans to seek happiness in unity, an appeal embedded in the traditional Mande concept of *djibe:*

> If a wife is a true partner
> In the home
> We call her "djibe"
>
> "Djibe" is the name we give
> The white horse and honesty
> Sincere and united neighbours
> We call "djibe" too
>
> Africans, let us be "djibe"
> Let's try and find
> Happiness in unity

The affirmative character of indigenization as a cultural dynamic should not be overstated, of course. In defining a position against essentialism, it is important to avoid an equally idealist theorization of indigenization as cultural "dialogue," a theorization that, in its hurry to celebrate the syncretic tendencies of contemporary African cultural practice, would "forget" about imperialism altogether, or bracket it as a "political" phenomenon, without implications for the putatively autonomous sphere of culture. Chinua Achebe has pointed out that one cannot talk about "cultural exchange in a spirit of partnership between North and South," because "no definition of partnership can evade the notion of equality" and because there is no equality in prevailing North-South relations.[13] The point here is that, if we wish to speak of contemporary African music in the light of anti-imperialist cultural struggle, it is necessary for us to begin by conceding the effectivity and reach of imperialism. This reach is not total; if it were, there would be no countering it. But, if it is not total, it is nevertheless extensive, both in material and in ideological terms. Billy Bergman, for instance, has drawn attention to the role played in the "Third World" by

> the big five multinational record companies – CBS, EMI, Poly-
> gram, WEA, and RCA – with their complex system of subsidiar-
> ies and licensing arrangements. . . . They record local music
> and distribute it to local and, sometimes, international markets.
> Then they also promote and distribute Top Forties American
> and British hits with the same fervor that such music is pro-
> moted in the United States and Europe. The clout these multi-
> nationals have has been documented by musical economists
> Wallis and Malm: "Using hundreds of promotion men and over
> a thousand salesmen, [EMI, for example] . . . has the power to
> stimulate demand both in quantity and quality and to meet the
> demand when sales accelerate."[14]

The adverse ideological consequences of this general state of affairs have recently been demonstrated in South Africa in the aftermath of the release of Paul Simon's album *Graceland* in 1986. In *Graceland,* as South African musician Johnny Clegg has observed, Simon "basically presented to the world an image of South African music that [was] . . . sixteen, twenty years old. That music . . . you don't hear it any more. . . . There's a time warp. And young black musicians are being told by the record companies, 'Look, guys, you've got to go back twenty years, because that's where the market is now.' They feel quite resentful."[15] The crucial point here is that *Graceland* has been so suc-cessful internationally that, even though there has been little re-surgence of interest in its style of music in South Africa itself, the big recording companies in the country have spent a considerable amount of energy in the intervening years pressuring sometimes reluctant local musicians to put out music in the *Graceland* idiom and making it difficult for them to get contracts otherwise. The net result has been a restrictive channeling of creative energies and a compounding of the already exploitative relations between black South African musi-cians and record producers in the country, the vast majority of whom are white.

The effect of *Graceland,* in short, has been to contribute to the *under-development* of black South African music. The immanent trajectory of the development of this music has been put under threat of desta-bilization from without, since there are now powerful voices in the

country calling for the production of music in accordance with the
world system's dominant consuming interests, those in Europe and
the United States. It is this fact, more than any other, that renders
Graceland frankly imperialist.

There is in the work of Simon, David Byrne, Paul McCartney, Brian
Eno, Lionel Richie, and many other influential musicians in the West
a profound insensitivity to the politico-ethical implications of cultural
appropriation across the international division of labor. Even in the
best of the work of these musicians – I am thinking, for instance, of
the brilliant and witty mock lament "Nothing but Flowers," on the
1988 Talking Heads album, *Naked* (Fly/Sire), or of any of the tracks on
Graceland – there is a distressing unilateralism of influence. While
"Nothing but Flowers" features Abdou M'Boup on congas, Yves
N'Djock on guitars, and Brice Wassy on shaker and has a distinctly
West African feel about it, it remains wholly and unrepentantly Euro-
American in its lyric reference. The discrepancy between the self-
conscious "One-Worldism" of the music and the unselfconscious
"First-Worldism" of the lyrics is discomfiting, and not in a productive
sense:

> Here we stand
> Like an Adam and an Eve
> Waterfalls
> The Garden of Eden
> *Two fools in love*
> So beautiful and strong
> The birds in the trees
> Are smiling upon them
> From the age of the dinosaurs
> Cars have run on gasoline
> Where, where have they gone?
> Now, it's nothing but flowers
> There was a factory
> Now there are mountains and rivers . . .
> We caught a rattlesnake
> Now we got something for dinner . . .
> There was a shopping mall
> Now it's all covered with flowers . . .

> If this is paradise
> I wish I had a lawnmower

It is hard to rid oneself of the suspicion that the organizing logic of this composition is that of advanced capitalist consumerism: as though from the center of the world system—his apartment in Manhattan— Byrne had selected diverse sounds, rhythms, and musical motifs from all over the world out of a catalog, and blended them into an exotic and hi-tech backdrop for his parodic, postmodern, but paradoxically *stabilizing* play on nature and culture.[16]

Similarly, while Simon draws his musical inspiration in *Graceland* not only from Sotho, Shangani, Zulu, and other South African musics but also from West Africa (Nigerian pedal steel guitarist Demola Adepoju plays on the title track and the popular Senegalese singer Youssou N'Dour is featured on "Diamonds on the Soles of Her Shoes"), Cajun Louisiana, and Chicano Los Angeles, his lyrics reveal a complete lack of cultural dialogism. Here, for instance, is the improbable opening verse from the *mbaqanga*-based track "Gumboots":

> I was having this discussion
> In a taxi heading downtown
> Rearranging my position
> On this friend of mine who had
> A little bit of a breakdown
> I said breakdowns come
> And breakdowns go
> So what are you going to do about it
> That's what I'd like to know
>
> You don't feel you could love me
> But I feel you could

There are even occasions in *Graceland* in which Simon's choice of lyrics seems actively to contribute to imperialist cultural assumptions about Africa and the "Third World." The album's opening track, "The Boy in the Bubble," begins as follows:

> It was a slow day
> And the sun was beating
> On the soldiers by the side of the road
> There was a bright light

A shattering of shop windows
The bomb in the baby carriage
Was wired to the radio

These are the days of miracle and wonder
This is the long distance call
The way the camera follows us in slo-mo
The way we look to us all
The way we look to a distant constellation
That's dying in the corner of the sky
These are the days of miracle and wonder
And don't cry baby, don't cry

In the context of the "armed struggle" in South Africa, in which the African National Congress scrupulously attempted to avoid the kinds of attack on civilian targets which would enable the state to brand it unproblematically as a "terrorist" organization, these lyrics are ill advised at best. And they are scarcely atypical. It is not for nothing, thus, that the hard-rock band Living Colour should have chosen to spoof Simon in the track "Elvis Is Dead" on their 1990 album, *Time's Up.* In the title track on *Graceland* Simon had sung of having

a reason to believe
We all will be received
In Graceland.

In "Elvis Is Dead," by contrast, one finds what music critic Jon Pareles calls "a sly reversal" of these lines. Living Colour sing, "I got a reason to believe we all *won't* be received at Graceland," an apparent reference, as Pareles notes, "to Presley's racist public statements" and to Simon's wholesale neglect of the question of race in the lyrics of *Graceland.*[17]

Graceland was produced by Warner Brothers Records. *Naked* was produced by Sire Records Company but marketed by Warner Brothers. Until fairly recently multinational corporations were responsible for almost all of the recording that took place in Africa, and it was only the superstars in the African popular musical firmament – musicians such as Manu Dibango, Franco and Tabu Ley – who were able to exercise any creative control in the production, distribution, and marketing of their music. Today the situation is somewhat different: on the one hand, there has been a proliferation of small, predominantly privately owned recording companies in several African states; on the other hand, a number of European-based independent companies have emerged to challenge the dominance of the multinationals. It is these independents – labels such as Sterns, Earthworks, Globe-Style, Oval Records, Shanachie, WOMAD, and Discafrique – which have been largely responsible for the recent explosion of interest in African music among Euro-American listeners. To date, as Ronnie Graham has written, their contribution has been a positive one. Founded by individuals with "enthusiasm, imagination, a background in Africa and, most of all, access to 'progressive capital,'" they "have been able to make significant contributions to the promotion of African music while, in the main, correctly interpreting trends originating in Africa and throwing their meagre resources behind these innovations."[18]

Zimbabwe has been one of the African countries best served by the independent record labels. Doubtless, this is partly a matter of luck: the emergence of the independents, and of Euro-American interest in African music, happened to coincide with Zimbabwe's acquisition of political sovereignty in 1980 and the consequent burgeoning of the music industry in that country. But one should not underestimate the extent to which, reciprocally, Zimbabwe's widely publicized and internationally popular accession to sovereign statehood after years of struggle served as a catalyst, stimulating Westerners to listen to music from that country.

The recent history of music in Zimbabwe makes for a remarkable narrative. One can glean the centrality of the national liberation struggle merely from a casual recitation of the names of leading bands: Thomas Mapfumo and the Blacks Unlimited, the Bhundu Boys,[19] the Marxist Brothers, Ephat Mujuru and the Spirit of the People, the Fallen Heroes, Zexie Manatsa and the Green Arrows, Susan Mapfumo and the Black Salutarys, Robson Banda and the New Black Eagles, and many others. But before turning to the national liberation struggle it might be helpful to make a few prefatory historical remarks.

In the precolonial era the music of the Shona people in what would become Zimbabwe was founded on the mbira, a legendary instrument found in many parts of Africa and consisting of a set of between eight and fifty keys laid over a usually flat soundboard and typically placed in a box resonator or some other device for amplifying the sound.[20] Strongly associated with Shona religious and artistic practices, the

mbira was ruthlessly disparaged, in the years following colonial conquest, by colonial officials and European missionaries. Performers
often "found themselves subject to intense religious indoctrination as
well as ridicule and abuse for being mbira players."[21] As a result of
these pressures, Paul Berliner has written,

> Mbira music suffered a decline in popularity in certain parts of
> the country. . . . It would appear . . . that for a period of time
> the older generation of mbira players had difficulty finding
> members of the younger generation to whom they could im-
> part their knowledge of mbira music. Young Shona students
> . . . had had a negative image of traditional African culture
> instilled in them and they therefore shunned identification
> with the ways of the elders. Those individuals who showed
> musical skill gravitated toward the guitar rather than the
> mbira. . . . In a sense, for a generation of Africans the guitar
> and the mbira came to symbolize a dichotomy of life-styles and
> values. Africans associated the mbira with the poverty of the
> reserves and with things "unChristian" and "old-fashioned,"
> while the guitar represented the wealth and glamor of the
> cities and things "modern" and "Western."[22]

This dichotomy, characteristic of the years between 1920 and 1960,
and so obviously convenient for the purposes of colonial rule, was
challenged and eventually shattered by the rise of nationalism and
the coming of the liberation struggle in Zimbabwe. Anticolonial nationalists began to pay attention to the mbira precisely *because* it was
regarded with contempt by the colonial authorities, and when, during
the struggle for liberation, the countryside became the resistance
movement's center of gravity, the beauty and integrity of the mbira's
sound was, however belatedly, once again recognized.

Remarkably, however, the return to the mbira was not in this case a
mere nativist gesture. On the contrary, as the struggle intensified, an
astonishing fusion of mbira sounds and conventions, Western instru-
mentation, and modern means of communication took the war to the
remotest regions of the country. The fusion was called *chimurenga,* the
Shona word for "struggle," and *chimurenga* came to refer both to the war
of liberation and to the style of music which spread its message. From
outside the country every evening at 8 P.M. Radio Mozambique broadcast the liberation movement's news program, "Voice of Zimbabwe," on

shortwave and mediumwave. It was picked up throughout Zimbabwe, despite the efforts of the Rhodesian government to jam the signal, to restrict the ownership of transistor radios, and to market a new cheap transistor receiving only FM signals. The most popular feature of the "Voice of Zimbabwe" broadcasts was the "Chimurenga Requests" segment, in which listeners' written requests for *chimurenga* songs would be entertained. Most of these songs had been written by fighters in the various guerrilla bases in Mozambique and elsewhere. Usually traditional in structure and melody, they were sung in Shona, Sindebele, and other Zimbabwean languages and tended, as one might expect, to be explicit and lyrically direct:

> People of Zimbabwe
> Living under oppression
> The world is changing
> Arise! Arise![23]

Music from the "Chimurenga Requests" program was, of course, banned in Ian Smith's Rhodesia itself. In the mid-1970s, however, Thomas Mapfumo began to develop an "internal" variant of the form. At that time the dominant shaping influence on Zimbabwean pop music was Cuban-derived Congolese rumba. (Other major influences were American soul, funk, and rhythm and blues and South African township jive.) This Congolese sound, today called *soukous* (or, in much of East Africa, *sungura*), has been for the past two decades or so probably the most widely influential form of pop music in all of Africa. Its influence can be heard in Tanzania, Kenya, Mozambique, Angola, Cameroon, Senegal, the Ivory Coast, and elsewhere. Roberts has written of its "immense force and flexibility," adding that although *soukous* "at first sounds somewhat Latin American . . . there is actually nothing like it in the New World. It seems to have grown partly from localizing techniques . . . and partly from the playing on guitar of lines that, in Cuban music, were brass or sax lines."[24]

Yet, instead of basing himself on the sounds of *soukous*, Mapfumo predicated his music on the ancestral rhythms and cadences of the mbira, utilizing guitars that mimicked the mbira sound, producing driving guitar lines made up of discrete but cascading notes. Recording and performing in public in Zimbabwe, Mapfumo obviously could not duplicate the outspokenness of music from the Requests program. Here, too, however, confronted by the problem of censorship, he was able to formulate a tradition-based solution, for historically, as Paul Berliner has observed, ambiguity and innuendo have been central features in the performance of mbira music: "Since subtlety is an important element in the art of [mbira playing], performers strive to express themselves indirectly at times, and members of the audience must guess at the meaning of their words. It is not uncommon for individuals listening to a performance of mbira music to derive differing meanings from the singer's lines."[25]

This customary motif was tailor-made for incorporation into the underground *chimurenga* music pioneered by Mapfumo. Mapfumo himself attained enormous popularity in Zimbabwe in the late 1970s on the strength of a string of releases that alluded delicately or indirectly to the liberation struggle. These tracks were never played on the radio, but their indirection and apparent apoliticality was for the most part sufficient to ensure that they were not banned outright, and, despite the lack of radio play, and the total absence of publicity, several of them became best-sellers in Zimbabwe. One of these was "Pamuromo Chete" (These Are Mere Words), whose lyrics give some idea of the mode of address of Mapfumo's music in the 1970s:

> Some of our people, Lord,
> Live as squatters at the Market Square;
> Some of our people, Lord,
> Have no place to go;
> Some of our people, Lord,
> Are suffering;
> Some of our people, Lord,
> Are existing as strays.
>
> These are mere words.
> These are mere words.[26]

Mapfumo has said of this song that it "wasn't being sung directly": "I was telling Mr. Smith that there were people in such trouble that all his talking was mere words, talk without substance. He was saying that never in a thousand years would we have a majority government. And I was saying that people will fight for the freedom they want. . . . The people understood. They knew what I was talking about."[27]

Mapfumo was made to pay for his activism. He was continually harassed by the Rhodesian authorities. On one occasion he was detained for ninety days without trial. On another occasion he was kidnapped. He was forced to perform at political rallies for Bishop Abel Muzorewa, a conservative black political figure broadly aligned with the ruling white Rhodesian regime. And he was routinely summonsed to police stations and subjected to interrogation.

Since Zimbabwe's independence in April 1980 Mapfumo's career has gone from strength to strength. The independence period saw the release of several songs glorying in the success of the national liberation struggle and, in a more somber vein, attempting to weigh the continuing obstacles to prosperity. In "Ndamutswa Nengoma" (Drums Have Woken Me Up), for instance, Mapfumo sings:

> The sun has risen forever
> There will never be darkness again in Zimbabwe
> It has dawned forever
> Let's work together – let's have socialism . . .
> I have been asleep
> Drums have woken me up.[28]

Similar sentiments are voiced in tracks such as "Kwaedza Mu Zimbabwe" (It Has Dawned in Zimbabwe) and "Nyarai" (Be Ashamed), the former purely celebratory, the latter urging "reactionaries" to abandon their opposition to Robert Mugabe's new government.[29] Already by independence, however, Mapfumo was beginning to turn his commitment and political vision to the problems of postcolonialism in Zimbabwe. In "Chauya Chirizevha" (Rural Life is Back), composed before independence, for instance, he addressed the questions of reconstruction and of the return of citizens to their homes in the countryside:

> The Chief was really saddened
> Seeing all his people come back
> To rural life
>
> Some lost their legs
> Some died there (in the bush)
> Some died in their homes
> Some fled their homes because of the war
>
> Today the war is over
> For sure the war is over
> And finished, Chief.[30]

This extension in the reference of Mapfumo's music has continued throughout the 1980s and into the 1990s. The results can best be appreciated on *Corruption* and *Chamunorwa* (What Are We Fighting For?), two albums by Mapfumo and the Blacks Unlimited, released – to considerable fanfare – by Island Records' Mango subsidiary in 1989 and 1991, respectively. *Corruption,* in particular, offers a brilliant example of politically committed popular music making. Recorded at Shed Studios in Harare, the production values are extremely high. Mapfumo sings about the legacy of the liberation struggle in "Chigwindiri" (A Very Strong Person), but most of the tracks on the album are devoted to postcolonial issues of class division, political disunity, and public morality. Similarly, whereas some tracks, such as "Muchadura" (You Will Confess), are still instrumentally reminiscent of the electric mbira sound of *chimurenga* music, others sample freely from reggae, *kwela, mbaqanga,* funk, and *sungura* styles.

This tendency to reach out beyond the *chimurenga* sound to other musical styles, while retaining the political focus of *chimurenga,* typifies Zimbabwean pop music in the 1980s and early 1990s. One observes it, for instance, in the music of such outfits as the Four Brothers, Oliver Mutukudzi, the Jairos Jiri Sunrise Kwela Band, the Sungura Boys, Jonah Moyo and Devera Ngwena, and in the Bhundu Boys. Along with Stella Chiweshe, whose mbira-based sound has recently become very popular, the Bhundu Boys are, perhaps, the only Zimbabwean band whose fame and popularity, both within Zimbabwe and internationally, rivals Mapfumo's.

Like Mapfumo, they are committed to the political vision of a socialist Zimbabwe. Their superb third album, *True Jit* (Mango, 1988), for instance, is dedicated "to Robert Mugabe and the others who restored sanity to our country." Yet the Bhundu Boys sound nothing like Mapfumo. After all, the "jit" to which their album title refers is the name of a vibrant young people's music, heavily percussive and vocally melodic. The band's commitment to jit-jive, as Chris Stapleton has noted, puts them "at some distance from the elders of modern Zimbabwe pop, among them Thomas Mapfumo, who base their repertoire around the ancient mbira tradition."[31] Certainly, Mapfumo's mbira guitar style remains a heavy influence on a track such as "Chemedzevana" on *True Jit,* in which in counterpoint with the loping bass it provides the rhythmic anchor for the song's explorations into different musical domains. Yet the track is more noteworthy, perhaps, for its incorporation of elements from other southern and central African popular musics, a true case of "South-South dialogue." The jangling, bell-like guitar playing of the climax, for instance, is reminiscent of the guitar lines of Congolese *soukous,* as is the recognizably Latin-derived brass section.[32] By the same token the general pacing of the song recalls the temper of *marabi* music from South Africa.

Another track from *True Jit,* entitled "Vana" (The Children), is even more remarkable. Formally, like "Chemedzevana," the track is based not on the mbira sound but, instead, on *soukous,* although it employs in addition the call-and-response chorus of male voices which, in various modes, accompanied and unaccompanied, represents one of the distinctive features of southern African music in general. Yet, if the track therefore has a *transnational* feel to it, it is nevertheless clear that what is involved is not in any sense a postindependence dissipation of *chimurenga* music into a depoliticized "Afropop." On the contrary, "Vana" might not at first sound like *chimurenga* music, but lyrically it is entirely about *chimurenga.* It is composed in Shona but features one verse in English, declaimed over a solid rhythmic groove to the accompaniment of a tense, high-pitched, staccato guitar line, echoing like machine-gun fire:

> This song is dedicated to all our brothers and sisters
> Who were fighting for our liberation in Zimbabwe
> Who fought and died in the bushes of Zimbabwe
> The lions were eating the children
> They were left to be swollen by the sun
> When this song was sung, vana (the children)
> Of Zimbabwe were fighting for our liberation
> My friend Theo didn't come home
> But I knew we would overcome in the struggle.

The sustainedly melodic passages of this track are predicated on traditional melodies of the kind that were taken up and modified by fighters during the years of the liberation struggle. One notices also the characteristically indirect and metaphorical quality of the lyrics – "The lions were eating the children / They were left to be swollen by the sun" – and the self-conscious internationalism achieved not only through the use of English but also, more specifically, through the allusion to universally recognized progressive slogans such as "We shall overcome." Within the Zimbabwean context, in short, "Vana" – like the brilliant "Viva Chinhoyi" on *Pamberi!*, the fourth album by the Bhundu Boys (Mango, 1989) – might be said to represent an attempt to consolidate the gains of the revolution by extending the range of *chimurenga* music and broadening its musical vocabulary.

In Western media the mass marketing of Afropop and the recent incorporation of African, Caribbean, and Latin rhythms and styles into Euro-American rock music is often described as a welcome development, on the grounds that it has helped to breathe new life into an otherwise increasingly sterile cultural domain. Perhaps the claim that African pop music has helped to revitalize its Euro-American counterpart is true (although a glance at Top Forty charts or at radio playlists far from persuades one that this is so). But to argue thus is to assume an exclusively First-Worldist perspective. It is also preemptively to domesticate African pop music, to consign it in advance to secondary status, as an auxiliary phenomenon – paradoxically, indeed, *as a phenomenon within Euro-American pop music.* Ultimately, it seems to me, this kind of argument is incompatible with a progressive, internationalist politics.

Certainly, a good deal of the Afropop that is currently being recorded and marketed for Western consumption *can* appropriately be categorized under the rubric of Western pop music. What is true of the music of David Byrne or Paul Simon is true, too, of much contemporary Afropop. As Jane Kramer has written, with reference to France:

> There are English and American music critics who say that the African groups that Parisians like so much are really ordinary rock groups – guitar, bass guitar, keyboard, and drums – with the native instruments thrown in like spice, for flavor. Certainly there is not much harmonic complexity in most of the African music you are likely to hear on [the radio] . . . or find on cassettes [in music stores]. . . . The international circuit that Parisians talk about can take the rhythmic – really the polyrhythmic – complexity that African music does have and reduce it to French pop standards, to a kind of rock monotone. Unless a group is tough and confident . . . it can make that music as banal as elevator songs.[33]

A similar point has been made, with a nod toward Max Horkheimer and Theodor Adorno, by the South African musician Johnny Clegg. In an interview recorded in 1988 Clegg referred to the culture industry, or, as he called it, the "Western cultural monster which feeds off anything new, takes it, perverts it and reduces it to a common denominator, and then markets and sells it."[34]

Yet one needs to proceed carefully here, for many Western popular music critics, anxious to establish their credentials by voicing their opposition to the culture industry, have moved to take up a position that is disturbingly undialectical and even reactionary. Consider, for instance, the terms of Richard Gehr's recent critique of Clegg himself. Writing in the avant-gardist *New Trouser Press Record Guide*, Gehr trashes Clegg's music with the band Juluka, dismissing it as "a mush of sweet, laid-back California style harmonies over a loping backbeat, with mild anti-apartheid sentiments."[35] And Clegg's more recent music with his new band, Savuka, receives still harsher treatment. According to Gehr, it is "even more Western-oriented. The slicker production of *Third World Child* relieves it of the simple, unassuming emotionality of township music. The self-conscious, breast-beating lyrics of the title track and 'Berlin Wall' suggest that Clegg's gunning for the Nobel peace prize while attempting to forge a calculated commercial sound. Too bad Paul Simon beat him to the bank."[36] This is a deplorable piece of criticism, displaying a profound ignorance of Clegg's work and of South African culture and society generally. Against Gehr, it is perhaps worth repeating that Clegg has been among Paul Simon's firmest and most articulate critics in South Africa, and it is certainly worth insisting that there has been nothing remotely "mild" about the "anti-apartheid sentiments" of Clegg's music over the course of the past fifteen years. On the contrary, such tracks as "Asimbonanga (Mandela)" (We Have Not Seen [Mandela]), on Savuka's *Third World Child* album (EMI, 1986) – with its recitation of the names of Mandela, Steven Biko, Victoria Mxenga, and Neil Aggett, political activists silenced or murdered by the apartheid regime – or "One (Hu)Man One Vote," on *Cruel, Crazy, Beautiful World* (EMI, 1989), written in memory of the assassinated university lecturer David Webster, are as tough, politically committed, resourceful, and Afrocentric as any of Thomas Mapfumo's *chimurenga* releases.

Yet my purpose in quoting Gehr's broadside is not so much to protest its insufficiency as criticism, patent in any event, as to draw attention to the inadequacy of the way of thinking about African popular music which it exemplifies. For it is clear that what Gehr dislikes above all about Clegg's music is its fluent integration of "African" and "Western" musical idioms. Gehr does not complain about the fact that Savuka, a South African band, has added guitar techniques from Zimbabwe, Malawi, and elsewhere on the continent to its fundamentally South African mix. But he strongly objects to the "Western-orientation" that he sees as being the necessary consequence of Savuka's use of synthesizers, folk-rock harmonies, and multitrack recording facilities. It seems that there is a little bit of the ethnomusicological purist – and, indeed, of the orientalist – in Gehr. He likes his Afropop not only "simple" and "unassuming" but also uncontaminated by the commercialism of Western pop.

In its dogmatism this way of thinking is unhistorical and does violence to the essentially hybridic form of *all* African pop music today. Celebrating the African pop music that he *does* like for its alterity, its otherness from Western pop, Gehr paradoxically exoticizes it, thereby contributing to a situation in which African pop music is afforded only ghettoized airplay on specialty radio and television programs or written about only in isolated feature articles. The existence in music stores throughout the United States of shelves marked International testifies to the pervasiveness of this latently essentialist conception of African (or, for that matter, "world") music. To be labeled world music, it would seem, is to be categorized above all through reference to its *difference* from the prevailing Western forms; it is not rock, not rhythm 'n' blues, not soul, not reggae (a rich irony here, of course, given the fact that most reggae music is still produced in Jamaica by Jamaicans), not punk, and not jazz.

Revealingly, Johnny Clegg himself has provided the appropriate response to this First-Worldist way of conceptualizing African pop music. In an interview recorded in 1988 Clegg described his musical "vision for the future" as being "to create and construct music which is based in the African experience. . . . My personal project is to define my African identity in the continent . . . and to communicate this with the world and my fellow Africans."[37] A skeptic could, of course, argue that, as a *white* South African – however radical and committed to a nonracial South Africa – Clegg's "African identity" is scarcely likely to be representative. The substantial validity of this objection should be conceded. Tracks by Savuka such as "Third World Child" (on the album by that name) and "African Shadow Man" and "Human Rainbow" (on the album *Shadow Man* [EMI, 1988]) clearly bespeak a restricted and, in the context of Africa at large, ungeneralizable subject position. Yet in another interview of 1988 Clegg insisted that the internationalization of "African experience" was a daily reality not only for himself but for all African musicians. Referring specifically to the South African scene – but to the South African scene *tout court*, not merely to the white South African scene – he argued: "What the new music is drawing on is not only, any more, the South African music experience, but the international one. People must understand and realise that we are exposed day and night to international music." Musicians in South Africa today, he continued – and one thinks of such figures as Ray Phiri of the band Stimela or Condry Ziqubu or Ladysmith Black Mambazo, for example – tend to celebrate, rather than deplore, their internationalization, which they do not in the least regard as corresponding to their subordination to imperialist social imperatives or to the logic of consumer capitalism: "We do not want to be straight-jacketed politically by apartheid. . . . So there's been a reaction against this. . . . Young people now [are saying], we speak English, we sing in English, and we're part of that whole, international culture. And . . . our music is reaching out to touch the soul and the spirit of that international music community, to be part of it."[38]

This formulation of the aspirations of *producers* of African pop music – echoed, incidentally, in the thinking of such musicians as Salif Keita of Mali and Ray Lema of Zaire – seems compelling, not least because it accords neatly with the views of many of the music's Western-based *consumers*, enthusiastic followers of Afropop. Most Western listeners, of course, tend to know little about social developments in Africa. They are initially attracted to African pop music because they find its sound exciting. What particularly stimulates them, I want to suggest, what enables them to find enjoyment in Afropop, is precisely its hybridity. Because it is a hybrid form, Afropop typically strikes Western listeners as simultaneously strange and familiar, accessible and inaccessible, opaque and immediately intelligible. This simultaneity – the relative alterity of Afropop, on the one hand, and the fact that it is "Euro-friendly" (to use the delightful term that one sees quite often today), on the other – is arguably the source of a pleasing intellectual challenge to Western enthusiasts, who endeavor, in exploring and sampling different Afropop sounds, to render these more and more comprehensible.

The music industry in the West attempts to exploit this passion on the part of Western consumers of Afropop—or, more generally, world music—by promoting world music as a new cultural resource waiting to be "discovered." It invites Western consumers to exoticize world music, to transform it into the musical equivalent of the "new" international cuisines, to which we in the West have been introduced as a direct consequence of our various imperial misadventures and which we like to sample once every now and then for a culinary change of pace. The code name for this strategy is "cultural pluralism," which, as Abdul JanMohamed and David Lloyd have recently argued, is "the great white hope of conservatives and liberals alike":

> The semblance of pluralism disguises the perpetuation of exclusion, in so far as it is enjoyed only by those who have already assimilated the values of the dominant culture. For this pluralism, ethnic or cultural difference is merely an exoticism, an indulgence which can be relished without in any significant way modifying the individual who is securely embedded in the protective body of dominant ideology. Such pluralism tolerates the existence of "salsa," it even enjoys Mexican restaurants, but it bans Spanish as a medium of instruction in American schools. Above all, it refuses to acknowledge the class basis of discrimination and the systematic economic exploitation of minorities that underlie postmodern culture.[39]

In light of this analysis the ideological implications of taking up the challenge posed by the hybridity of world music seem to me potentially considerable, for, ultimately, world music cannot be represented as a supplement to Euro-American music. Rather, it carries the potential to subvert the ideological parochialism of Euro-American music, not, of course, at the level of the music industry itself (this would be to claim far too much) but, instead, in the minds of a large audience of listeners and enthusiasts in the West. To those Western enthusiasts who, following the lead of British rock musician Peter Gabriel,[40] have heard enough to embrace the concept underlying it, world music is not to be thought of merely as a convenient name for a sprawling body of music deriving from Yemen or New Zealand or Brazil or Cameroon—in short, from anywhere but "here." It is, rather, the name of a movement that cannot be accommodated at all within the ideological universe of Western popular music. For what makes it *world* music is precisely its latent tendency to contribute to the dismantling of the subject of Western popular music, a subject whose identity rests squarely upon the political economy of empire. To listen to world music as a Western consumer is, in these dialogical terms, a distinctly subversive practice, for it is to allow oneself to take seriously the suggestion of a world free of imperial domination. Free of imperial domination, note–not "on the other side of the imperial divide." The proposal is not that we listen to world music for what it can tell us about life "over there" but rather, that we listen to it for what it can suggest to us about radically different ways of living *over here*, ways of living which are unimaginable under prevailing social conditions.

NOTES

I have taken the title of this chapter from a phrase in *Nervous Conditions*, the splendid first novel by the young Zimbabwean author, Tsitsi Dangarembga (Harare: Zimbabwe Publishing House, 1988). Near the beginning of the novel, Dangarembga has her central protagonist, Tambudzai, speak of "the new rumba that, as popular music will, pointed unsystematic fingers at the conditions of the times" (4).

1. Ayi Kwei Armah, *The Healers* (London: Heinemann Educational Books, 1979), 308–9.
2. Deborah James, "Musical Form and Social History: Research Perspectives on Black South African Music," *Radical History Review* 46, no. 7 (1990): 309.
3. Ibid., 313.
4. Francis Bebey, *African Music: A People's Art*, trans. Josephine Bennett (Westport: Lawrence Hill, 1975), 1.
5. John Storm Roberts, *Black Music of Two Worlds* (New York: Praeger Publishers, 1972); David Coplan, *In Township Tonight! South Africa's Black City Music and Theatre* (London: Longman, 1986).
6. Roberts, *Black Music*, 259. See also John Collins and Paul Richards, "Popular Music in West Africa," in *World Music, Politics and Social Change*, ed. Simon Frith (Manchester: Manchester Univ. Press, 1989).
7. Andrew Tracey, quoted in Billy Bergman, *Goodtime Kings: Emerging African Pop* (New York: Quill, 1985), 32.
8. Andrew Goodwin and Joe Gore, "World Beat and the Cultural Imperialism Debate," *Socialist Review* 20, no. 3 (1990): 70.
9. Salif Keita, quoted in Chris Stapleton and Chris May, *African All-Stars: The Pop Music of a Continent* (London: Paladin, 1989), 111. For a discussion of the social relationship between nobles and griots in Mande culture, see Christopher L. Miller, "Orality through Literacy: Mande Verbal Art after the Letter," *Theories of Africans: Francophone Literature and Anthropology in Africa* (Chicago: Univ. of Chicago Press, 1990), 68–113; see also 55 n. 51.
10. Stapleton and May, *African All-Stars*, 113.
11. Ibid., 112.

12. Nii Yamotei, liner notes to *Soro* (1987).

13. Chinua Achebe, "Impediments to Dialogue between North and South," in *Hopes and Impediments: Selected Essays 1965–1987* (Oxford: Heinemann, 1988), 15.

14. Bergman, *Goodtime Kings*, 19.

15. Johnny Clegg, interviewed on the television documentary production "The Sounds of Soweto," dir. Barry Coetzee (Picture Music International, 1988).

16. This play is overdetermined by the design of the album cover, which features a framed portrait of a chimpanzee (the frame presumably signifying "culture" and the chimp "nature"), and by the album's title, which gestures toward the distinction, made famous by John Berger, between nakedness and nudity (see *Ways of Seeing* [London: British Broadcasting Service and Penguin Books, 1986], 45–64).

17. Jon Pareles, "Righteous Rock; Issues You Can Dance To," *New York Times*, 26 August 1990, 23.

18. Ronnie Graham, *The Da Capo Guide to Contemporary African Music* (New York: Da Capo Press, 1988), 22, 20.

19. *Bhundu* is a slang term for *bush* in southern Africa.

20. See Paul Berliner, *The Soul of Mbira: Music and Traditions of the Shona People of Zimbabwe* (Berkeley: Univ. of California Press, 1981), 4, 10.

21. Ibid., 240.

22. Ibid., 240–41.

23. "Muka! Muka!" quoted in Julie Frederickse, *None but Ourselves: Masses versus Media in the Making of Zimbabwe* (Johannesburg: Ravan Press, 1982), 104. I have drawn extensively from Frederickse's indispensable study in my account of Zimbabwean music in the national liberation struggle.

24. Roberts, *Black Music*, 253.

25. Berliner, *Soul of Mbira*, 177.

26. "Pamuromo Chete," quoted in Frederickse, *None but Ourselves*, 107.

27. Thomas Mapfumo, quoted in ibid., 108.

28. Thomas Mapfumo and the Blacks Unlimited, "Ndamutswa Nengoma," on the compilation album, *Viva Zimbabwe!* (Carthage, 1983).

29. Both tracks are included on Thomas Mapfumo, *The Chimurenga Singles, 1976–1980* (Meadowlark, 1985).

30. Thomas Mapfumo, "Chauya Chirizevha," on *Chimurenga Singles*.

31. Stapleton and May, *African All-Stars*, 221.

32. In the context of a track like "Chemedzevana" Billy Bergman's observation of the similarities between *chimurenga* music and Congolese *soukous* is particularly interesting: "As in Congolese music," Bergman writes, *chimurenga* "harmonies are filled out by horn lines and the dance momentum is effected by a quasi-rumba bass. But the guitars are even faster and more twangy than in Zaire" (*Goodtime Kings*, 120).

33. Jane Kramer, "Letter from Europe," *New Yorker*, 19 May 1986, 112.

34. Clegg, interviewed in "Sounds of Soweto."

35. Richard Gehr, entry on Savuka/Juluka/Johnny Clegg, in *The New Trouser Press Record Guide*, ed. Ira A. Robbins (New York: Macmillan, 1989), 304.

36. Ibid., 305.

37. Johnny Clegg, interview on the television documentary production "Johnny Clegg," dir. Julian Caidan (Picture Music International, 1988).
38. Clegg, interviewed in "Sounds of Soweto."
39. Abdul JanMohamed and David Lloyd, "Introduction: Toward a Theory of Minority Discourse," *Cultural Critique* (Spring 1987): 9–10.
40. In "World Beat and the Cultural Imperialism Debate" Goodwin and Gore note the extent of Gabriel's commitment to the promotion of world music, citing, for instance, "his support for Britain's WOMAD organisation, and more recently . . . his participation with the Real World record label and recording studio" (67).

6 Late Landings

Reflections on Belatedness
in Australian and
Canadian Literatures

Carolyn Masel

> At work Rose read commercials and the weather forecasts,
> answered letters, answered the telephone, typed up the news,
> did the voices in Sunday skits written by a local minister, and
> planned to do interviews. She wanted to do a story on the
> town's early settlers; she went and talked to an old blind man
> who lived above a feed store. He told her that in the old days
> apples and cherries had been tied to the boughs of pine and
> cedar trees, pictures taken of them and sent to England. That
> brought the English immigrants, convinced they were coming
> to a land where the orchards were already in bloom. When she
> got back to the station with this story everybody laughed; they
> had heard it so often before.[1]

This wonderfully succinct anecdote is a case study in miniature,
involving both an exposition and an appraisal of the state of a particular culture. According to its judgment, the local culture is deemed to
be healthy, insofar as a local story thrives; the problem is, rather, one
of belatedness, since its being so well known means that the story is
no longer tellable. Because it is already disseminated, it can no longer
be broadcast. Yet its belatedness is, in a sense, a sign of its authenticity.

In the following exploration of some contemporary writers' responses to belatedness I consider this construct not in the sense made

famous by Harold Bloom – a condition of anxiety to be worked through as an oedipal conflict – but as a condition of the postcolonial writer in relation to place. It is an anxiety about the colonial experience, about arriving too late, about a perceived lack of authenticity in relation to place. If one considers the close relationship between topos and topic, it may hardly seem surprising that, in the two bodies of literature I am considering here, place should not be mere "setting" but should actually constitute a preoccupation. What is intriguing is the persistence as a dominant cultural construct of a set of anxieties about how to settle, own, and live in a land and that, moreover, these anxieties should be manifested so similarly in two countries whose landscapes are so different that they might be characterized as opposites and whose colonial histories are comparable only in the broadest terms.

Comparable features and points of equivalence in the two cultures are easily rehearsed. Both countries reserve actual places as places of peculiar authenticity: the North in Canada and the Outback (the Bush) in Australia. These huge and topographically various sites are reserved places of sacred character, irrespective of the fact that the large majority of people have no familiarity with them whatsoever. In Australia most of the population lives in vast suburbs sprawling out from the cities, while in Canada most people live within twenty-five miles of the United States border; hence, various metonymies for the authentic landscape, bearing the equivalent cultural freight, are often substituted for the landscape itself. The most common of these is the weather.[2]

Furthermore, in both countries the cultural anxiety about one's relation to the land is heightened by the presence, or else the hauntings, of precolonial populations, whose closer daily contact with the landscape they inhabited has meant that they have been inscribed by their postcolonial successors as more authentic dwellers in the landscape. While the Noble Savage conception that informed earlier generations' views of aboriginal populations has largely disappeared, the anxiety it induced has not; indeed, it has been much exacerbated both by ecological concerns and by recent land claims and/or constitutional demands made by the First Peoples in Canada and the Koori (Aboriginals) in Australia, in the course of which very different conceptions of ownership of and relationship to the land enter the public arena. The problem for postcolonial writers is that the landscape has, in effect, been hierarchized, and that, collective postcolonial guilt aside, the place or places of authenticity are perceived to be debarred from postcolonials of nonaboriginal extraction.

Whether that set of anxieties about belonging which constitutes belatedness is an internalization of a collective cultural experience or whether it is a cultural construct, itself belatedly inserted into a collective history, is ultimately unknowable. In either case it manifests itself as almost a compulsion to replicate narratives of immigration and settlement, or narratives whose structure imitates that pattern. Of course, it could be argued that, since large-scale immigration is still occurring in both countries, the concern with immigration and associated themes should hardly surprise us. In an obvious sense this is irrefutable, yet to content oneself with this reflective model of literature is to make all kinds of assumptions about the literary status quo which are, or ought to be, problematic. Why, for example, should social realism have been privileged for so long over other narrative styles? Why should it be preferred to other modes in literary treatments of place? There are no answers per se to these questions, but the very fact that social realism *has* been the overwhelmingly preferred literary mode in both Canada and Australia until very recently ought to prompt them.[3]

The story that Rose collects has the feel of the genuine settler's anecdote, being a rather fateful version of beggar-my-neighbor, putting one over on the Old Country, the underdog's revenge. And, like all jokes that cast their practitioners as underdogs, its strategy is ultimately defeatist. The ineffectuality registered here has its source in Canada's "difference": its unrecognizable trees, its extreme climate, its shorter growing season. As a practical joke, its consequences are extreme, its object being to seduce the English with their own greed. It is a tale of punishable ignorance, a quest for a second, improved Eden ending in exile in the coldest of hells. Why it should be intended to be so punitive is an interesting point of speculation. Possibly it stems from envy of what has been forgone: superior growing conditions, an easier life. Possibly it is desperate loneliness. Or is it possibly the malice of the damned, in which the greed of the English immigrants would replicate the first settlers' own? It seems to me that the duping of the English may well involve some such notion of Nemesis, or justice, and that, if this is the case, the ability to make such a judgment must rest on a claim to know, in some significant sense, both places. England and Canada are seen from a perspective, a moral vantage point, which is beyond either place.

The joke on the first settlers, while quintessentially Canadian, is of the kind that an Australian would easily understand – Hell, in both countries, being any one of a number of possible extremes of rugged- ness of terrain or climate, as in Henry Lawson's vision of the Bush as a landscape of attrition. But, if a life spent in Australia or Canada has lost for many its obligatory punitive capacity, the sense of a double consciousness has persisted. Judith Wright, whose work celebrates the harshness of Australian landscapes, published an essay in 1965 entitled "Australia's Double Aspect," in which she testified to the per- sistence of Europe in the Australian consciousness.[4] Twenty-five years later David Malouf, talking about his novella *Fly Away Peter* (1982) in a radio interview, makes a similar point: "If you live in Europe you know which part of the world you're living in and you don't have to think always that at the other end of the globe, there is another hemi- sphere. If you live in Australia you live in that hemisphere but you're *always* aware that there is the other half of the globe; that is, that Eur- ope is always part of the consciousness of your being in Australia."[5] It should be remarked that the kind and degree of your consciousness of Europe will depend on who you are – on your immediate circum- stances, including your education, quite as much as your actual cul- tural inheritance. In order to claim a heritage you have to be able to recognize it. And the crust of historical consciousness is generally much thinner than Malouf acknowledges here. For one thing, uncom- fortable histories, with all their cultural insignia attached, have a habit of disappearing. Sally Morgan's book *My Place* (1987) recounts the painstaking discovery of her Aboriginal ancestry, involving her in a reconstruction of her great-uncle's, her mother's, and her grand- mother's early lives in the brutally racist institutions of the state. It is an autobiography in which are embedded three smaller autobiog- raphies; it is very much a work of salvage and, finally, a stubborn cel- ebration of her heritage.

Interestingly enough with regard to my concerns here, the initial, misread sign that she has to decode is the color of her skin:

> One day, I tackled Mum about it as she washed the dishes.
> "What do you mean, 'Where do we come from?'"
> "I mean, what country. The kids at school want to know

what country we come from. They reckon we're not Aussies.
Are we Aussies, Mum?"

Mum was silent. Nan grunted in a cross sort of way, then got
up from the table and walked outside.

"Come on, Mum, what are we?"

"What do the kids at school say?"

"Anything. Italian, Greek, Indian."

"Tell them you're Indian."

I got really excited then. "Are we really? Indian!" It sounded
so exotic. "When did we come here?" I added.

"A long time ago," Mum replied. "Now, no more questions.
You just tell them you're Indian."

It was good to finally have an answer and it satisfied our
playmates. They could quite believe we were Indian, they just
didn't want us pretending we were Aussies when we weren't.[6]

Significantly, the solution here is the deployment of that catchall term
Indian, which in this context would be understood to mean "coming
from the Indian subcontinent" but which also has connotations of the
indigenous through analogy with American "Indians." The Koori are
the "Indians" of Australia, and their history since colonial times is
comparable to that of Native Americans. Unwittingly, Sally's mother
has hit on an appropriate pun to disguise her Aboriginal heritage.
More obvious is the irony that, according to the hierarchized criterion
of authenticity mentioned earlier, this family is more Australian than
most. What prevents this fact from even being suspected by Sally's
schoolmates is the expectation of a narrative of immigration and settlement. In Australia any saga of immigration and settlement is more
easily recognized than any originary narrative of place, let alone a
saga of displacement, in which the generations, systematically abused,
adopt silence about the past as a last, defensive tactic. Morgan's four-
voiced autobiography points up the necessity of the oral tradition as
an alternative to the whitewashing of white historical writing, which,
for example, leaves "blank" the identity of her mother's father. Aboriginal kinship structures provide an alternative paradigm of owning/be-
longing felt to be missing from postcolonial Australia.

The writers discussed here all consider narratives of immigration
and settlement to be cut deeper than any other form of cultural inscription. And all of them see such narratives as being still viable in

the sense of being an informing principle. But, it should be said, this is not the whole of viability. Alice Munro, as we have seen, implies strongly that such narratives are no longer recountable, at least not in the form of any kind of art. It is not that such stories as the one Rose collects in *The Beggar Maid* (1980) are moribund – far from it: they are well known, even commonplace. Only Rose mistakes the relic-like condition of the raconteur for the condition of the story. In fact, the local joke, with an extra twist, is once more played out against an outsider; Rose, though Canadian, is sufficiently foreign for it to work. Trying to participate in an insider's joke, she reveals the lack of insider's criterion of judgment. In view of the debate in recent years about whether Canada can be said to have a body of national literature, or whether "Canadian literature" in fact consists of regional literatures, we can read Munro's claim that it is local, or regional, culture that is the true cultural unit and that, furthermore, this "authentic" culture is not readily interpreted by an outsider. In her job as a radio presenter Rose has a complex status, being not herself a representative of the community she serves yet the instrument of a communal authority. The insurmountable problems she faces are analogous to those faced by a writer. These involve not only the choice of which stories to tell – the question of which stories are still viable – but also the larger question of how to represent a people to itself, how to tell the stories of a place in a way that will be meaningful to the people who dwell in it. And, indeed, Alice Munro, as Rose's creator, who knows that Rose's venture as a folklorist is bound to fail, constructs herself as more belated even than Rose.

Even in such a case of explicit demurral from the theme of immigration's being a national theme, however, it is arguable that the demurral displays certain key characteristics of the case it purports to dispute. In *The Beggar Maid* Rose, as a child, longs for glamour and success on a scale that her native small-town Ontario cannot envisage. Yet in each of the environments of her adult life – whether the rain-soaked melancholy of Vancouver or the isolation of the Canadian Rockies or the sophistication of Toronto – she is constantly striving to feel less of an outsider. Her inability to feel settled anywhere is the heart of the problem.

Mavis Gallant must also be numbered among those who think in specifically regional rather than national terms. In her fine collection of Canadian stories, *Home Truths* (1981), Canadian culture is indeed

defined as a conglomeration of various equally "authentic" cultures –
of equally authentic *lives* – and these various cultures are defined in
relation to, and frequently in conflict with, one another, or with gen-
uinely "foreign" cultures. As she remarks in her introductory essay: "I
have sometimes felt more at odds in Canada than anywhere else, but
I never supposed I was any the less Canadian."[7]

In "The Ice Wagon Going Down the Street" two of her Canadian
characters encounter each other in Geneva, when Agnes comes to
supervise Peter in an office in the information service of an international agency in the *Palais des Nations*. Margaret Atwood has remarked
that the North in Canada and the Outback in Australia are places of
the unconscious, places of quest.[8] But it could also be said that the
complete anonymity of thorough internationalism performs an analogous function – that this office in Geneva is a postmodern sort of
Arden: "In Geneva Peter worked for a woman – a girl. She was a Nor-
wegian from a small town in Saskatchewan. He supposed they had
been put together because they were Canadians; but they were as
strange to each other as if 'Canadian' meant any number of things, or
had no real meaning."[9]

Agnes and Peter's fleeting relationship provides one answer to the
question of what being Canadian and having nothing in common
might mean. But their first meeting is not an auspicious one, for Peter
is not prepared to acknowledge that the "world of difference" between
them is a Canadian construction and no longer pertinent. His superiority seems to him intrinsic and self-evident, and, until Agnes's arrival, he has been able to rely on it to ensure him the exclusive patron-
age of the rich and powerful. Peter emblematizes Agnes as a mere
mole, whereas he and his wife are "peacock parents," watched by
wrens, their children:

> Lucille and her nieces are much the same – sandy-coloured,
> proudly plain. Neither of the girls has the father's insouciance
> or the mother's appearance – her height, her carriage, her thick
> hair, and sky-blue eyes. The children are more cautious than
> their parents; more Canadian. When they saw their aunt's
> apartment they had been away from Canada nine years, ever
> since they were two and four; and Jennifer, the elder, said,
> "Well, now we're home." Her voice is nasal and flat. Where did
> she learn that voice? And why should this be home? Peter's

answer to anything about his mystifying children is, "It must
be in the blood."[10]

This half-joking yet unexamined claim of genetic superiority masks,
of course, a history of social privilege. The source of Peter's massive
self-assurance lies in his family history, just as Agnes's lack of confidence has its source in hers. But, as Peter has already noted, that history is a specifically Canadian legacy; it is irrelevant to his and his
family's present lives in Geneva, and these lives must therefore be
mythically as well as financially constrained.

Ultimately, the question of what being Canadian might mean depends upon the extent to which Agnes's and Peter's separate stories
can be made comprehensible to one another. When, on her second
day at work, Agnes produces a large black Bible, the process is under-
way, for Peter Frazier is shocked to recognize in her "the true heir of
the men from Scotland," proclaiming their daunting message: "You
can begin, but not begin again."[11] But to be able to actualize Agnes in
his imagination Peter has to go back to the deep memory of childhood. By interweaving this deep memory of himself into Agnes's narrative of childhood, Peter becomes the small child in Agnes's arms,
whose presence does not count, on the morning when she rises earlier than everyone on the prairie farm to steal a moment of solitude.
Peter, belatedly, steals this visionary moment.

All this occurs on a symbolic level; in actual terms the consumma-
tion of this brief relationship, which will leave each feeling forever
bereft of the other, is a private conversation in their office, on the
morning after an embarrassing fancy-dress party. The details of this
conversation are withheld, but here, just where one might have expected a revelation, Gallant lightly sketches a tentative definition of
the minimum they share as Canadians:

> Agnes and Peter were too tired to speak after that morning.
> They were like a married couple in danger, taking care.
>   But what were they talking about that day, so quietly, such
> old friends? They talked about dying, about being ambitious,
> about being religious, about different kinds of love. What did
> she see when she looked at him – taking her knuckle slowly
> away from her mouth, bringing her hand down to the desk,
> letting it rest there? They were both Canadians, so they had
> this much together – the knowledge of the little you dare admit.

> Death, near-death, the best thing, the wrong thing–God knows
> what they were telling each other. Anyway, nothing happened.[12]

This generalized minimal formulation may at first seem disappointing, yet its very evasiveness may be telling. For the definition of Canadianness rests, ultimately, on the cryptic phrase "the knowledge of the little you dare admit," which might mean that you know, deeply, a little of the truth or else that you know that you cannot afford to admit very much. In either case, the salient feature of this knowledge of the little you dare admit is its high seriousness. This listing of the items touched upon–"death, near-death, the best thing, the wrong thing"–can be read mimetically, beginning, in an almost naively direct way, with the most private and serious topic and immediately hopping nervously toward the social. The last defensive sentence–"Anyway, nothing happened"–closes the door, summarily, on the reader.

Like Munro, Gallant claims the importance of the region as the primary unit of culture, yet for both writers the case for the nation is essentially the case for the region writ large. Agnes and Peter, seeking both authentication and betterment in Europe, discover that the originary moment of selfhood, which is also the moment of self-fulfillment, is irrevocably past and that their adult lives constitute a species of exile. Whatever the explicit claims of Munro and Gallant about regionalism, the sense of irrevocable exile and the closely related problem of settlement inform the deepest structures of their narratives. To this extent these two Canadian stories approximate the condition claimed as the *Australian* writerly condition by Judith Wright and David Malouf. This is not to suggest that a consciousness of Europe is intrinsic to the Canadian psyche (such a claim, I have suggested, is, in any case, questionable in relation to the Australian psyche), but there is a similar sense of unsettledness, almost of displacement, of not having quite landed, put down roots–which may, paradoxically, result in a need to rehearse individual stories of settlement, claims to rootedness.[13]

Thus, in both countries a sense of "here-ness" involves a collective sense of "there-ness," of a place from which one's family might have come. It is not so much the fact of difference that interests me here (though all the writers considered here affirm difference as fundamental to the national psyche) as the question of the *direction of the narrative pathway* between differing entities. For it would seem that not

only the mental habit of comparison but also the experiential direction of immigration – from there to here – has persisted long beyond
each country's colonial era and remains, in various internalized forms,
a distinctive characteristic of contemporary Australian and Canadian
writing. Moreover (as Derrida has reminded us), the movement from
there to here can also be read temporarily to mean the movement
from then to now.

Two well-known writers, Canadian Margaret Atwood and Australian David Malouf, best exemplify this pattern of the here-and-now's
involving the then-and-there in its particular relation to a problematized landscape. Both would agree that belatedness may be as much
a matter of place as of time, whereby the land itself becomes an arena
of conflict, a problematized topos where authenticity, within limits, is
striven for; the early settlers' desires to possess the land, to settle it,
to be at home on it, have modulated into a more metaphysical struggle to speak authentically out of a landscape. But, while both writers
exhibit that persistent sense of belatedness which informs each of
their nation's psyches, their responses to it are quite different.

Atwood has, on several occasions, tackled the problem of authenticity in relation to aboriginality, which, I have suggested, is essentially
a problem of hierarchization. In *Surfacing* (1972) there is a moment in
which the narrator-protagonist, consumed by returning grief and lack
of food, has an authentic experience of place:

> Slowly I retrace the trail. Something has happened to my eyes,
> my feet are released, they alternate, several inches from the
> ground. I'm ice-clear, transparent, my bones and the child
> inside me showing through the green webs of my flesh, the
> ribs are shadows, the muscles jelly, the trees are like this too,
> they shimmer, their cores glow through the wood and bark.
>
> The forest leaps upward, enormous, the way it was before
> they cut it, columns of sunlight frozen; the boulders float, melt,
> everything is made of water, even the rocks. In one of the lan-
> guages there are no nouns, only verbs held for a longer
> moment.
>
> The animals have no need for speech, why talk when you
> are a word
>
> I lean against a tree, I am a tree leaning

> I break out again into the bright sun and crumple, head against
> the ground
>   I am not an animal or a tree, I am the thing in which the
> trees and animals move and grow, I am a place[14]

Atwood is claiming for her narrator an intrinsic connection between language and nature, an authentic relationship that is a new knowledge of self in the world. It is as if the English language itself were being remodeled so as to become a more appropriate vehicle of transcendence, as if the speaker were feeling her way toward a sacred language, and was prepared to break the confining strictures of English grammar to this end. There would seem to be an impulse toward a nounless language of process, the light punctuation or the absence of it pointing toward a language of nonclosure.

An interview given some six years after the publication of *Surfacing* throws some further light on this language of process, linking it to the nonsubstantive perception of the land enjoyed by certain of the First Peoples:

> There are a number of Indian languages which are very interesting. In one of them there are no nouns. What we would call a noun is a variation of a verb. So that you don't say, "A deer is running across a field." You say something like, "Fielding . . . or something which is being a field is manifesting something which is being a deer." That is, the whole language is composed of verbs. The mode of linguistic expression mitigates against seeing objects as distinct from their backgrounds . . .
>
>   It seems to me that English, on the other hand, and to some extent all European languages, see nouns as hard, separate, distinct, contained things. They are separate from verbs.[15]

There is, I think, a problem of self-perception here. Insofar as she purports to mimic certain Indian languages, Atwood seems *automatically* to privilege Indian culture over English-Canadian culture – that is, irrespective of any claim either culture might make to achieve a worthy perception. She thereby debars forever the English language from the place of perceptual clarity, condemning it to second place, perpetual eccentrism, even rank imperialism, should it ever attempt to depict a visionary state.

What Atwood claims about a certain Indian language in her interview approximates very closely what the linguist Benjamin Whorf claimed about certain Indian languages (chiefly the Hopi and the Algonquin) in the 1950s. According to what has come to be known as the Sapir-Whorf hypothesis: "We all, unknowingly, project the linguistic relationships of a particular language upon the universe, and SEE them there."[16] Language is, indeed, a two-sided mirror. It may be that Indians' nonsubstantive language renders the landscape as a kind of process. On the other hand, an English speaker's perception of a particular Indian language as being nonsubstantive does not make it so. Indeed, in the example Atwood has chosen it might be argued that the Indian language cannot really lack a substantive function, since a deer that cannot be specified as separate from its background cannot be hunted. The Indian language may not have nouns, as an English speaker knows them, but its substantive function may be differently marked (as linguists say). But all of these criticisms only apply insofar as Atwood makes out her enterprise to be a pale imitation of something better – that is, only insofar as she hierarchizes perception, problematizes authenticity.

The anxiety about authenticity manifested here is, however, only a kind of by-product of the transformation to self-transcendence. Self-transcendence – becoming a place or a tree leaning – involves the characteristic movement backward in time which is my concern here. In this case we go back to the precolonial era, and the result is unequivocally restorative: "The forest leaps upward, enormous, the way it was before they cut it." For Atwood knowing where you are is generally always a matter of knowing how you got there. The movement backward in time, while not always restorative, is always necessary. This pattern is apparent in any number of her novels, informing, for example, her penchant for flashbacks – indeed, informing, at the deepest level, the whole cartographic cast of her imagination. But perhaps it is her poems that, being shorter, tighter structures, manifest this pattern most clearly. In fact, we might view them as maps or even as the places reached by mapping. For brevity's sake, here I shall deal with some poems from two of her volumes: *Two-Headed Poems* (1978) and *Interlunar* (1984).[17]

"Nothing New Here" (*Two-Headed Poems*, pp. 24–25), is concerned with one kind of belatedness, for being belated can mean arriving late but also actually being overtaken by lateness: being rendered obsolescent. In this case the speaker's sense of obsolescence is linked with her perception of the past. Her memories of hard work in a bush garden and her sense of the unremitting need for work have outlasted any sense of the fruits of her and her partner's labors. The cycle of the seasons, experienced as repetitions of violence, defeats any impulse toward self-betterment. Only the enemies of cultivation burgeon, proliferate inexorably, whether hail or slugs or weeds. There is a sense of displacement from an urban norm, instanced as a norm of commercial surety: ". . . thistles blossom, their flowers / as purple as if I'd bought them." But learning the names of the weeds, "Ragweed, pigweed, milkweed," is no charm against their encroachment. Only personal endurance, both in the sense of lasting and in the sense of hardening, can avail against the violent fertility of this bush garden:

> Our love is clumsier
> each year, words knot
> and harden, grow sideways, devious as grass.

This is quite positive for the wary-voiced Atwood. Words join, conjoin, compose a pattern and record of growth like the knots in a tree, or, more convolutedly, like love knots. Words, too, proliferate like grass, inevitably recalling Whitman's interpretation of language as a token of democracy, although here words are valued, rather, as tokens of persistence –"devious as grass." And the poem's final note of equivocal triumph is very reminiscent of Mavis Gallant's formulation at the end of "The Ice Wagon Going Down the Street." You have to, and you do, make do with the partially achieved, with shattered wholeness, disillusionment:

> Our blunted fingers,
> our mouths taste
> of the same earth, bitter and deep.
> (Though this is also what we have
> in common; this broken
> garden, measure
> of our neglect and failure, still
> gives us what we eat.)

The fifth section of "Solstice Poem," from the same volume, is a foil for "Nothing New Here" in that it is predicated on a *failure* to believe in the repetition of the cycle of the seasons:

> In this dark
> space of the year, the earth
> turns again toward the sun, or
>
> we would like to hope so.

The mechanistic turning toward hope in these lines seems all the more automatic for occurring at the end of the poem: an empty gesture required by the poem's rhetoric. This is the dark season of Atwoodian irony, when a *politeness*, almost, of diction masks fear, a crucial failure of the human spirit. In the terms of this bleak poem, however, whatever small force might be summoned by the feebly preferential locution "would like to hope" still counts as hope. All the same one wonders if there is not something quite melodramatic (even if wryly so) about the thought of having to hope, rather than to trust, that the earth will continue to turn. Yet, arguably, this is the very difficulty that epitomizes the long winter in Canada.

The poem's bleakness of vision, however impersonally cosmic it may seem, is very carefully constructed so as to implicate human action. The first stanza situates the house "in a dying orchard," squeezed between a "tributary of the wilderness" and a road. Within this fragile, doomed environment the speaker's daughter "dances / unsteadily with a knitted bear," an image that evokes for me Earle Birney's famous poem "The Bear on the Delhi Road" (1962). Atwood herself includes this poem in her selection from Birney for *The New Oxford Book of Canadian Verse*.[18] In Birney's poem two Kashmiri men teach a real bear "to lurch with them / in the tranced dancing of men." In capturing the bear and teaching it to dance, the captors have effectively captured themselves, becoming slaves to their work. In Atwood's poem the dancing bear is a toy bear, as if to suggest that no wild beasts now dwell in that so-called wilderness where the family has its home. Indeed, in comparison with the Birney poem, Atwood's poem is antimarvelous, an active diminishment of the wonderful. In her second stanza the child's father is described as a "onetime soldier"; at the end of the next their pagan celebration of the solstice is described as "our fools' picnic . . . our fragile golden / protest against murder." The proximity of these images makes it seem highly unlikely that this "protest against murder" could be made in any abstractly ideological – that is, innocent – sense. While the knowledge gained from past experience informs the present desire for peace, it also underscores the improbability of peace's lasting. The most anyone can hope for is not to be the victim of one's own praxis, or, for that matter, anybody else's.

There is a sense in which this poem works like *Surfacing*—and not merely like the passage I have cited but like that novel as a whole. In terms of their large structures the point is the same for both works: that in order to come to terms with the present, you have to go backward in time, seeking to know how you yourself are implicated in the web of history and taking responsibility for it, no matter how belatedly. Like "Nothing New Here," the fifth section of "Solstice Poem" is very much a meditation on the theme of repetition. While the repetition that promises the passing of the season is cause for hope, however, the repetition of language has made it less and less useful. "Worn language," overused, emptied of meaning, obfuscates not only our intention but also our perception, rendering both obsolete and ineffectual. However, the poem goes on to say, the cries of the birds outside are "rumours," muted annunciations of hope (or at least of change); unfortunately, they are as yet unintelligible.

"Marsh, Hawk," one of the finest poems in the volume, further elaborates some of the same themes. Just as in the fifth section of "Solstice Poem" the "onetime soldier" participates in the family's "protest against murder," so in this poem the individual participates in the collective violence against the landscape:

> Diseased or unwanted
> trees, cut into pieces, thrown
> away here, damp and soft in the sun, rotting and half-
> covered with sand, burst truck
> tires, abandoned, bottles and cans hit
> with rocks or bullets, a mass grave,
> someone made it, spreads on the
> land like a bruise and we stand on it, vantage
> point, looking out over the marsh.

Just as in "Solstice Poem" the cries of the birds remain incomprehensible to the family, so here "guttural swamp voices" utter their oracular syllables, which are yet too "boring" to merit the restless listener's consideration. The marsh landscape importunately pelted with rocks "eludes" its perceivers. But, even as we attempt to force it to respond, we know that "intrusion is not what we want." And, indeed, in formulating more precisely what vision it is that we seek—while gazing upon the landscape and simply observing what is happening in front of our eyes – an epiphany is seen to take place. This revelation consists of, or occurs by means of, a hawk rising. Grammatically speaking, the move is from the optative to the indicative, a move so subtly effected that it is not certain whether or not the poem's speaker is herself conscious of being in the visionary state she speaks of seeking.

Tantalizingly, epiphanies may occur, even to white, English-speaking Canadians who are, Atwood asserts, singularly ill-equipped by their linguistic heritage to seek ontological illumination. In the "Snake Poems" section of the later volume, *Interlunar*, she continues her diagnosis of this particular Canadian linguistic condition. In "Lesson on Snakes" (9), for example, she makes the point, more blandly than in "Marsh, Hawk," that a violent response is

> a bad answer
> to anything that gets in
> what you think is your way.

The point here, as in "Marsh, Hawk," is that you can never know what your way ought to be. Going carefully is your best option. Moreover, violence – in this case the kind of violence that is habitually directed against snakes – is itself revealing. It involves tools, a "hoe or crowbar," which, while they are misappropriated in their killing work, nevertheless appropriate the corpse they create, rendering it *useful*: "a twist of slack rope."

Atwood is a strong advocate of snakes' otherness:

> Alone among the animals
> the snake does not sing.
> The reason for them is the same
> as the reason for stars, and not human.[19]

Communication with the other may, in any given instance, be more than you can take. In *Surfacing* encountering the other is barely tolerable, resulting as it does in a paradoxical unblocking of the self: a deed represented as painful, necessary, and, ultimately, liberating. "The White Snake" (*Interlunar*, 15–16) is a poetic parable about the receiving of a vision of otherness. According to legend, the eater of the snake will understand the language of the animals. The poem follows out the horrible logic of this promise, whereby the revelation received looks very much like empathy, a realization of what has been done to the snake *in the snake's terms.*

Fortunately, there are other ways to treat snakes. Acknowledging their otherness means keeping your own consciousness; employing the language of metaphor may be enough to maintain an appropriate distance:

> O snake, you are an argument
> for poetry:
> . . . .
> a thin line moving through
>
> that which is not
> time, creating time, . . .
>
> . . . a movement
> from left to right,
> a vanishing. . . .
>
> O long word, cold-blooded and perfect[20]

In this poem the function of language is not appropriative. The snake is said to be so many things in such quick succession that it retains its potential to be anything. Language is only its slippery skin, a fictive approximation, linear and directional.

What is true of snakes is true of places. In all of the works I have examined Atwood diagnoses violence as *the* human ill; indeed, she goes so far as to represent it as integral to the human self. But whereas in *Surfacing,* self-transcendence is achieved through the merging of self and sacred place, in her later work she tends to warn against seeking such a merger and to recommend maintaining one's distance. The following lines, from the poem sequence *Daybooks I* (*Two-Headed Poems,* 27), address explicitly the issue of belatedness in relation to Indian culture:

> Midnight: my house rests
> on arrowheads and toebones,
> scraps of raw fur, a cellar
> scooped from the trashgrounds
> of whatever ancestors once also
> passed through time here,

shedding themselves piecemeal
in their long trek to sunset.

Things we are leaving:
bushel baskets and broken glass,
a knitted hand squashed flat,
potatoes that sprout and rot,
a rubber foot . . .

The word *trashgrounds* in the first stanza is interesting, *trash* being an American rather than a Canadian locution. (The Canadian *garbage* would give *garbagegrounds,* a rather baroque word for *dump.*) *Trash-grounds* is an invented word, self-consciously modern, suggesting some specialized amenity, even as a transient life-style is explicitly affirmed. It balances, to my ear, the slight archaization of the modern artifacts in the second stanza: "a knitted hand" for a glove, "a rubber foot" for a galosh or flipper. (And might not "potatoes," too, suggest toes of a kind, coming as they do between a hand and a foot and echoing the *toebones* of the preceding stanza?) The point is that the speaker of *this* poem can participate in an activity begun by the First Peoples. They are the speaker's ancestors by virtue of having "passed through time" in the same place as she. She does not privilege their culture over her own per se but is able, rather, to find her own cultural equivalence, adding artifacts from her life to the general human debris.

The case for David Malouf is much the same as that for Atwood in that the question "Where am I?" almost always involves the corollary question "How did I get here?" This is not to say that there are not other ways of answering the question "Where am I?" but the historical answer seems to be the one that predominates; purely geographical thinking is very rare in both authors. Moreover, in both cases, the speaker usually ends up where she or he started – that is, in the present, facing the future. And, furthermore, the encounter with the past (whether a personal or a collective past) seems not only to have located the self in the present but also to have given it some presentiment about the future, which is that it is likely to be brief, fragile, and perilous.

We can find this characteristic structure in all of Malouf's work to date. One of the most concise and least complicated examples comes, in fact, from his recent book, *The Great World* (1990). Here is part of the narration of the central journey, the primary trajectory, of the protagonist's mother:

> She would remember the journey to Keen's Crossing for the
> rest of her life, perhaps because she was to make it just the
> once. Every detail of it remained new for her.
>
> Years later, towards the end, on a windy day in August, she
> would climb the bluff behind the Crossing and be astonished to
> see that Sydney, a place she thought of as worlds away, further
> even in some ways than England, had all the time been visible,
> just thirty miles from where she was. She could have gone up
> there and looked at it any day of her life. Its outer suburbs by
> then were already climbing the far side of the ridge.[21]

The positioning of this passage close to the start of the novel is noteworthy. Insofar as it describes Digger's mother's bridal journey, this
seems quite natural in a book that looks, at this point, as though it is
going to be shaped around the life of a protagonist. (It is, in fact, shaped
around the lives of two.) Nevertheless, from the very beginning the
authorial use of the future tense shows her perspective to be limited
and hints strongly that this limitation is as much moral as temporal.
The authorial voice, with the perspective of hindsight, projects in the
future the completion of the inscription that she is about to begin. Her
Englishness is also pertinent, for she functions as an archetypal figure,
whose long, single journey inscribes for all time the linear, directional
pattern of immigration and settlement. Her forward-facing is willful,
immutable, and tantamount to a moral stance. This willful attempt to
forget her journey – which has nevertheless been indelibly scored in
her memory – is an exercise of power, albeit limited. It is not the entire
past she refuses to confront but, rather, only that section of it which
represents her acquiescence in exile; Sydney is "worlds away, further
even in some ways than England."

In contrast with this willed forgetting, both Malouf and Atwood
make much use of involuntary forgetting, the unconscious repression
of the past. In Atwood's case the unblocking of memory is often crucial
to the larger plot; indeed, this seems as true for *Cat's Eye* (1988) as for
Surfacing (1972). For Atwood memory is the keystone of romance. It
hardly needs to be said that repressed memories are often painful ones
and that the recovery of repressed material may mean a sudden access
of pain. In such circumstances the encounter with the past may well
be forced, negotiated only if and when the present becomes unbearable. Paradoxically, it would seem that when, under the pressure of an

intolerable present, the past is confronted the result is restorative. We have already seen one example of this in Atwood's *Surfacing*, when the grief-burdened narrator has a transcendental vision. In *The Great World* a very similar thing occurs when Digger, Malouf's protagonist, takes refuge in fever from the prisoner-of-war camp at Changi:

> When he found Ralphie's water-tin, the water he lapped up was the water of life – cool, sweet, slaking this thirst he had been tormented by, which was not the thirst of his body but of what his body had left when it shook him off.
>
> He lapped and lapped – Ralphie didn't mind, didn't begrudge him the water he got from the dried-up bowl; or the bone either, which was alive with maggots. He got his teeth into it, defying the flies. It filled the hunger in him, fed some earlier body than the one he had abandoned, and did him good. Some animal part of him, which he loved as he had loved Ralphie, and which *was* Ralphie, wolfed it down, maggots and all, took the strength from it and was enlightened. He felt the strength gather in him; and lightly, on all fours, began to run light-footed over the earth. Under the moon, past bushes that lay low before him so that he could leap over them, across plains that burned but did not blister. He ran and ran and had breath for it, and came in the early morning down the track to Keen's Crossing.
>
> He woke feeling refreshed and fed. His dreaming body had fed his thin, racked frame, slaked its thirst, licked him into life again.
>
> "I'll live," he thought, "this time. I'll live."[22]

While both authors share the view that, in extremis, an encounter with the personal past may have a restorative effect, Malouf is clearly distinguishable from Atwood in that he evinces no anxiety whatsoever about his protagonist's right to assimilate the other. In *Surfacing* only almost total self-abnegation results in self-transcendence, whereas in the passage just quoted the child Digger's love for his dog, Ralphie (which *affirms* the past self), gives him the right to take on Ralphie's body, to appropriate his water and maggoty bone. Ralphie's body is Digger's own body re-membered and the rotten yet life-giving bone the telos of Digger's whole identity.

Malouf's lack of anxiety about appropriation – which, I would suggest, is the obverse of his lack of anxiety about authenticity – operates in terms of place as well. Instead of seeking to graft his perceptions of landscape onto imagined precolonial perceptions of it, as does Atwood, Malouf makes a fundamental claim for postcolonial perception – makes, indeed, a claim so universalist that it might as well be essentialist: "First houses are the grounds of our first experience. Crawling about at floor level, room by room, we discover laws that we will apply later to the world at large; and who is to say if our notions of space and dimension are not determined for all time by what we encounter there, in the particular relationship of living-rooms to attic and cellar (or in my case under-the-house), of inner rooms to the verandahs that are open boundaries?"[23]

The implications of this suggestion are clearly too far-reaching for us to follow through here; indeed, Malouf has devoted a whole book to this specific purpose. Nevertheless, we might well ask, for example, how we are to reconcile the universalist and, hence, egalitarian claims made above, by which the first perception of architectural space is naturalized in the imagination and all subsequent perceptions of spatial relation assimilated to it, with the seemingly contradictory claim that in Australia "you're *always* aware that there is this other half of the globe which is Europe." On the one hand, there would seem no more obvious evidence of a European-derived culture in Australia than architectural evidence, and the ludicrous incongruity of European architecture in the context of an Australian landscape (and particularly in the context of his native Brisbane) is something that Malouf refers to on other occasions. Yet this is not strictly what he is claiming here; indeed, he would appear to be claiming that a contrary naturalizing impulse predominates. And, if this is the case, we must ask how a consciousness whose whole drive is to assimilate and naturalize what it perceives may register a persistent and oppositional otherness. Is "Europe," for example, merely the residue of that naturalizing process, the unassimilable other that perpetuates the assimilative appetite? Or is Europe manifested as a form of cultural anxiety? And, if this is so, then to what extent is the cultural anxiety that is born of the perpetual consciousness of Europe encoded in spatial terms? Is the Europeanness of the source of that anxiety recognizable as such, or does that anxiety register more vaguely, as, say, simple incongruence or else as anxiety about the past, priority, history? Do characteristically Australian perceptions involve a consciousness of belatedness?

As we can see, there is a very wide range of interpretative possibilities available to Malouf within his seemingly simple scheme and, moreover, an almost infinite potential for contradictory interpretations at any given point. It seems worth delineating also a second set of possibilities that stem from his universalizing of the personal: "First houses are the grounds of our first experience." One effect of this universalization is, without doubt, to sanctify childhood as the kernel of the whole personality. The child's tendency to assimilate the world around him or her may, indeed, be thought to constitute a form of personal expansionism, an expansionism that is condoned because it is involuntary and natural: "Set loose in a world of *things*, we are struck at first by their terrible otherness. It drives us to fury. For a time, while we are all mouth, we try to swallow them, then to smash them to smithereens – little hunters on the track of the ungraspable. Till we perceive at last that in naming and handling things we have power over them. If they refuse to yield their history to us they may at least, in time, become agents in ours. This is the process of our first and deepest education."[24] The thought expressed at the beginning of this passage is not far from Emersonian solipsism in, say, "Circles." But in Malouf's account the strong impulse to assimilate the world appears to undergo a modification: a process akin to sublimation, whereby what is under scrutiny is named rather than being anonymously engulfed. Nevertheless the self that he envisages is still essentially cumulative.

Perhaps the most important consequence of this cumulative self is its irreversibility. The self can acquire layers but may not shed them. This means that remembering a past self has limits; one cannot do it fully, since one cannot un-remember experience acquired. Even one's own past body is irrevocably out of reach. From this it might seem that the act of remembering, even if effected without nostalgia, must result in a sense of belatedness – a surplus of experience – registering in the remembering consciousness. However, Malouf is careful to assert, memory always has a totalizing function, and, while it is this quality that prevents us from accurately remembering the past (since we cannot forget experiences acquired between then and now), it is also this quality that made past experiences complete in themselves – although that completeness is lost to us in the present. Since it cannot truly separate itself from its past, the self, in its irrevocable accumulation, stands facing the future. Hence, it resembles – that is, *any* self resembles – Digger's mother in her willed forward-facing stance, keeping Sydney always behind her, except that, ultimately, her will is superfluous, for the past is irrevocable without any effort; moreover, it is mercifully so. This trajectory from there to here, or from then to now is, it should be clear by now, the very same as that faced by Margaret Atwood's protagonist-narrators and lyric subjects.

One further consequence of Malouf's conception of the growth of the self is of crucial importance here: if a person's very early perception of space is indeed formative, and if all initial spatial perceptions are sacred, then no one starting place is intrinsically better than any other. Any place can be the sacred center of the universe. This fundamental claim about the primacy of individual perception enables Malouf to explore the staging of what look like reversals of immigration narratives: that is, journeys to that other hemisphere that is Europe which are yet *not* returns—as, for example, in *Fly Away Peter*, which "very much works out . . . that business of your having to move from precisely the place where you are most settled, to the other end of the world, in a kind of reverse migration."[25] Here is the protagonist, Jim Saddler, reflecting on memory:

> It amazed him, this. That he could be watching, on a warm day in November, with the sun scorching his back, the earth pricking below and the whole landscape dazzling and shrilling, a creature that only weeks ago had been on the other side of the earth and had found its way here across all the cities of Asia, across lakes, deserts, valleys between high mountain ranges, across oceans without a single guiding mark, to light on just this bank and enter the round frame of his binoculars; completely contained there in its small life . . . and completely containing, somewhere invisibly within, that blank white world of the northern ice-cap and the knowledge, laid down deep in the tiny brain, of the air-routes and courses that had brought it here. Did it know where it had arrived on the earth's surface? Did it retain, in that small eye, some image of the larger world, so that it could say *There I was so many darknesses ago and now I am here, and will stay a time, and then go back*; seeing clearly the space between the two points, and knowing that the distance, however great, could quite certainly be covered a second time in the opposite direction because the further side was still visible, either there in its head or in the long memory of its kind.[26]

Since a personal aesthetic is bound to have wider ideological implications when its possessor is a much admired maker of postcolonial culture (involved, as others studied in this volume are, in taking the exact cast of perceptual reckonings about the world), it is worth attempting to assess the political connotations of what Malouf is doing here.[27] We might read this passage as an allegory of perception. The sandpiper attains its identity through cartography; its future is only ensured by remembering the past. Each journey is an acquisition, an expansion of the field of perception which adds to the store of experience of the species. Indeed, there seems to be no palpable difference between memory as an instrument of survival and memory as an instrument of empire. In fact, the congruence of solipsism and a fundamental imperialism of perception might seem to be an inevitable consequence of Malouf's cumulative conception of the self.

Before we level any serious charge against Malouf, however, we should recognize a crucial distinction between his expansionist aesthetic and the expansionism that is part and parcel of any paradigm of imperialism. In all of the examples of Malouf's work which we have examined expansionism is represented as a two-way process: while we are still children we discover that if the things we have attempted to consume "refuse to yield their history to us they may at least, in time, become agents in ours." What is true for food is true for language and landscape. Imperialism, on the other hand, eschews assimilation, seeking rather to keep the Other other. Control is asserted in order to prevent infiltration; hierarchical structures are constructed or appropriated so as to ensure the dominance of the colonizing agency. It might be argued that, in the fable of the sandpiper, the cartographic project only pertains to a migratory bird, a bird being a traditional emblem of thought and possibly the most innocent paradigm of imaginative perception Malouf could have chosen. But, if the point of the allegory is to indicate what Jim Saddler can imagine rather than what a sandpiper might perceive, then the cartographic project properly applies to Jim Saddler. Yet I would ultimately place the fable of the sandpiper on the safe side of the expansionist/imperialist divide because of its method, which is questioning, speculative, even wondering. In the last analysis it is the spirit in which one maps the world which is the essential thing. The attribution of something like a race memory to the bird, however, should give us pause. "The long memory of its kind"–a cumulative memory of other places–returns us (almost as reflexively as the migrating bird) to the Australian collective memory of some other place.

The case against Malouf (if there is one to be made) is nowhere so clear as in *The Great World*, which contains some intriguing meditations on the ways in which a child assimilates information, the relevance of one's early style of perception to later life, and the relation of language to both of these. In this passage the child Digger pits his way of looking at the world against that of his mother, who is a materialist by temperament and a grocer by profession:

> "I'd watch out if I was you," she warned him. . . .
>
> What she was really warning him of was the difference between what she called reality, or duty, or fate . . . and a hunger he had, and which his father had too, for something that began where her reality, however clear and graspable it was, left off. . . .
>
> What it had to do with was the sheer size of the world, and the infinite number of events and facts and objects it was filled with. Things you could touch and smell, but other things too that were just thoughts; which were real enough, and could even be put into words and turned this way and that, but you couldn't see them.
>
> There was no set of scales in existence that could measure all that, and no number of little paper bags would be enough to contain it, but your head could. That's what he had seen. Your head. Which was the same shape as the world, and really was the world, only on an infinitely small scale; an inch to a million as on the globe he loved to look at, where the tip of your finger could cover an area of thousands of square miles, and whole cities with millions of people in them, but only because in your head you could *see* this.[28]

On the one hand, this is evidently a conflict between an empirical view of the world and a dreamer's view of it, between a view that parcels things out and one that seeks to retain a holism of perception. It is hardly an even contest, being so clearly weighted in Digger's favor. On the other hand, Digger's assertion that "your head . . . really was the world" strikes me as an extraordinary claim. It is variously interpretable – as the result of a child's solipsism, a kind of phenomenological hubris that empowers the imagination, or even as a religious view of one's head and the world's being coeval. The shrinkage of the world to a model of the globe and the gigantism of Digger's gesture toward it are somewhat alarming. Yet that gesture is itself harmless; what Digger loves to do with the world is to look at it. Arguably, his attitude to the world is even self-reflexive, since his insight derives from his looking at himself looking at the world, watching his fingertip on the surface of the globe. Moreover, his gesture is one of pointing or tracing, not of grasping; the imaginative impulse is directed outward: the point is to envisage the cities with millions of people in them. Whether Digger can envisage a million other centers of consciousness is, however, another question. Moreover, we are left unenlightened about what his "covering" them might mean. This is a difficult case to adjudicate.

Notwithstanding all of this, there can be no doubt that valorizing the perception of the individual is one way of solving such culturally encoded problems as priority and belatedness. Indeed, it might be argued that such problems will never arise, that they are in fact preempted by the terms of the investigation (since any first perceived place is as formative as anywhere else). It comes as no surprise that both Malouf and Atwood should favor symbolism and archetypes, for these are the proven tools of the universalizing impulse. There may also be some connection between both authors' subscription to a universalizing aesthetic and the fact that both are essentially monologic, or, rather, monovocal, since they do write dialogues and think dialogically. Yet Atwood's characters, while they are clearly distinguishable from one another, all seem to use the same style of personal utterance: the same shocking casualness, the same chopped cadences. Malouf also speaks all of his characters' innermost thoughts in something like his own voice: slow, meditative, with a perfect ear for the natural rhythms of Australian speech and a faultless use of local idiom. The common touch: Malouf and Atwood both have it. Their interest is in the ordinary, representative man or woman, the exemplary figure, the case.

One way of confirming what Malouf and Atwood have in common is to compare them with someone who writes very differently. Such a comparison is bound to raise more questions than it answers, yet it may also help us to define the limits of each of their enterprises. Two Australian writers, Elizabeth Jolley and Peter Carey, suggest themselves as appropriate foils for Malouf and Atwood; since, however, my concern at this point is merely to point a contrast, Jolley alone will suffice. The most striking difference between her writing and Malouf's and Atwood's lies in her ability to handle a very wide variety of idioms. Like Poe, perhaps, she is rather a ventriloquist, and her mastery of idiom is an intrinsic part of her method. And, perhaps also like Poe, her inspiration lies closer to Chaos than either Malouf's or Atwood's:

> We're having this dumb play at school Falstaff or something
> I was supposed to be the Sheriff of London but the bell went
> before my part came on and as it was the long weekend Hot
> Legs let us go before the bell stopped.[29]

> "I have always . . . how you say . . . sweet teeth," Mrs Schultz
> sat back happily. She kicked off her shoes. She turned to me. "I
> am not . . . how you say . . . my beast till night then my beast
> comes out, at midnight! Schultzi always said it. My Schultzi
> was, how you say, a goof, he buy me presents all the time and
> I never like."[30]

Jolley's primary interest in the carnivalesque, in clowning and grotes-
querie, is subversive, antagonistic. Her *heteroglossia* (to use Bakhtin's
term) is a means of fracturing wholeness, by which process, it would
seem, creative energy is released, semantic play set in motion. Malouf,
by comparison, is a lawmaker. So, in the last analysis, is Margaret
Atwood, although her narrator-protagonists have first to pass through
a movement of dislocation from the world, during which its evils are
diagnosed, until they can reach a point of crisis which precipitates the
starting point of a new order.

But, although they are possessed of radically different tempera-
ments and concerns, Jolley and Malouf share, as Australians, a preoccupation with landscape. According to Malouf, the great Australian
theme is possession. He calls his novel, *Harland's Half Acre* (1984), "a
very Australian book," "because it's about the whole question of who
possesses the land, and how you possess the land. And in the end what
he [the artist, Frank Harland] discovers of course is that you possess
things through the imagination. You possess them by taking them into
your consciousness, and into your spirit. And not by actually putting
down money and buying them."[31] Jolley would appear to concur with
all of this: "The landscape of my writing is not to be found clearly on
any map. . . . A picture of the sea or even the sharp rise from the
coastal plain which is characteristic of the southern part of Western
Australia, as well as many other regions, is based on something seen
but not seen in a sharply defined geographical location."[32] Like Malouf,
Jolley would appear to consider the idea of possessing land as largely
an imaginative activity – indeed, even an imaginary one. All of the
stories in her collection *Five Acre Virgin* (1976) are about possessing
land, although very few of the characters actually own any. In Jolley's

canon agricultural property is a locus of urban and, more especially, of immigrant dreaming: you have to have yearned for it for a consider- able time before it can ever be yours. Being on the land not only re- leases characters from such urban constrictions as poverty, class, and legality; it may also result in a minor miracle – for example, a dreamed- of reformation of a character. Such a change is effected in the person- ality of the Prince, whose mother has contrived to give her family the opportunity to live on the land that economic necessity has forced her to sell. According to the "gentlemen's agreement" that she secures from the new owners, the family is allowed to plant and harvest one crop. She chooses a jarrah forest, an Australian hardwood that takes forty years to come to maturity.

To use Jolley as a foil for Malouf and Atwood, contrasting her acute sociolinguistic ear and exuberant heteroglossia with their lyric simplic- ity, is inevitably to reveal more of disparity than similarity. Such a contrast can perhaps also be read, however, as an index to the sheer variety of creative possibilities available to writers approaching the twin themes of immigration and settlement. For these themes con- tinue both to be a rich source of stories and to constitute a shaping principle – flexible yet deeply inscribed in the cultural bedrock.

NOTES

1. Alice Munro, *The Beggar Maid: Stories of Flo and Rose* (Harmondsworth: Pen- guin, 1980 [first pub. in 1978 as *Who Do You Think You Are?*]), 146.

2. The example that most readily comes to mind is the French Canadian song, *"Mon pays, c'est l'hiver."* Since this chapter deals only with English Canadian lit- erature, I hope French Canadians can forgive this single appropriation.

3. In Australian literary history the departure from this mode is, arguably, pre- cisely datable. In 1974 Peter Carey's short story "The Fat Man in History," pos- sibly Australia's first carnivalesque story, was published. Carey also wrote Australia's first Utopian novel, *Bliss* (1981), and Australia's first pastiche, *Illy- whacker* (1985).

4. The essay forms the introduction to her book *Preoccupations in Australian Poetry* (Melbourne: Oxford Univ. Press, 1965), xi–xxi.

5. David Malouf, Interview for BBC's radio program, *Meridian*, 20 April 1990.

6. Sally Morgan, *My Place* (1987; reprint, London: Virago, 1988), 38–39.

7. Mavis Gallant, *Home Truths: Selected Canadian Stories* (1981; reprint, Toronto: Macmillan, 1987), xiv.

8. In Jim Davidson, ed., *Sideways from the Page: The Meanjin Interviews* (Mel- bourne: Fontana/Collins, 1983), 106.

9. Gallant, *Home Truths*, 115. This story is reprinted in *The Secret Self/2: Stories by*

Women, ed. Hermione Lee (London: J. M. Dent, 1987); and also in *Overhead in a Balloon and Other Stories* (London: Faber, 1989).

10. Ibid., 108.

11. Ibid., 118.

12. Ibid., 133.

13. Judith Wright's family saga, *The Generations of Men* (Melbourne: Oxford Univ. Press, 1959), is, in my view, precisely such a work.

14. Margaret Atwood, *Surfacing* (1972; reprint, London: Virago, 1979), 181.

15. In Davidson, *Sideways from the Page*, 94–95.

16. Benjamin Lee Whorf, *Language, Thought, and Reality: Selected Writings of Benjamin Lee Whorf*, ed. John B. Carroll (1956; reprint, Cambridge: MIT Press, 1965), 262.

17. Margaret Atwood, *Two-Headed Poems* (Toronto: Oxford Univ. Press, 1978); *Interlunar* (Toronto: Oxford Univ. Press, 1984).

18. Margaret Atwood, ed., *The New Oxford Book of Canadian Verse in English* (Toronto: Oxford Univ. Press, 1982).

19. Atwood, "Bad Mouth," *Interlunar*, 11–12.

20. Atwood, "Psalm to Snake," *Interlunar*, 17.

21. David Malouf, *The Great World* (London: Chatto & Windus, 1990), 14–15.

22. Ibid., 137–38.

23. David Malouf, *12 Edmondstone Street* (1985; reprint, Melbourne: Penguin, 1986), 8–9.

24. Ibid., 9.

25. Malouf, *Meridian* interview.

26. David Malouf, *Fly Away Peter* (1982; reprint, Melbourne: Penguin, 1983), 19–20.

27. Malouf was, for instance, the inaugural recipient of the prestigious Pascall Award in 1988.

28. Malouf, *Great World*, 27–28.

29. Elizabeth Jolley, *Stories* (Melbourne: Penguin, 1989), 4. These were first published as two separate collections, *Five Acre Virgin* (1976), and *The Travelling Entertainer* (1979), by Fremantle Arts Centre Press, Fremantle, W.A.

30. Ibid., 82.

31. Malouf, *Meridian* interview.

32. Jolley, *Stories*, 310–11.

7   Prisoners and Spiders Surrounded by Signs

Postmodernism and
the Postcolonial Gaze
in Contemporary
Australian Culture

Patrick Fuery

Toward the end of Peter Carey's *Illywhacker* (1985), when Herbert Badgery, the key illywhacker in a land of illywhackers, is living with his family in the enormous pet store, he inserts a window in his room on the fourth floor so he can look out onto Pitt Street. A month later a neon sign is erected around this window, and Badgery becomes obsessed by the nature of these things. Most important of all for him is his own image in the window from the position of others; he tries to make other people stand in his place so he can test appearances, but the task falls mostly to his young grandson Hissao:

> So it was Hissao whom I persuaded to stand there instead. I would have him stand on my Danish Deluxe. He would jump up and down on it – I didn't mind that – and I would make that interminable journey down the stairs – I always forgot what floor I was on – and go and stand and look at him.
>
> I was using him, of course, but not in any way that was harmful to him. I was looking at him, but imagining myself as a passer-by and looking up to see ME in there. The question is: how would you take me, sitting there in my chair, neon lit, surrounded by these swirling signs? Am I a prisoner in the midst of a sign or am I a spider at its centre?[1]

Every culture is set up and sets itself up in a window, surrounded by signs, to watch and be watched. In a sense it is the interplay of the window, its surrounding signs, and the position of the passerby which determines the culture. Carey's vision of Australia is precisely mirrored in his fictions as a culture setting itself up in an attempt to see its true nature. The difficulty is the distractions – the lies, the surrounding signs, the distortions, the convoluted narratives and ways of speaking them. There can be no truth, only gestures toward it and attempts to determine it, which is why the idea of the illywhacker becomes so central not just to Carey's fiction but to a whole textual order of Australian culture and even the culture itself. One of the central issues is why the act of distortion is so significant to the cultural perspective in Australia: why does it act as such a fundamental determining process? The answer lies in part in the choice between being the prisoner or the spider in the sign. Australia as a postcolonial culture is constantly engaged in the idea of the gaze and in how it should look at its own signs and signifying practices. It sets up images of itself and watches them like the passerby on the street below.

The central concern here is how certain types of representations occur in the textual system of Australian culture with specific reference to the idea of a cultural gaze and how the gaze is part of the formation of signs that demonstrate an Australian sensibility. To describe a rubric for a cultural gaze is an impossible task in itself, complicated even further by the multicultural dimensions of Australian society. I will concentrate here on a specific type that is in many ways central to the understanding of contemporary Australian cultural identity and textuality. In the first instance I wish to speak of a cultural gaze and of how the gaze operates in a cultural context. It is then possible to consider a particular type of cultural gaze which has developed in Australia which is a combination of postcolonialism and postmodernism.

The concept of the *gaze* is used here in terms of recent critical theory, in particular, the psychoanalytic models of Jacques Lacan. Essentially, this is the gaze not simply as a mechanism of perception but of a larger (often social) process that actually determines the subject itself. For Lacan the gaze is not an innocent activity but, instead, the positioning of the subject in relation to the object and other subjects. The subject gazes but is also gazed at, and it is this sense of being gazed at by another which determines the whole sense of being for Lacan.[2] In terms of the issues at hand this sense of being determined by the gaze (the subject's own gaze and the gaze of the other) is extended to the idea of a cultural gaze – that is, a particular way of looking at the world and the culture itself and at the same time feeling positioned in a particular way through the gaze. In this sense the gaze is as much about how things mean as how they are actually "seen." For this reason we can speak of the gaze as a type of discourse; it is controlled, mediated, determined in a type of language system.

Augenverdreher – Eye-Twisters and the Empty Eye

The choice Herbert Badgery offers, between the prisoner trapped by the signs that surround and determine him or her or the spider that utilizes those same signs to trap others, is a form of twisting the gaze to being trapped or trapping. But, of course, every gaze is twisted, and every reading through the gaze is twisted. There cannot be a transcendental untwisted gaze, a Platonic ideal gaze fixed to an ideal untwisted object; the image on the cave wall is twisted many times, but eventually it passes as the actual, the unmediated. The cultural gaze becomes the naturalized way of viewing the world from a particular perspective. This passing over to seem like the actual, the real, is why the gaze functions as an order of discourse.

Eye-twisting is a fundamental part of the discourse of the gaze, so fundamental in fact that the very activity of the gaze itself must be seen as *augenverdreher*.[3] The action of the gaze puts a forced construction on all that it meets because this is how the discourse operates. When we see something totally new we rub our eyes, we blink rapidly, we twist our head to one side to try to assimilate the unfamiliar (the defamiliarized). But what we really try to do is draw the new into the old twist, the established discourse, the familiar pattern of the culture. But the old twist doesn't seem like a twist because it is in the ordering principle, a hermeneutics, rather than just an act of perception. Narratives – ways of telling a culture to itself and to others – do not seem to twist the gaze, and yet this is precisely what they do in a constant and direct fashion, so much so that events, histories, acts of interpretation, become twisted into narratives so that they fit more easily into the act of gazing.

A fundamental aspect of eye-twisting – of constructing things in a particular way – is that certain ways of representing, and even certain representations themselves, become privileged. This tends to produce a corpus of images, narratives, ideas that eventually form the cultural model. Australian culture, like other cultures, becomes recognizable through a (relatively) clearly defined set of signs; we only have to look at a travel brochure to be reminded of this. The forced constructions of the gaze privilege one set of presences over any other, usually because of the social and historical basis of the twist. Even though there are many senses of the present and the absent, the twist of presence is limited and the range of absences veiled from the gaze.

What comes to be represented (the presences) and how is a complex process; in many ways it cannot be mapped because of the possible range of influences and processes of selection. We must be satisfied with some of the implications of the selection here, rather than the history of their development. What is significant about these selections, and their subsequent representations, is that the discourse of the gaze makes the selection process invisible. This means that often the cultural gaze becomes tied to the perceived knowledge of the culture. This has the effect of making the ideologically based selections seem somehow "natural." Michel Foucault, in dealing with the relationship of power to knowledge, can be used to contextualize this point: "In appearance, or rather, according to the mask it bears, historical consciousness is neutral, devoid of passions, and committed solely to truth. But if it examines itself and if, more generally, it interrogates the various forms of scientific consciousness in its history, it finds that all these forms and transformations are aspects of the will to knowledge: instinct, passion, the inquisitor's devotion, cruel subtlety, and malice."[4] Historical consciousness read as a form of cultural gazing is the sociocultural and ideological gaze twisted, and the twisting that occurs to create the mask of neutrality is of the same order that positions all gazes, both literal and metaphorical.

The centrality of absence and presence to the discursive function of eye-twisting is related to another process that figures the gaze in terms of desire and subjectivity: the emptying of the eye. This phenomenon involves the Lacanian distinction between the gaze and the eye, which in turn has its basis in the idea of scopophilia. Freud's concept of scopophilia as the opposite of, but referentially connected to, exhibitionism is based at least in part on Jean-Martin Charcot's idea of *scotomization*, of *scotome scintillant* and its *éblouissement de ténèbres*.[5] There is the historical (and political) complicity of scotomization and repression here,[6] but it is possible to put to one side these difficulties and see how scopophilia relates to this notion of privileged presences and absence and the cultural gaze, which in part implies a connection with repression.

The other side to these issues of repression and representation is that of desire. The twisting of the eye and the emptying of the gaze operate through the correlative system of subjectivity, culture, and absence/presence. Eye-twisting is the interplay of presences – the instigation of one set of presences over any other set – and the emptying of the gaze is the fear of losing the signifier of the self, translated into the loss of the gaze. In both of these processes desire is a significant feature, in terms of the operation of the gaze and the systems of representation. This is especially true of the formation of a cultural gaze. For Lacan these issues of desire and representation are centered on the action of the gaze, the subjective position of the eye and the temptation of the lure. We can read these in terms of Lacan's own emphasis: the scopic drive and desire, the desiring subject and the gaze.

The scopic drive is directly connected to the action of desire and the positioning of representations. The scopic drive is not about the subject's relationship to the object, as first might appear to be the case; rather, it is about the subject's relationship to desire. Desire, Lacan constantly reminds us, is the desire for the other, and its operation in the scopic is no exception. To this extent drives are systems of meaning for the subject; they basically make something meaningful because of their centrality to the subject. It is this combination of meaning and desire which locates the operation of the gaze in systems of representation: how things are represented, how things are positioned in order to be read, and so on. In terms of cultural gazes this same operation is extended so that whole systems of representations and ways of making sense are developed. It is now time to consider how this operates, concentrating on a type of cultural gaze in the Australian context.

The Postmodern and Postcolonial Gaze

Neither *postmodern* nor *postcolonial*, as critical terms, have fixed definitions. At best they operate, in their own discursive/analytic situations, in terms of a shared agenda, but most of the time they are contentious points of debate. It is beyond the immediate concerns of this chapter to engage in the difficulties of the definitions or theoretical operations of either concept, but this does not negate their critical use here. The central point of investigation is a particular type within a larger order of discursive practices. This type is designated as the gaze determined through a historical and cultural order as well as a set of textual practices. Both postmodernism and postcolonialism have been described as either a historicocultural order or a paradigm of textual practices, and both have occasionally been seen as a combination of the two. This is particularly significant when the two are combined to examine a cultural phenomenon. What I wish to argue is that there is a particular type of gaze, as discursive practice determined through the scopic drive, in contemporary Australian culture which is a combination of postcolonial identification and postmodern practice and that this gaze is one of the fundamental and central aspects of textuality and cultural identity. The central orientation of this function is to facilitate certain ways of looking (i.e., the function of presence) which come to determine a sense of the cultural gaze and, in many instances, the cultural identity itself.

To describe a particular type of cultural gaze in the Australian context as a combination of the postcolonial and postmodern is not arbitrarily to join two critical issues but, rather, to acknowledge a dynamic interplay in the production and reception of a number of textual systems. This interplay must be seen as relatively equal so that a potentially difficult methodological issue is avoided. It would be almost impossible to try to distinguish which of the two is more of a determinant than the other, or even if one determines the other. Undoubtedly, this does occur (e.g., a postmodern text is such because it emphasizes in some way the postcolonial issue and vice versa), but for the moment this can be put to one side, and the aspect of combination can be seen as the more significant factor.

The type that is of concern here, to sum up, is a combination of a postmodern and postcolonial textual system constructed through the gaze, which has been defined as an operation of representation and desire as well as perception. It is the action of gazing at the texts, in its broadest sense – the "culture" itself is a text, made up of multiple texts – which draws attention to the particular nature of representation and reception.

The object of the gaze, and subsequently the gaze itself, for most (if not the entire time) of Australia's white history has been the concept of a cultural identity. What signs declare themselves to be Australian; what signs exhibit some phenomenological sense of "Australianness"; what signs lend themselves to such a reading? These are difficult textual issues made all the more difficult because of the self-reflexive and self-conscious register in which they are articulated. The concept of postcolonialism adds to these difficulties because it restates a key hidden agenda: what is the "post" of postcolonialism, and what does it produce through the interplay of absences and presences of representation? Essentially, it becomes an issue of comparisons, of measuring one set of discourses against another because to be "post" something (historically, ideologically, textually) is to acknowledge, at least in the first instance, a preceding articulation, or system. Postcolonialism cannot simply mean, however, the insertion of a set of discursive practices after the abnegation of an earlier set, or even the reinsertion of any earlier system. The reason why it cannot be this is because it is a transformational process, and the things that are transformed are precisely the signifying systems that constitute the culture. The postcolonial environment in Australia may have involved a revival in the production (through replication or review) of originary Aboriginal texts, but these will always be seen in terms of the European other. They carry with them, concomitant with or overlaid, a political gesturing about two hundred years of colonialism. Similarly, texts produced by the non-Aboriginal sections, the diverse multicultural strata, which reflect a sense of Australianness can be measured against a different system of colonialism and postcolonialism. In this sense there is not a single homogeneous postcolonial perspective in Australia but, rather, multiple heterogeneous ones. Of all these two stand out: the white-Aboriginal relationship in terms of colonialism (of the past and continuing) and the English/European–Australian relationship in terms of colonialism and postcolonialism. A third model, current cultural colonialism from the United States, is a further significant development.

Gradual shifts in cultural paradigms mean that a concept of postcolonialism cannot be read as one system replacing another. In this sense *post* is a misnomer. A more likely scenario is that there is an inmixing of ideological and textual systems, and a sense of the postcolonial develops out of the merging paradigms of representation and interpretation. This inmixing forms a central part of the absent-present qualities of the cultural gaze. It must be remembered that Australia is a culture that still attempts to produce English country gardens in a land dominated by desert, while also coming to terms with its own multicultural (European, Aboriginal, Asian as well as British) identity.

The signs used to represent Australia – the Australianness of particular objects, images, icons, and words – are formed not simply in their material basis but also in the way they are positioned through the gaze. We might want to "see" kangaroos, deserts, chopped slang, antiauthoritarian attitudes, beach culture and ANZACS as signs of Australia, but it is just as important to remember that it is also the twisting of the gaze which makes these signs Australian. It is the gaze, the ways of seeing and representing, which confirms or denies the Australianness of the sign both within the culture and for those who observe from outside.

In order to keep manageable the consideration of postcolonialism and postmodernism as aspects of the gaze, the discussion will be limited to two examples that can been seen as significant to recent issues of and attempts at cultural representation. The two examples I wish to concentrate on are, first, historicism and pastiche and, second, the operation of simulacra as/in spatial diegesis. In keeping with the overall concept of a cultural gaze, these two textual constructions, and their reception, can be seen as examples of the ways in which representation and interpretation occur in a postcolonial/postmodern condition in a number of recent Australian texts. This allows some flexibility in the sense of the text being seen as produced and/or received as postmodern and postcolonial.

Postmodernism and History: Historicism and Pastiche

Fredric Jameson offers perhaps one of the strongest arguments for forging a link between postmodernism as a critical method and as a cultural indicator when he attempts to resolve some of the difficulties of the term. Jameson suggests that postmodernism is not another attempt at historicocultural homogeneity: "This is, however, precisely why it seems to me essential to grasp 'postmodernism' not as a style, but rather as a cultural dominant: a conception which allows for the presence and coexistence of a range of very different, yet subordinate features."[7] This offers a number of parallels to the sense of postcolonialism discussed earlier. It is not the solidification of a cultural order but, rather, the opposite: a fragmenting of the (hegemonic) system of representation and interpretation. Postcolonialism, at least in the Australian experience, is the collapse of a single (which may only be in appearance) cultural order for a fragmented one that attempts to hold multiple and divergent views. The multicultural basis of Australian society feeds the postmodern sense of pastiche because it requires the binding together of diverse, sometimes oppositional, systemic orders. Postmodernism and postcolonialism permit, encourage even, this operation of pastiche, which is not to suggest some sort of textual egalitarianism but, rather, a condition of textual production and, perhaps, reception.

The rise of postmodernism and postcolonialism as critical terms and historical conditions occurs at around the same time in Australia. The idea that Australia may be moving toward some sort of postcolonial cultural gaze and, consequently, identification becomes foregrounded around the early 1970s, and this is mirrored in particular in the cinema of the time. At first glance this might seem contradictory; if anything, the films made during this period (1970 to the early mid-1980s) are dominated by a backward look, based on Australia's white history constructed through (largely) English eyes. This immense discursive practice of representing the past can be seen, however, not as an attempt to bolster images of a colonial past in the midst of a postcolonial surge – that is, some sort of ideological clash – but, in fact, as a fundamental part of the postmodern reading of the culture and history and the developing sense of postcolonialism. Jameson argues that a key part of postmodernism is "the nostalgia mode (or *la mode rétro*)," in which the past is reinvented within current concerns; this is the "colonization of the present by the nostalgia mode."[8] To be postmodern the requirement is that the reinvention of the past operates as pastiche. Christa Buerger argues that there is a loss of history in postmodernism, so that the time frame "restlessly wanders between present and the past, indiscriminately retrieving its aesthetic forms from the imaginary museum of the cultural tradition."[9] This is precisely what takes place in a great deal of Australian cinema at this time and, to a certain extent, is still taking place in both the films and literature.

This is not to argue that all the films constructed as historical pieces made in this period are postmodern by virtue of this rereading through the nostalgia mode;[10] a postmodern text is not simply a product of nostalgia. In order, however, to read the phenomenon of this large group of texts operating as a form of postcolonialism it is necessary to accommodate the postmodern. What is being argued, in effect, is that the political rereading of these texts as postmodern historical pastiche alters the seemingly inherent colonialist celebration (i.e., the colonial power settling/cultivating/taming the Great Southern Land) to one of a historical reinvention in terms of postcolonialism. It is precisely this form of historical rereading which occurs in Peter Carey's *Illywhacker* and *Oscar and Lucinda* (1988), particularly the latter, which contains as its narrative structure a metadiscourse about the operation of colonialism and history in Australia's past. A great deal of the Aboriginal literature written during this period reflects similar issues, with the emphasis shifting to historical pastiche and white history's categorizing and temporalizing of Aboriginal culture and sensibilities. In terms of the cinematic texts it is the culture's obsession with its past and the deconstruction of history which allows for a postmodern reading.

The effect that this had on the cultural gaze is that it was twisted by the nature of the texts and their excessive historical quality. Australia's past, in particular the colonial past, became more significant than the present, and it was not until the mid-1980s that the present was substantially tackled. It was history as pastiche which defined the culture's present and, to a certain extent, still does. The sense of the contemporary was made absent through this cultural gaze and was only reintegrated when the postmodern nostalgia mode was somehow seen as part of the present: the absent past becomes fundamental to the interpretation of the present. Jameson argues: "These restructure the whole issue of pastiche and project it onto a collective and social level, where the desperate attempt to appropriate a missing past is now refracted through the iron law of fashion change and the emergent ideology of the 'generation.'"[11] In Australia's case the missing past needed to be reinvented because it was deemed essential to the sense of a cultural identity. It is this sense of a lack of cultural identity which directly connects the postmodern historical pastiche to postcolonial ideological issues in Australia, as particularly manifested in the cinema.

The gaze is directed to a consideration of the culture's past in a strikingly self-conscious fashion. This gaze is highly postmodern because of its concern with the (cultural) past; this is in keeping with Lyotard's idea of the future anterior. Postmodernism is "working without rules in order to formulate the rules of what *will have been done*. . . . *Post modern* would have to be understood according to the paradox of the future (*post*) anterior (*modo*)."[12]

The historical, nostalgic mode that dominated Australian culture was necessarily postmodern in design because it contained the fragmentation of cultural presences within the context of a missing past. These texts (particularly the films) never really represented a past in a strictly historical sense but, rather, declared a phenomenological pastness about themselves, and it is this essential sense that connects the postcolonial and the postmodern. The Australian cultural gaze has become a postmodern and postcolonial one through this historical self-reflexivity in a historical absence. The domination of these texts led to a cultural gaze that attempted to make sense of the present, to make the present even, by returning to the past. Because this can be read in terms of postmodernism, however, this historical excess forms a fundamental and crucial part of Australian postcolonialism.

Cultural Simulacra as/in Spatial Diegesis

This gaze, which still operates as a cultural model of representation and interpretation, is linked to another configuration of postmodernism and postcolonialism in contemporary Australian culture. The postmodern condition is indicated by the constant and excessive production of images of the self – in this case, the cultural self. Replication, duplication, and representation create a body of texts that become indicative of the process of image making, rather than of what the images themselves might be or how they might be operating. Fundamental to this process is the simulacrum: "It is for such objects that we may reserve Plato's conception of the 'simulacrum'– the identical copy for which no original has ever existed."[13] Simulacra, it would seem, are an essential part of the postcolonial condition because of the cultural referentiality involved. When a culture attempts to represent itself, its own "culturalness," the images become crucial to the ideological and historical sense of the society. In Australia's case (multicultural and postcolonial) simulacra operate in the interplay of absences and historical pastiche. This does not mean that in this postcolonial and postmodern condition the signifiers are necessarily emptied, rather that the representational quality is stressed. One hesitates to designate these signs as metanarratives (or even Lyotard's idea of *petites histoires*). There are certain gestures toward their becoming such, however, in a number of texts.

Both the novel and film versions of Carey's *Bliss* (1981) engage in the simulacra of contemporary Australian culture. There are continual references to the United States (perhaps the archetypal culture of simulacra) which operate as a type of mapping of Australian culture in a postcolonial context. In this way Harry Joy and Honey Barbara's "return" to the Bush at the end of the narrative reflects, at least superficially, an idyllic rejection of the more recent cultural colonization of Australia by the United States.[14] This same pattern and operation of simulacra takes place in the two *Crocodile Dundee* films (cultural simulacra being the journey to the city and the eventual return to the Outback). What is perhaps more significant, and more firmly based on the interplay of postmodernism and postcolonial identities and conditions, is the return to Carey's motif of the shifting position or unreliable nature of the narrating voice. In all three of Carey's novels (*Bliss, Illywhacker,* and *Oscar and Lucinda*) the narrating voice is used to trick the reader in some way, most often through lies and deceptions. Perhaps of greatest significance in this schema of duplicity is that one of the most common deceptions operates through the interplay of family generations; history and storytelling combine to trick the reader and distort the sense of truth and the past. Truth, narrating voices, history, and generations become simulacra, and their urgency is made all the more pressing through the overdetermination of the signs. This in itself is seen as part of the Australian culture: to lie and trick is often seen as an honorable and admirable trait. Compare this to perhaps one of the most heinous of cultural crimes in Australia, which is to "dob in a mate" (to inform the figure[s] of authority). Truth is something to be wary of and to avoid, while lies are seen as a bonding between friends and a show of trust. Such an inversion produces a peculiar attitude toward simulacra.

Simulacra are also demonstrated in the representation of spatial diegesis in a great many post-1970 Australian films.[15] This is particularly significant in terms of the sense of a cultural gaze because the ways in which a culture looks at and represents its own spatial configurations indicate how the ideological, historical, social, and cultural frames operate within that social order and how a culture constructs its own spatial dimensions through the gaze in terms of absence and presence. For Jameson this relationship of space, culture, and representation illustrates a key operation of the postmodern. The space of the city in Australia is mostly presented as the other – a lack or absence in a land dominated by the Bush, desert, and beaches. While this may be topographically correct (in terms of proportions of land use), it creates a cultural consciousness that is opposite to the reality for the vast majority of Australians.

Being one of the most highly urbanized countries in the world means that "the Bush" remains as mysterious to the land's inhabitants as it is to those who view from further out. It should be noted that the Bush operates in a polysemic fashion, and at a broad paradigmatic level, so that a great many signifiers have been developed to represent it. The common feature of these signifiers is that they present the natural environment in a particular ideological fashion and as (politically) distinct from the city or suburbia. In this sense the Bush is bushland, scrub, desert, rain forest, mountains – in short, all of the environment not transformed into urban dwelling space – and is paradigmatically tied to beaches and even the sea. There are also a group of signs which operate between the two. Examples of this include the road, the country town, the beach in its urban context (cultivated yet still natural), the pasture lands. This form of spatial diegesis can be read as simulacrum (in the postmodern sense) because it is linked to a nonoriginary representation and because it is directly tied to an intense and crucial production of signs in a great many texts.

The significant difference that has taken place in the postmodern and postcolonial text is that this distance from the nonurban areas is acknowledged and sometimes investigated. This has led to a shift in the construction of diegetic structure of space in the Australian cinema and, consequently, to an ideological shift in its reception. Spatial diegesis as a form of postmodern simulacrum has been central to postcolonial consciousness and textual representation. This can be demonstrated by comparing three films that were made within a space of fifteen years of each other.

Nicholas Roeg's *Walkabout* (1971) is quintessentially "English" (which here stands for the non-Australian) paranoia of the Australian Bush. It is represented as a harsh and destructive environment that is totally alien to any white eyes, but in particular to any non-Australian eyes. What is significant about this is not the relative truths or errors of such a representation (the Bush/desert certainly is a hostile and potentially deadly place) but, rather, that it feeds into a whole signifying practice that needs to be positioned against its binary opposite – the Bush as metaphor for the Australian cultural character. It is this interplay of opposites (hostility vs. open friendliness, alien vs. known, city vs. Bush, culture / the cultured vs. nature / the natural) which is investigated in a similar fashion in Ted Kotcheff's *Wake in Fright* (1971). Both films, significantly made by non-Australian directors, represent Australian spatial diegesis as fundamentally life-threatening and psychologically destructive. The same concept is developed in Colin Eggleston's *The Long Weekend* (1979) and, in an urban setting, Peter Weir's *The Last Wave* (1977), with the difference being that in both these films it is white

Australians (from the city) being threatened by their own environment. In a similar fashion George Miller's *Dead Calm* (1989) combines a threat from the environment (the sea, which paradigmatically stands in for the Bush here) and outsiders (a psychopathic American).

A fundamental difference between this last example and Roeg's film is that it lacks the recouping idea of the Australian character – that is, that mixed in with the hostility there is also a "friendly" side to the Australian environment. In *Walkabout* the abandoned children survive because they meet an Aborigine, although his exact positioning in terms of threat and safety is often ambiguous. *Wake in Fright* plays with the sense of the Australian humor, placing it in a much more sinister, carnivalesque register. This dark side of larrikinism – so often designated as part of the Australian (male) character – contains an element of horror within the supposed friendliness of the joke. Weir's *The Cars That Ate Paris* (1974) is similar because it shows the small Outback community united in playing the joke on others. This violent "humor" is often related to the depiction of Australian masculinity and at its most extreme demonstrates a strong misogynistic tendency.

The idea of spatial diegesis represented as totally alien and hostile shifts somewhat in Weir's *Picnic at Hanging Rock* (1975). Here the elements remain constant (Anglo-European figures from the universal City cast into the unknown Australian Bush), but there is a shift in the sense of the threat from the landscape. Although there is the same sense of tragedy and psychological scarring, the Bush (metonymically presented here as Hanging Rock) also has its positive elements, which are not necessarily mediated. The unknown becomes the central feature of the spatial diegesis, and in particular the metaphor of sexual knowledge, the escape from Victorian repression, the transition from child to woman, from English conservatism to postcolonial sexuality, and so on. This same sense of the transformation of one feminine sexual identity to another (the unknowledgeable, inexperienced girl to the sexually aware woman) also occurs in *Walkabout*; nature becomes symbolic of sexual liberation, particularly for women. In one sense this can be related to the phallocentric figuring of the Outback: it is ultimately a man's place, especially an Australian man's place.

In *Picnic at Hanging Rock* Miranda's disappearance does not hold the same paranoid and negative qualities that are to be found in similar films on this subject. The postcolonial gaze in this sense has transformed the totally negative spatial diegesis of the Australian Bush into something that holds both the negative and positive. The Bush is still unknown and alien, is still represented in terms of the other, but now there seems to be something worth knowing about in that unknown. A distinction needs to be made, however, between this transformation of the environment as something "liberating" and how this idea of liberation is essentially male orientated. The discourse of the Australian environment is still male dominated and positioned in terms of a specific subject – that is, white, male, Anglo-Celtic, and from a particular paradigm of colonialism and postcolonialism. Beyond this perspective is marginalization and the marginalized.

The inmixing of threat and pleasure, of seeing the natural environment as a mixture of sexual transformation and yet also part of the patriarchal order, as threatening and yet also containing a form of humor, produces a curious blend of compelling desire and repulsion which in many ways comes to signify Australianness. A further variation of this occurs in films such as John Duigan's *The Year My Voice Broke* (1987) and Gillian Armstrong's *My Brilliant Career* (1979). Here the noncity environment (rural, small country town) threatens only in terms of its closeness, its finite feeling. The limitless Bush has been replaced by a static, clearly defined country town, but the two operate within a closely linked sense of spatial diegesis and simulacra. This is also true of perhaps one of Australia's most postmodern of films, Miller's *Mad Max* (1979),[16] in which the country towns harbor the murderous bikie gangs. The same can be said of Weir's earlier film *The Cars That Ate Paris*, which also sets up a particular relationship between the individual, machinery, and the environment (City, country, Bush).

The country town sits between the City and the Bush, neither one or the other, European or "natural" Australia, raw or cooked. But the country town of *The Year My Voice Broke* does not have the same sense of the surrounding Bush as perilous (as in *Walkabout*) or the harshness of city life (e.g., the drug culture of *Monkey Grip* or *Dogs in Space* or urban poverty such as *Mouth to Mouth*) or romance (as in *The Man from Snowy River*). Instead, it undercuts the "wide-open spaces" with a feeling of stasis and entrapment. The transition of the gaze which takes place here is spatial excess as simulacra to spatial limitations. Which is not to say that there is a shift in cinematographic style; the Australian environment still invites long panning shots, constant references to depth and unlimited space. Rather, there has been a change in the paradigmatics of the signs. Simulacra still operate – images are produced which demand to be read as signs of Australia, even if they have no referential origin to the textual or the reader – but they have altered the relational context of reader to the represented sense of culture and land.

Postmodern/Postcolonial Seduction

Baudrillard offers the following on the nature of seduction: "Seduction is not that which is opposed to production. It is that which seduces production – just as absence is not that which is opposed to presence, but that which seduces presence, as evil is not that which is opposed to good, but seduces good, as the feminine is not opposed to the masculine, but seduces the masculine."[17] I would like to add to Baudrillard's list by saying that the postcolonial is not that which is opposed to colonialism but, rather, that which seduces colonialism, and the gaze is not that which opposes a set of discourses but, instead, that which seduces discourse, all discourse. The postcolonial gaze in Australia is seductive because it represents an attempt to engage in the difficulties of a missing – or, at the very least, unspoken – cultural identity. This seductive nature has, in part, a sense of the postmodern for a number of reasons. It operates to draw attention to the act of gazing itself, of discovering what it is to have a (cultural) gaze and how systems of representation operate within this sense. This is the Lacanian search for certain objects (the *objet petit a*) which might somehow constitute cultural sensibility. What becomes more and more evident as the examination of the gaze itself takes place is that it is the process of twisting the gaze which constitutes the cultural identity, rather than any extraordinary set of signs taken as distinctly Australian. It is not the figure in the window, surrounded by signs, which constitutes the postcolonial agenda but, rather, the gaze of the figure who determines whether the simulacrum is a prisoner or a spider. In doing so, the gaze is seduced from one set of ideological paradigms to another.

NOTES

1. Peter Carey, *Illywhacker* (London: Faber & Faber, 1985), 545. Subsequent references are to this edition.
2. Lacan deals with the relationship of the gaze to the formation of the subject in a number of texts. Of particular interest in these issues are his *Four Fundamental Concepts of Psycho-analysis*, trans. Alan Sheridan (1977; reprint, Harmonds-

worth: Penguin, 1986), in particular the seminars under the heading "Of the Gaze as *Objet Petit a*"; and his book *Freud's Papers on Technique, 1953–1954*, trans. John Forrester (New York: W. W. Norton, 1988), in particular the seminars under the heading "The Topic of the Imaginary."

3. Freud uses the term *augenverdreher* – the twisting of the eyes – in reference to a patient of Tausk, who claimed that her lover was an "eye-twister": "She could not understand him at all, he looked different every time; he was a hypocrite, an 'eye-twister' (*augenverdreher*), he had twisted her eyes; now she had twisted eyes; they were not her eyes any more; now she saw the world with different eyes" (Sigmund Freud, *On Metapsychology–The Theory of Psychoanalysis*, trans. James Strachey [Harmondsworth: Penguin, 1984], 203).

4. Michel Foucault, *Language, Counter-Memory, Practice: Selected Essays and Interviews*, trans. Donald Bouchard and Sherry Simon (Oxford: Basil Blackwell, 1977), 162.

5. See, in particular, J. M. Charcot, *Leçons sur les maladies du système nerveux, Oeuvres complètes* 3 (Paris, 1887).

6. See Elizabeth Roudinesco, *Histoire de la psychanalyse en France*, vol. 1 (Paris: Seuil, 1985), for a discussion of this development. Scopophilia is the pleasure derived from looking and has become one of the central issues in film theory, especially in terms of feminism, in recent years.

7. Fredric Jameson, "Postmodernism, or the Cultural Logic of Late Capitalism," *New Left Review* 146 (1984): 56.

8. Ibid., 66, 67.

9. Christa Buerger, "The Disappearance of Art: The Postmodern Debate in the United States," *Telos* 68 (1986): 97.

10. There were a great many of these types of films produced. A short list includes: *Breaker Morant* (1980), *Caddie* (1976), *The Chant of Jimmy Blacksmith* (1978), *Eliza Fraser* (1976), *Gallipoli* (1981), *The Getting of Wisdom* (1977), *Mad Dog Morgan* (1976), *The Man from Snowy River* (1982), *My Brilliant Career* (1979), *Newsfront* (1978), and *Picnic at Hanging Rock* (1975).

11. Jameson, "Postmodernism," 66.

12. Jean François Lyotard, *The Postmodern Condition: A Report on Knowledge*, trans. Geoff Bennington and Brian Massumi (Minneapolis: Univ. of Minnesota Press, 1984), 81.

13. Jameson, "Postmodernism," 65.

14. This "return" became a significant part of the Australian cultural myth, illustrating the tension between urbanization / city living and the ideological figuring of the Bush. Part of this myth (in a semiotic sense) is the sense of the real and the false – that cities are lies and reality somehow rests in the Bush. Films such as *Crocodile Dundee* and *The Cars That Ate Paris* take this seemingly universal idea and expose it to a sense of antiauthoritarian rule bending so that the population of the Bush are truth twisters in their own right. Herbert Badgery explains about cities in *Illywhacker:* "I showed him, most important of all, the sort of city it was – full of trickery and deception. If you push against it too hard you will find yourself leaning against empty air. It is never, for all its brick and concrete, quite substantial and I would not be surprised to wake one morning and find

the whole thing gone, with only the grinning façade of Luna Park rising from the blue shimmer of eucalyptus bush" (547). This awakening takes place constantly throughout the literature and films of Australia, as if the grip on the land by the cities is very tenuous and quite imaginary.

15. Diegesis in film theory refers to the particular ways film constructs its representational systems. In this sense it is tied closely to the way narrative is devised.

16. For an interesting reading of the central figure in *Mad Max* as postmodern hero, see Christopher Sharrett, "Myth, Male Fantasy, and Simulacra in *Mad Max* and *The Road Warrior*," *Journal of Popular Film and Television* 13, no. 2 (1985): 82–91.

17. Jean Baudrillard, *The Ecstasy of Communication*, trans. Bernard and Caroline Schutze (New York: Semiotext(e), 1988), 58.

8 Politics and the Individual in the Modernist Historical Novel

Gordimer and Rushdie

Jonathan White

What used to be called the historical novel has moved increasingly into present history, or, at least, has had as a premise certain ideas or questions about what has produced the historical present. One other feature of writers of whom this is so – and one could begin a long list with names such as Gabriel García Márquez for Latin America, Christa Wolf for Central Europe, Nadine Gordimer for southern Africa, and Salman Rushdie for the Indian subcontinent – is that protagonists in their novels have become hyperrepresentative of national evolutions and destinies. This is so even to the point where we might want to claim that, for all their differing degrees of modernism, postmodernism, magical or other realism, many such novelists have challenged traditional history with what one critic has called "history from the inside."[1] The challenge is of crucial importance in an age when the novel, as a form of conventional entertainment and, hence, source of ideas and "knowledges about" particular events or places of recent times, far outstrips all other modes of academic or popular history. (One could even claim that televisual modes of narrating the emergence and especially the emergen*cies* of modern nation histories owe more to the novelist's tracing of events within character than to any of the various dense textures of academic historicism.) If what I am claiming is largely true, then the consequences within educational realms are enormous. An important aspect of the practical achievement of the

"end of history"– as distinct from its mere pronouncement as an ideological theme – is the inadequate inculcation within today's secondary
schools of what Nietzsche called "critical history."[2]

The political or historical novel may have a major role to play in
redressing such an inadequacy. Many students who have already well
and truly "given up" history and who also, one could claim, are only in
a minimal sense politicized by their education to a given point, can
and, in my experience as a university teacher of literature, actually do
become radicalized – or perhaps we should only for the moment say
infected – by voices that have been listened to attentively in their reading of particular novels. Colleagues and numerous acquaintances attest
that much or even most of what they know about history is gleaned
from the novel genre as basic source. Indeed, I would go so far as to
claim that certain novels have been written with this consideration –
the novel as an alternative way of *doing* history and politics – upper-
most in mind.[3]

Much of what I have to say in what follows is by way of accounts of
two cases in point, Nadine Gordimer's *Burger's Daughter* (1979) and
Salman Rushdie's *Midnight's Children* (1981). These two novels make for
especially interesting contrast because they were written more or less
contemporaneously during the latter years of the 1970s,[4] are both conscious of the (quite different) modernist modes they are deploying, and
are pushing very hard (the one solemnly, the other through a set of
ongoing comic hyperboles) notions of their protagonists as *loci* of
most, if not all, of the main events in their two different national histories: postcolonial India in the case of Rushdie; and, for Gordimer,
South Africa, a country in which she has elsewhere claimed that the
legacy of "nineteenth-century colonialism . . . reached its ultimate expression, . . . the ugliest creation of man," apartheid.[5] Both novels are
hence about consequences of colonialism in a direct sense. They are,
in interestingly different ways, political novels – Gordimer's openly so,
like almost all her other writings; Rushdie's in such colorfully man-
nered ways that the forthrightness of his critique of modern India
might at first be mistaken for mere literary *jouissance* (or "a mixture of
condiment and oratory," to adopt the book's own phraseology [210]).
What cannot be overstressed, however, is the openness of each novel's
invitation to its readership, to come to know in as full a sense as possible the nation being written about. Novel ways (in a literal sense) are
created of telling over its recent history as well as of making complex

guesses about its future. With whatever differences the two cases both do this via interest in a protagonist (Rosa Burger or Saleem Sinai), for whom next developments in the *nation's* destiny are always also of crucial *personal* importance.

It is wise to spend most time establishing the distinct achievement of the two separate texts. But I begin by means of a contrast with another contemporary writer, Christa Wolf, exercised by quite a different (and, as it happens, nonpostcolonial) national history, that of Germany during and after the Nazi era. None of these writers in whose works national and personal histories are fused simply repeats the phenomenological or ontological presuppositions of any other. There is similarity aplenty but also grand-scale difference. Both are important.

In some ways we do well to begin with reminders of how divorced the lives of individuals may be from momentous events of contemporary history. And, since our concern is with how the modern novel has taken on the role of witness to the shaping histories of our era, it is appropriate to consider what it might posit to be the problems that emerge when the destinies of individuals remain *un*marked by important goings-on around them. One of the novelists who has had to inspect the implications of such a possibility most forcibly is precisely Christa Wolf, who in a novel such as *A Model Childhood* (1983) is having to face the pain of German guilt for Nazi concentration camps which came into being already partly occluded from history. I do not mean at this point to enter a larger debate about how much responsibility should be shouldered by individual Germans for the Holocaust but, rather, simply to show that the moment in that novel which is, so to speak, the historical and political crux of the text, records, hauntingly, an absence of the individual from history. The point being that an absence *from* history is experienced by the individual herself as an absence *of* history. History only exists as remembered or recorded experience. Someone to whom that experience has not happened, and whose knowledge of its having happened to others is hazy or missing, is subject to a complex form of ignorance which is itself, Wolf would seem to be arguing, historical in form. Everything will subsequently depend on whether individuals – who are in the book representatives of the experience and absence from experience of the wider nation – meet an opportunity for recording what (however previously occluded) *has taken place already*. Moreover, the emphasis on *location* in that ordinary English expression is also important: doubly so for the passage from Wolf's novel in which the whole weight of modern German history comes to bear in the question "Where on earth have you all been living?":

> In case it's no secret, what did they accuse you of?
> I'm a communist, said the concentration-camp inmate.
> Nelly was to hear all kinds of new sentences that day. How important were the fires burning in the dark with impunity compared to this man who openly accused himself of being a Communist?
> I see, her mother was saying. But that wasn't reason enough to put you in a concentration camp.
> Nelly was surprised to see that the man's face was able to change expression. Although he was no longer able to show anger, or perplexity, or mere astonishment. Deeper shadings of fatigue were all that remained accessible to him. He said, as though to himself, without reproach, without special emphasis: Where on earth have you all been living?
> Of course Nelly didn't forget his sentence, but only later, years later, did it become some kind of motto for her.[6]

Nelly and her mother are ignorant, not of the existence of concentration camps as such, but of the extent of their functions; of the breadth of the categories they were an attempt to obliterate. Their ignorance is in part conditioned by the fact that considerable measures had been taken by the Nazis to *obliterate the obliterating processes* (even if still further measures, as Stephen Greenblatt, among others, has forcibly pointed out, were a meticulous recording of just who and what were being destroyed).[7] A wedge has been driven deep into the "integrity" of the nation's experiencing of its own history, if, as the novel shows us was possible, some people could be having what for them were happy and idealistic childhoods, including just such activities as committed involvement in the Hitler Youth Movement, with only very occasional occurrences that hinted at another reality *in their midst*; while another set of people – precisely that other reality itself – not only experienced the full horror of what happened but also were left completely unable to account for the *absence from where they themselves were* of the majority of the German population, by whom they were nevertheless, and paradoxically, surrounded. In the above passage what we see happening, in 1945 after the collapse of nazism, is that the two parts of the same history – each of which has functioned more or less without reference to the other; indeed, has only been possible as a reality because Nazi ideology has successfully kept them divided by intricately constructed walls of ignorance – are beginning to fit together, as previously mutually-absent-to-each-other complements. A fuller history of the epoch in question is henceforth possible. It will be a painful process to write that history, since at every point it will involve matching up elements of the two "complements," which had previously operated in isolation from each other. Only some people will have the moral will to engage in the matching-up process, since at all points it will involve facing aspects of that fundamental question of *location*, such as: "Where was I when all these horrors were occurring?" Christa Wolf is one writer who has engaged very fully in the process in question.

Her notion of the positioning of the individual in relation to the state or nation during the epoch of nazism is a special case. Nazism itself is fortunately a special case, except in the sense implied by Walter Benjamin when he says that "the tradition of the oppressed teaches us that the 'state of emergency' in which we live is not the exception but the rule."[8]

But what is changed if we turn from this extreme example, of individuals within a modern European history cut off from the horrifying experiences of others in their very midst to a world such as Nadine Gordimer normally writes of? Her fiction tirelessly documents a reality in which a state of emergency is indeed all too clearly the rule. Or the world of Salman Rushdie, with so much comic fantasy in its way of claiming the individual as the focal point of national destiny that some, who fail to see how the fantasy complements a still deeper level of realism, accuse the novelist of abrogating history altogether? At the basis of Gordimer's representations lies not so much the shock felt by Wolf, at how much that is felt by others can escape the notice of individuals not engaged in the direct experiencing processes, but rather a kind of reversal of this: namely, a particularly sharp *prise de conscience* on the part of individuals at the suffering of others and the political will in consequence of this to intervene in the struggle for change. By no means all the characters in Gordimer's fiction come spontaneously to the anti-apartheid movement, or come to it at all for that matter. But even when they do not her fictions are concerned with documenting the evasions and almost conscious turnings away that do at least constitute a kind of knowledge and source of embarrassment.

In brief, a great deal of *Burger's Daughter* is cast in terms of a differential of attitudes to suffering. This encompasses at the most unfeeling end of the spectrum a family of Afrikaner farmers, the Nels, cousins of the Burgers, who accept unthinkingly what Rosa in the wake of her father's death sees with wistful skepticism as "that condition of a healthy, ordinary life: other people's suffering"–an ordered life of "black people out in the street and white people in the shade of the hotel stoep" (61). In the middle of this gamut of differing reactions there is the perfectly well-meaning white liberalism of a Flora Donaldson, someone with "managerial kindness and the tact of a well-off woman who fellow-travels beside suffering as a sports enthusiast in a car keeps pace alongside a marathon runner" (95). And then–more skeptically on Gordimer's part–there are the attitudes of the various European left-wing intellectuals with whom Rosa has affairs, such as Marcus, the Swedish filmmaker of her father's life, for whom "from his safety, from his welfare state where left-wing groups were like mothers' unions or Rotary Clubs, and left-wing views did not imply any endangering action, being the lover of Lionel Burger's daughter for a month or two was the nearest he would ever get to the barricades" (64–65); and Bernard Chebalier, the French schoolteacher she meets in the south of France in the second part of the novel, who damns himself and his like from his own mouth ("You don't know how careful we are, we French Leftist bourgeoisie. So much set aside every month, no possibility of living dangerously" [274]) and who uses the big words "'Oppress.' 'Revolt.' 'Betray' . . . as people do without knowing what they stand for" (276).

Problems begin when, like Wolf, Gordimer has her characters face a paradox. In her case it is the one best put in one of the epigraphs she uses, Wang Yang-ming's dictum that "to know and not to act is not to know" (213). In point of fact, the project of the novel is to see the protagonist Rosa through and beyond the terms of such a paradox, or, to put it differently, the horns of such a dilemma. Rosa's eventual casting of her lot with the politics of the anti-apartheid struggle – hence, her taking on the full burden of her political inheritance in relation to suffering – is something she only comes to after an initial attempt to "defect." Late in the novel, upon her return to South Africa, after having sought to construct a kind of apolitical idyll in the south of France, she will come to the conclusion that "no one can defect" and that the sum total of her existence is "about suffering. . . . How to end suffering. . . . And . . . ends in suffering" (332) – suffering, note, no longer seen and accepted merely as that of others but her own as well, and therefore universal.

To see how Gordimer gets thus far in her political analyses, however, we need to backtrack to the premises of *Burger's Daughter*, to those realities that at its opening are offered as givens in South Africa. The novel is the story of a young woman whose father and mother, longtime members of the Communist party and committed to fight for the overthrow of racism in South Africa, eventually die in the struggle, leaving Rosa, the daughter, either to take up or abandon the political inheritance of her upbringing. The novel's opening book both firmly establishes essential details of that upbringing and shows the crisis of commitment faced by Rosa when she no longer has an immediate family to define her political responsibilities for her (as they had done in her youth), but, instead, must find a will from within herself to continue in the same tradition (9–210).

We first see Rosa as a schoolgirl, waiting, along with a group of others, outside a prison, where her mother has been detained (not for the first time) for her latest political activities. In only its third sentence the novel comes out with what would seem a revealing pun: "Imagine, a schoolgirl: she must have somebody inside" (9). Those words, "somebody inside," primarily indicate that she must have a member of her family inside the prison. But there is a more elusive hint in them, of Rosa's possessing a developing personality in her own right, behind and within the schoolgirl exterior. This double sense is of vital importance, especially if one supposes that only one of the two meanings – the more obvious one – seems intended at the level of the deadpan, noncommittal, and only half-observant language in which many of the doings of Rosa are told. What we have, in other words, is a narrative style that enacts a point of view at best only half-aware of what is going on and what is at stake. The reader must observe a curiosity of his or her own, to win from this kind of language a set of fugitive insights which, when they *are* caught, need to be seen as nothing less than the orders of public (political) experience as these are felt intimately at the level of the individual. The reader is hence enrolled from the very beginning as engaged political interpreter, of a reality in the face of which not to seek some deeper understanding could only imply acceptance of and complicity in its continuance.

Important for our dealings with Gordimer, this role of the reader answers to a case she has made for the writer, as a being "in whose sensibility is fused what Lukács calls the duality of inwardness and outside world."[9] The "outside world" is what anyone might see, represented by what I have called the voice of the "deadpan" narrator in *Burger's Daughter.* "Inwardness," on the other hand, is what writer and reader alike must strenuously reach for. It coheres, in just such language acts as elusive puns. Indeed, Gordimer has laid claim to a special sensibility in writers, in a passage that represents her at her most Wordsworthian: "Writers, looking pretty much like other human beings, but moving deep under the surface of human lives, have at least some faculties of supra-observation and hyperperception not known to others. If a writer does not go down and use these – why he's just a blind fish."[10] While one might have some doubts about a certain *old-fashionedness* of this Wordsworthian-sounding case about special sensibility in the writer, it does, in *conjunction* with what I am positing as a complementary active role for the reader, suggest not a privileged aesthetic percipience but, ultimately, a collaborative reaching for a world of extended awareness, including the exercise of a canny political consciousness. It is in the practice of the fiction rather than in the sometimes disappointing theoretical formulations by Gordimer that this world is most fully realized.

Our present example helps show how this works. Rosa's developing political consciousness (the "someone inside" who is herself) is a clear case of a being acted upon by events. She is thus early positioned for the reader as the person about whom the overall epigraph of the book – Claude Lévi-Strauss's "I am the place in which something has occurred" – needs to be understood. That is why, furthermore, the pun on the word *"inside,"* unstressed and not even consciously intended though it may be, can bear the exemplary weight I am loading onto it in this initial move into interpretation of the novel. Totally unlike Wolf's protagonist Nelly, for whom concentration camps had been an "elsewhere," only able to be fully located in relation to the self in the immediate historical aftermath of the collapse of nazism – however they might figure later in her life (and more widely) as a guilt haunting the German nation – for Rosa the prisons of the apartheid regime are real material edifices for harboring dissidents such as her parents but also places *inside herself,* where events from the material world are replicated as *occurrences within consciousness.*

This internalizing of the political reality is a tendency she inherits from others, most notably from her parents. Early in the novel we come to realize that they likewise had been loci of political events. Lionel Burger, her father (and, notably, the other person figuring in the novel's title), who is eventually tried and found guilty of state conspiracy, makes an address from the dock as a last opportunity for "bearing testimony once and for all" (24) before being sentenced to life imprisonment ("And here life means life" [28]). In it he gives a synopsis of the events and attitudes that went to the forming of his Luther-like protest, "Here I stand. *Ich kann nicht anders*" (26). In a text that Gordimer herself has called a "novel of ideas,"[11] Lionel Burger's speech reads like the fundamental tenets of faith, his own set of theses pinned to the doors of the state's political edifice. The following are just a few salient extracts from it, worth quoting for their relevance to all that follows in the novel by way of his daughter's coming to take such a stand in her own right:

> He spoke for an hour. ". . . when as a medical student tormented not by the suffering I saw around me in hospitals, but by the subjection and humiliation of human beings in daily life I had seen around me all my life – a subjection and humiliation of live people in which, by my silence and political inactivity I myself took part, with as little say or volition on the victims' side as there was in the black cadavers, always in good supply, on which I was learning the intricate wonder of the human body . . . I found at last the solution to the terrifying contradiction. . . . That my people – the Afrikaner people – and the white people in general in our country, worship the God of Justice and practise discrimination on grounds of the colour of skin; profess the compassion of the Son of Man, and deny the humanity of the black people they live among. . . . My covenant is with the victims of apartheid. The situation in which I find myself changes nothing . . . there will always be those who cannot live with themselves at the expense of fullness of life for others. . . . I would be guilty only if I were innocent of working to destroy racism in my country." (24–27)

No selected highlights can do justice to this speech, which acts as a marker in the novel for ideas close to Gordimer's own in her vocation as a writer. Insofar as it is a speech in justification of Burger's continued membership of the Communist party, however, it is imbued not so much with Gordimer's own personal history, as with that of a real-life model for Burger, the Transvaal High Court judge Bram Fischer. Fischer had been tried for his membership of this outlawed organization in a major trial of the mid-1960s. Gordimer seems to have been fascinated by his case. She wrote an article about the trial, published in the *London Magazine* in March 1966, which reads like a strong foretaste of the novel we are considering.

Indeed, it is time to say a little more about the novel's place in history. For not only does its inception in the Bram Fischer trial help us to understand its own textual dealings with that history. The way it too was dealt with by history, upon publication in 1979, as a text first banned and then rapidly but revealingly unbanned, when the storms of international protest grew too strong for the South African authorities to withstand, tells us much about the national context that the novel itself is an attempt to represent. What the next passage in this argument will not very fully broach, however, is the treatment of Rosa, which, being in my opinion the most truly original aspect of the way Gordimer has *internalized* the complexities of a history and made them manifest within character, I will leave till a little later, where its contrast with the sheer extravaganza of Rushdie's (in any case more publicly vaunted) handling of history and politics may be the more telling.

The case of Abram Fischer, QC, is unquestionably the spark for this novel. Or, rather, Fischer's perceived heroism, seen and documented by Gordimer in the 1960s, is one historical precedent for the "theme of the novel," which, by her own later reckoning, came to Gordimer "as a question: what is it like to be the daughter of a hero, in a country where social strife still produces the hero-figure?"[12] Fischer stood for Gordimer as a real historical example of such a hero. As "son of the Judge President of the Orange Free State (one of the old Boer Republics) and a highly-respected and successful member of the Johannesburg Bar,"[13] he was the clearest prototype from reality for Lionel Burger. Like Burger a self-confessed Communist, he was none the less for that a "'son of the soil,' a true Afrikaner, born and bred," whom "not even the Afrikaner Nationalist-governed State that prosecutes him for alleged treason would deny . . . that status."[14]

This motif resurfaces in the novel in a young Afrikaner apologist's conversation with Rosa about Burger. "Brandt Vermeulen did not need to tell her her father could have been prime minister if he had not been a traitor. It had been said many times. For the Afrikaner people, Lionel Burger was a tragedy rather than an outcast; that way, he still was theirs" (186). Gordimer had, of course, changed her hero's profession from the barrister of the prototype into that of a doctor. His experiencing of the consequences of apartheid would be none the less for that change, as the earlier quotation from Burger's speech from the dock will amply demonstrate.

In 1963 Fischer had acted as defense counsel in the famous Rivonia trial, the state's prosecution of the High Command of the African National Congress (ANC), which led to the life sentences passed on Nelson Mandela and the others then found guilty. In 1965 Fischer himself was on trial along with thirteen others, for being a member of the banned Communist party and for state subversion. Exceptionally, because of his standing as a QC, he was granted bail and even given leave to represent a client in London. But upon his (to many unexpected) return to South Africa he slipped bail for some ten months and lived clandestinely in white suburbs of Johannesburg until recaptured. What in the novel figures as Burger's speech from the dock had its equivalent in a real public letter from Fischer written while in hiding, in mitigation of his having slipped bail. In it he too takes the opportunity of making an outright critique of racial oppression under apartheid and prophesies "appalling bloodshed and civil war" unless the "whole intolerable system is changed radically and rapidly."[15]

Close though this all is to the unfolding of Burger's attack on apartheid, it is in incidental details of the courtroom and the contrasting privileged life-style that Fischer has forgone in making his political stand that Gordimer found some of the most salient inspiration for her political novel of a decade later. Here is a small sample of her account of the resumed Fischer trial of 1966:

> In "G" Court they sat divided, according to the law and custom
> of the country, in the tiny public gallery that held a maximum
> of about thirty. A barrier separated white spectators from black.
> Every time Fischer turned from the court with its panoply of
> policemen, Special Branch men in plain clothes, lawyers, court
> officials and journalists ranged along the walls, he faced the
> social pattern of apartheid that had brought him to his present
> situation: stripped of his profession, alone, arraigned of trying
> to change that pattern even if, in the end, violence were to be
> resorted to in order to do so. . . . His fellow white South Afri-
> cans, indifferent to the quality of life on the other side of the

colour bar, living their comfortable lives in the segregated suburbs where, once, he too had a house with a swimming pool
and among whom, last year, he lived as a fugitive, express
strong opinions about what he has chosen to do with his life.[16]

This should stand as ample evidence of how much not only of the
events of history but also of its material texture and grain Gordimer
could first transcribe as the reality of Fischer's trial and then transmute
into the heart of her fiction. (Quite apart from the trial scene itself, she
makes the Burgers' "house with a swimming pool" into a main symbolic motif of the novel.) Changing the living QC Fischer into the doctor of the novel, Lionel Burger, does not invalidate the substantive historical validity of her text: in almost every respect it also permits her
to deepen it. (Bram Fischer's public letter is, for instance, in the final
analysis a lot less interesting than Burger's speech, as an argument on
the evils of racial oppression.) As Gordimer was to pronounce in a
speech delivered in New York in the early 1980s: "Nothing I say here
will be as true as my fiction."[17] And elsewhere, in self-commentary con-
temporaneous with the writing of the novel: "In the writing, I am acting upon my society, and in the manner of my apprehension, all the
time history is acting upon me."[18] Despite appearances, it is in many
respects the first part of that claim—"In the writing, I am acting upon
my society"—that is so extraordinarily bold. Unguardedly (rather than
immodestly, surely), Gordimer is saying that her own writing *counts
historically* in the anti-apartheid struggle.

As why should it not? We get too used to assuming perhaps that the
written word can make little difference in our advanced technological
industrial world, bound and structured as it is by the forces of Capital.
But, if there is truth in the claim made in the novel by Lionel Burger's
first wife ("It's strange to live in a country where there are still heroes"
[100]) and repeated by the author in her synopsis of the novel ("a country where social strife still produces the hero-figure"),[19] then Nadine
Gordimer, too, given the particular political themes of all her writing,
is subject to that truth, no less than the real QC Fischer or the fictional
doctor she wove from that reality. In this respect Gordimer is herself
a further prototype for the figure of Lionel Burger, more deeply embedded—a deeper genealogy, so to speak— than even Bram Fischer.

For a start this hypothesis helps us make more sense of the author's
preoccupation with the destiny of a daughter figure—and one for

whom, futhermore, France is the most significant *elsewhere*. Gordimer herself had a daughter living in France throughout this period, so it was her own main foreign point of reference. In short, her family – she and her daughter at the very least – cannot but be seen as the main figures of what I have called the "deep genealogy" of Lionel Burger and Rosa in the novel.

More important than this matter of finding from where exactly in national and personal history the novel's themes and details are taken is the corollary point that was being made above: that South Africa in the period of history dealt with – essentially, the period following the Sharpville massacre of 1960 and including the Rivonia trial of 1963, Bram Fischer's real trial of 1965 and 1966, and Lionel Burger's trial of the early 1970s in the novel – is perceived as a country in which individuals (lawyers, doctors, and, important for the case I'm making, writers) can make their mark. For, if Gordimer wrote out of the conviction that fiction could itself *count historically*, then, to return to one of this chapter's initial claims, the modern political novel such as *Burger's Daughter* had potentially a major role to play in helping produce the future out of the present.

Those who were originally responsible for having *Burger's Daughter* banned in South Africa seemed not unaware of this potential. On 18 July 1979 the Directorate of Publications produced its banning order. The main report called *Burger's Daughter* a "political novel" whose "theme is black consciousness and organizing for the coming black revolution."[20] Apart from the revealing note in that form of words – that the directorate accepted black revolution as a perhaps inevitable eventuality – there is a general accuracy in using the term Gordimer herself uses to describe its genre, that of the political novel. But the directorate is inaccurate (presumably ill informed) about the Black Consciousness movement. This movement's extreme wing excluded whites from participation in the struggle against apartheid. It is really only treated in one or two episodes: at a party in one of the black townships, where Rosa is made to feel uncomfortable on the basis of her race alone by a group of black youths; and in her late-night telephone conversation in London at the end of part 2 of the novel, in which she is rejected and abused by the black companion of her Burger home upbringing, Zwelinzima Vulindlela ("Baasie," as she had known him then). Later, in nonfictional writing of the early 1980s, Gordimer mentions with relief "the phasing out or passing usefulness of the extreme wing of the Black

Consciousness movement, with its separatism of the past ten years."[21]

The Directorate of Publications listed what it saw as a host of misrepresentations of South African society in *Burger's Daughter*. Gordimer duly refuted that they were such, in a detailed section of the riposte published by Taurus Publications the following year, *What Happened to "Burger's Daughter"* (the best source for all documentation of the banning and subsequent unbanning). Only in a minority report in Afrikaans appended to the Directorate's banning move, by one of the Afrikaner members of the panel especially shocked by thoughts about the potentially detrimental effect of the novel on the South African public, was the felt danger of its publication acknowledged outright. Three of the points of this minority report were the following:

> 7. The book creates a dangerous image of the South African situation to a broad spectrum of the R.S.A. [Republic of South Africa] reading public. . . .
>
> 11. As a matter of fact the value of the book as a product of the mind seems to lie in the insight that it gives into the psychological cravings and complexes from which the writer suffers.
>
> 12. The effect of the book on the public attitude of mind is dangerous in all aspects.[22]

In English translation it is hard to get quite the feel of this hard-line Afrikaner fear and mistrust of *Burger's Daughter* in the minority report. But what is striking is that, for all the tone of paranoia in which these points are put, they perhaps, severally and in combination, get near the mark. The power of such a novel does indeed lie in how it manages to take a readership right into the mental terrain of the writer's "cravings and complexes," so long as we understand that these are no more nor less than Gordimer's very strong beliefs about the iniquities of the status quo in South Africa under apartheid. This is the fundamental respect in which she differs from the writer of the minority report, and it is why he will imply that she suffers from psychic abnormality, whereas we might interpret that suffering as an inevitable consequence of seeing the "complexes" of the situation in South Africa as she does and her resultant compulsion to communicate "cravings" for change. In short, the way the minority report sees the novel as "dangerous in all aspects" (the three points quoted climax in that frightened remark in the third) is actually a strong tribute to the felt political power of this text. As such, they show no liberal ingenuousness of the kind Gordimer herself, in reflecting on the nature of politics in the novel, is too much stuck with. Her main definition of the genre (in defense of this particular instance) had been to see it as "a novel of ideas" which "explicates the effect of politics on human lives."[23] The minority report is closer to Stendhal's remark that politics in a work of literature is like a pistol-shot in the middle of a concert.

On the assumption, therefore, that the Afrikaans minority report was closer to perceiving the political effectiveness of Gordimer's text than even the author, then what in particular did it have to fear?

In essence, it had to fear the nation itself, as represented, and the protagonist Rosa, as representative. For the inevitable logic of Lionel Burger's, and Gordimer's own, personal histories of coming to the anti-apartheid struggle (we may recall here Burger's turn of phrase, "I would be guilty only if I were innocent of working to destroy racism in my country") unfolds in Rosa's story. And that story is at once a reading of the public realities of South Africa and a way of showing how these are internalized by a given individual.

Many important scenes of *prise de conscience* operate as virtual parables within the mind of Rosa as they are happening. I will mention only two, both of them among the most striking in the novel. The first is the harrowing climax to part I, the scene in which Rosa comes across a cart driver mercilessly beating his donkey. It unfolds in a "place" so unofficial, so unmapped, as to constitute an extreme locus of what the state at a public level has sought not to recognize. Rosa is progressively described as driving lost, "in one of those undefined areas between black men's hostels and the mine-dumps on the outskirts of the city," through a landscape of impoverished black lives "in what had been condemned and abandoned by the white city," amidst "places that don't appear on any plan of city environs"–"places that don't exist" (206–7). This last, ironically *metaphysical* definition of the setting preludes the scene of torment – the cart driver whipping his donkey – described in such a way that it becomes within Rosa's mind a metonymic parable of the whole gamut of suffering caused by oppression in South Africa, itself then laid bare in the writing:

> The entire ingenuity from thumbscrew and rack to electric
> shock, the infinite variety and gradation of suffering, by lash, by
> fear, by hunger, by solitary confinement – the camps, concentra-
> tion, labour, resettlement, the Siberias of snow or sun, the lives

of Mandela, Sisulu, Mbeki, Kathrada, Kgosana, gull-picked on
the Island, Lionel propped wasting to his skull between two
warders, the deaths by questioning, bodies fallen from the
height of John Vorster Square, deaths by dehydration, babies
degutted by enteritis in "places" of banishment, the lights beating all night on the faces of those in cells. (208)

To return to the minority report, we might say that it was one more
move by whites to banish the above reality to realms of "nonexis-
tence." It disapproves of publication precisely because the novel re-
trieves all that suffering from the "nonplaces" to which it is typically
banished and gives it a location and visibility. The location is at once
Rosa's mind and the text of the novel; for the purposes of this argument
those two are one. They can only be that because of the stylistic
devices on Gordimer's part which make them so for extensive sections
of the novel. We note, for instance, how naturally the figure who is a
creation of the novel, Lionel Burger, assumes *his* place in Rosa's mind
(the text), along with the other (nonfictional) suffering listed. The outer
world of South Africa and the inner world of Rosa's direct apprehen-
sions of it – or Gordimer's textual representations of it, as we had better call them – have become indistinguishable. Given the politics of
those representations, it is no wonder that they were a cause for concern to a member of the Afrikaner establishment.

Interestingly, in political terms, at this stage Rosa herself cannot
stand the pressure of seeing so much and knowing that their own people have made the peasant cart driver what he is: "I drove on because
the horrible drunk was black, poor and brutalized. If somebody's going
to be brought to account, I am accountable for him, to him, as he is for
the donkey." Unable to live with herself for being a member of the ruling white race, which perpetuates black subjugation –"Every week the
woman who comes to clean my flat and wash my clothes brings a child
whose make-believe is polishing floors and doing washing"– she is
determined to use the passport she has gained by careful compromises
with Brandt Vermeulen, a young apologist for the Afrikaner establishment, and simply leave South Africa. "After the donkey I couldn't stop
myself. I don't know how to live in Lionel's country" (209-10). So, the
end result of this particular parable of suffering in South Africa is to
drive her away.

Another parable-like incident happens to her soon after her arrival
in France. Its details can be quickly summarized, though the signifi-

cance to be won from them is more difficult, in part because she does not go so far herself in interpreting them, as in the case of the donkey incident.

Having arrived in Paris, where her skin coloring makes her actual origins indistinguishable—"If I'd been black that would at least have given the information I was from Africa. Even at a three-hundred-year remove, a black American" (231)—Rosa catches someone trying to filch her pocketbook in the crowded Rue de la Harpe. She seizes the hand of the pickpocket, a black man, presumably from Francophone West Africa: "The face was young and so black that the eyes, far-apart in taut openings, were all that was to be made out of him. Eyeballs of agate in which flood and volcanic cataclysms are traced; the minute burst blood-vessels were held in the whites like a fossil-pattern of fern" (233).

Though this reads all too like a continuance of colonial notions of the primeval otherness of primitive black Africa, the point of the rest of the passage is that it reenacts in miniature a drama of decolonization. First of all, the complementarity of Rosa and the pickpocket, white and black Africans coming together in the crowded anonymity of Paris, is stressed: "He was what he was. I was what I was, and we had found each other." Strangely though, by contrast with the donkey episode, at first the black is figured as oppressor and the white as victim: "pickpocket and victim, that's all, nothing but a stupid tourist with a bag, deserving to be discovered" (233). Interestingly, too, she is figured thus as victim, *even though* for the instant that she holds his hand grasped tightly he is ostensibly in her power. These reversals of conventional roles are continued in the idea of the black "discovering" the white, the obverse of imperial convention. We enter a kind of agnostic terrain, where it is impossible to say which of black and white will retain domination over the other.

This duality of being dominant or dominated continues in the rest of this *tableau vivant* of the stages of decolonization. Rosa speaks to the black man, but not in any language "that would have meaning for him." She lets go of him, and he moves away in the crowd: "His fear of me melted to a presence of connivance and contempt: because if I wouldn't denounce him while I held him, no one need believe me now that I had set him free" (234). The idea of her "freeing" him reinstates the conventional roles of white and black, at the moment of independence being granted: just as the "connivance and contempt" of his gaze as he drifts off into freedom seems to complete a precise metonymy of the attitude of formerly colonized to former colonizer. Even the denunciation of him which she does not commit could be thought of as a token of that point having been reached when the oppressor, in colonial pairing with the oppressed, can no longer, for moral reasons that have become instinctual, go on asserting dominance.

The incident is as graphic and disturbing as anything in the book, in the comfortlessness of its account of interaction between Africans of different races. One could find plenty of more ideologically straightforward incidents in the novel, ones in particular inclining Rosa toward the activist tradition of her parents which she eventually takes up in part 3. The importance of the pickpocket incident, however, seems to lie in its multiple reversals of power, as Gordimer envisages new orders of racial experience which confuse even her (or, to say the least, show her retaining notions of black primitivism based on the otherness of pigmentation alone – attitudes that cannot merely be passed off as those of her protagonist). It is an incident that seems to hold no optimistic prognosis for the decolonizing aftermath of independence. It unsettles, by refusing to conform to our notions of a progressive politics for Africa, and by putting in their stead the enduringly bitter image of a latter history based on "connivance and contempt." Desired political stances and outcomes are, by this reckoning, not to be arrived at by wishing, no matter how strongly. And, if Rosa commits herself to them, the novel keeps implying through to its closing sentences, it is with no guarantee of their coming to pass.

Thus far, I have sketched out how the text is forged of ties between national and personal histories and how it represents the public lived experience of South Africa as that is processed through the mind of someone still forming in political terms. Many of its further complexities have had to be omitted from this account. What I would stress is that this is a novel aware of its own – and any white person's – inevitable omissions, when it comes to representing the gamut of South African experience. The harrowing telephone conversation at the end of part 2 of the novel shows Rosa's black "brother" being utterly unfair to her, at the same time as the novel seems to be saying that he is only being so because the whole representation of South Africa to date (and in this judgment the text and its protagonist are not excluded as exempt) have been unfairly biased toward white experience: "Listen, there are dozens of our fathers sick and dying like dogs, kicked out of the locations when they can't work any more. Getting old and dying in prison. Killed in prison. It's nothing. I know plenty blacks like Burger. It's nothing, it's us, we must be used to it, it's not going to show on English television" (320).

The fact that we have in our hands a novel that can, so to speak, include the issue of its own inevitable omissions and limitations is a matter of no small consequence. Gordimer is in any case notably tough on herself in criticizing the degrees to which she has given voice to black experience: her achievements in this regard, here and in her writing generally, are far greater than she is willing to take credit for. I will not waste text on the racist obtuseness of critics who say she has no right to represent black points of view. She has answered such critics herself in convincing terms.[24]

Someone else who considers *Burger's Daughter* to be Gordimer's finest novel is Salman Rushdie,[25] to whom I now turn, for consideration of a very different modernist text but one that has its own distinctly inventive ways of linking national and individual histories and, by doing so, making politics an unavoidable consideration for its readers.

There is about some authors' writings – and very notably Salman Rushdie's – a prophetic cast of thought, whereby the future, which the present is hurtling toward, is every bit as important to historical consciousness as the past, out of which the present has emerged, distorted. Rushdie himself is now a figure prominently located within a charged recent past, problematic present, and ominous future. Each day sees new twists in the plot of his history. Nobody, not even he, contemplating his protagonist in *Midnight's Children*, so resoundingly "handcuffed to history," as Saleem Sinai pronounces himself to be on the first page –"my destinies indissolubly chained to those of my country" (9) – could have guessed that the author would become the focus not of a national but of an international affair, himself handcuffed to each side of a world historical rift between East and West, stretched almost to breaking point between different angular faces of Islam and of the Christian world. In 1985, talking in an interview about his character of the 1981 novel, Rushdie had come inadvertently near to prophesying his own destiny, in pronouncing that "he had to be un-housed, he had to lose the cocoon around him, and . . . be thrown into the middle of all this history that he claimed to be influencing. He then discovers, at the end of the book, that very far from being the controller of history he is a victim of it, and he never really recovers from this discovery."[26]

Although Rushdie never in his own person naively claimed to be influencing history, he too has clearly been "unhoused"—multiply unhoused in a literal sense, we gather—and thereby has lost any such cocooning from history which, like anyone else, he might reasonably have expected and laid claim to. Just as Saleem, he is now more "victim" than "controller" of his lot: a character in a larger, world novel, of which he is not really the writer but the written, very much a text rather than an author, and whether for him there will be anything like reprieve or recovery from his present predicament is still anybody's guess.

So much for the actual. I don't wish to make this an extended contemplation of all the repercussions of Rushdie's having written and published *The Satanic Verses*. The matter is treated extensively in other places. My own resolute interest is in the nature of history in Rushdie's writings, which I continue to believe is better discussed in relation to the earlier novel. *Midnight's Children*, as Rushdie stressed in a later interview mostly devoted to *The Satanic Verses*, "had history as a scaffolding on which to hang the book; this one doesn't."[27]

I began this section, however, with an allusion to the prophetic cast of Rushdie's historical consciousness and cannot entirely dismiss *The Satanic Verses* from consideration, without pointing to one or two prefigurations in Rushdie's earlier writings of what was to emerge in it and moments within that text itself of what was to emerge *from* it. So much is necessary if we are to begin to get a greater purchase on this protean term *history*, especially in relation to the phenomenon of prophecy which looms so large in all Rushdie's writings.

Since at least as early as his Cambridge days, where he sat the tripos in history, Rushdie had been fascinated by Islam, the main culture of his own upbringing, and by its major prophet, Mohammed. He had written a special-subject project on precisely Mohammed, Islam, and the Rise of the Caliph for part 2 of that degree. This material resurfaces piecemeal throughout writings as early as *Midnight's Children* but notably in succinct form on page 163 of that novel. Saleem is involved in explaining how he became a kind of radio-receiver station for hearing the other children born like him in the midnight hour of India's independence on 15 August 1947, the so-called Midnight Children's Conference, his own M.C.C. Elsewhere its 581 survivors (of the 1001 live births) are figured as a children's parliament, their number in fact the same as India's own parliament in Delhi and therefore hyperbolically called the "lok sabha or parliament of my brain" (227). (This is all part of the

elaborate historical fantasy of Saleem's life being a microcosmic replication of the nation's own macrocosm.) On this particular page, however, the analogy is not yet with India's *lok sabha* but with the way
earlier prophets – Moses, Mohammed, and Saint Joan are the examples given – hear voices. The crux of the passage in question as it bears
on Islam reads thus:

> Muhammad (on whose name be peace, let me add; I don't want
> to offend anyone) heard a voice saying, "Recite!" and thought he
> was going mad; I heard, at first, a headful of gabbling tongues,
> like an untuned radio; and with lips sealed by maternal com-
> mand, I was unable to ask for comfort. Muhammad, at forty,
> sought and received reassurance from wife and friends: "Verily,"
> they told him, "you are the Messenger of God"; I, suffering my
> punishment at nearlynine, could neither seek . . . assistance nor
> solicit softening words. . . . Muted for an evening and a night
> and a morning, I struggled, alone, to understand what had hap-
> pened to me. (163)

We have here and hereabouts in embryonic form much of what was to
offend in *The Satanic Verses*, including (not in the words quoted but on
the same page) the multiple "other-naming" of the prophet, first designated "Muhammad" but then in succession "Mohammed, Mahomet,
the Last-But-One, and Mahound." Here is the self-comparison with the
prophet which, with mock seriousness on Rushdie's part, elevates the
speaker Saleem to Mohammed's level, at the same time that it debases
the latter to the same ridiculousness as this snot-nosed nearlynine-
year-old. But, as if in prophetic anticipation of all the trouble that
was to follow publication of the later novel, here also is the attempt –
whether tongue-in-cheek it is heard to guess – to dispel any umbrage
being taken: "I don't want to offend anyone."

To say the least, the writing is full of risk. For some people there is
in all this only outrageous offense and for others merely a kind of de-
lectable cultural play. How may we get a clearer perspective on the
whole orchestration of such ambivalent cultural outrage/play in Rushdie's use of prophetic religiosity to expound a profane text?

Consider what he himself understands as the liberal possibilities of
Islam, as realized in his own upbringing within its culture: "I come
from a Muslim tradition, and in my family in the Indian subcontinent,
there was an absolute willingness to discuss anything, there were not

these anathemas, these rules, about what you must not talk about."[28] But Rushdie is not ingenuous in the matter of other Islamic traditions than his own, has always been able to see the difference between liberal and fundamentalist. I suggest that this must be so because, while writing under the self-license to "discuss anything," he is at some pains in most texts to draw the barb of any offense to more strict interpreters of the faith.

In trying so hard not to offend, however, he can tie himself up in apologetic sophistry and then, in quite another voice, expose his own profanations. Such seems to be the case in the highly revealing exposé of the disciple of his own name, Salman, in *The Satanic Verses* itself. Salman is upbraided by the prophet Mahound, just as his namesake, the author, will be by the Ayatollah Khomeini: "Your blasphemy, Salman, can't be forgiven. Do you think I wouldn't work it out? To set your words against the Words of God . . ." (374). It is an uncanny prefiguring of the Ayatollah's singling out of this Salman, for what was seen as *his* text's "words against the Words of God." Or else this is not uncanny at all, and Rushdie knew all along the kinds of risk his writing courted. In the light of such uncanniness or such knowingness – I suppose a third alternative would be uncanny knowingness – other remarks made by him as early as 1982 look a long way forward to the writing of *The Satanic Verses* and are curious, too, for focusing at their close on a kind of wish beforehand that it were not his future lot to have to write it: "At some point, the writing is going to perform the same migration that I did. Because otherwise it becomes spurious to spend your life living in the West and writing exotically about far distant lands, maharajahs. . . . I am very interested in writing about the idea of migration and the effect it has on individuals and groups. And somewhere, I think, there's an enormous novel waiting to be written, unfortunately."[29]

In one respect that term *unfortunately* would seem only to refer to the magnitude of the task of writing the novel which is recognizably, from this description, *The Satanic Verses* in anticipation. But *enormous novel* is itself a term with another meaning than sheer size. The enormity of its potential offensiveness would seem, however subliminally, to be making Rushdie of this 1982 interview wince in prophetic pain. Already then, to have to write the novel was to be under a kind of sentence.

All this makes Salman Rushdie more than ever like a character *written by* one of the autobiographical consciousnesses of his novels. For the earlier period of his career that thought quickly leads us back to Saleem

Sinai. In one local respect Rushdie *is* written by Saleem, in being casually included in a list Saleem gives of his schoolmates at the cathedral and John Connon Boys High School (this was the Bombay school that Rushdie did indeed attend in his pre-Rugby upbringing): "Naturally, the prefects had the pick of the ladies; I watched them with passionate envy, Guzder and Joshi and Stevenson and Rushdie and Talyarkhan and Tayabali and Jussawalla and Waglé and King; I tried butting in on them during excuse-mes but when they saw my bandage and my cucumber of a nose they just laughed and turned their backs" (233). Not surprisingly for such a cultural virtuoso as Rushdie, this slight mention of himself becomes a semiquotation of the way Hitchcock included Hitchcock (as in quotation) in some walk-on role or other in each of his films. Here Rushdie is just a more successful school contemporary of Saleem. At another level, however, Saleem is altogether modeled on the experiences of Rushdie's early Bombay years and family background. Saleem is both a translation of Rushdie's personal life into fantastic comic absurdism and a locus for the repercussions of every historical event of modern Indian history, a sort of comic lightning conductor for Rushdie's serious concerns with modern Indian history.

Let us inspect the two sides of that claim more closely. All that I have said so far urges us to further inquiry into the modern political novel's handling of recent history at the level of individuals.

Two early dealings with India's approach to the independence moment are important in what they say, the one about the reality of colonialism and the other about its legacy to the postcolonial epoch. They are, of course, both set prior to Saleem's actual birth, but any general points about the role of individuals within them hold good for him as well, the novel in its entirety bearing after all his unmistakable autobiographical imprint in almost every sentence, nowhere more so than in its *ante*-natal book 1.

My first example is the text's treatment of the Amritsar massacre. On 7 April 1919 at Jallianwala Bagh, Brigadier Dyer ordered his fifty crack troops to fire on a large crowd of Indians, who were observing one of the cross-India Hartal marches, which had been decreed by Gandhi "to mourn, in peace, the continuing presence of the British" (33). Hundreds were killed and hundreds more wounded.

Aadam Aziz, Saleem's maternal grandfather, has been literally led by his nose to witness the march. Thus far in the novel, a complex history of hybrid influences has gone to the making of Dr. Aziz, so he is already a highly overdetermined being to have as a spectator of a perfidious act of colonialism. As a "Europe-returned man" (as these very pages rub in) and one who, furthermore, is putting pressure on his wife to "translate herself" sexually into a greater Europeanness—"Forget about being a good Kashmiri girl. Start thinking about being a modern Indian woman" (34) – his is in large part a colonized consciousness and, hence, somewhat compromised when it comes to being constituted as a main witness to colonial brutality.

But not entirely so. He had smarted bitterly at his Heidelberg friends' notion "that India – like radium – had been 'discovered' by the Europeans": in fact, "this was what finally separated Aadam Aziz from his friends, this belief of theirs that he was somehow the invention of their ancestors" (11). So it is a piling of irony on irony that a combination of his large Kashmiri nose and his Heidelberg "doctori-attaché" case save him from being one more statistic in the Amritsar massacre. The case flies open when, ultrasensitive to impending danger, he sneezes violently. Forced to scrabble about on the ground for the treasures of his European medicine chest, he is out of the line of the rifle fire when Brigadier Dyer and his British let loose their "one thousand six hundred and fifty rounds into the unarmed crowd" (36).

On the one hand, Rushdie captures the perfidies of colonial oppression in every last syllable of Brigadier Dyer's complacent uses of the English language in congratulating his men: "Good shooting. . . . We have done a jolly good thing" (36). On the other, Dr. Aziz represents all India's protesting unacceptance of this colonial reality, in his shocked refusal to classify the event he has just witnessed as one that *took place* in the most literal sense. In answer to his wife's urgent questioning of the bloodstains on him—"But *where* have you *been*, my *God?*"–he responds, "Nowhere on earth" (36). This paradoxical insistence on *no* place is as important for Rushdie's protesting record of colonial brutality as my earlier attention to Christa Wolf's counterpointed place*ment* of different categories of people under Nazi rule or Nadine Gordimer's fascination with Lévi-Strauss's formula of *persons as places in which events occur,* leaving indelible traces.

My other main historical example from *Midnight's Children* evokes the colonial legacy to the postcolonial epoch, in all its copycat-producing splendors and elaborations. It is the story of how the descendant of the original dreamer of a "British Bombay," William Methwold, hands over villas of the estate he has built to their new Indian owners, in a way that exactly replicates the British government's own transference of power at the moment of independence. Methwold wants to hand over everything "tickety-boo,"–"absolutely intact: in tiptop working order" (97) – as, of course, do the British, the administration of an ordered (because colonized) India. The wives of the new Indian owners of Methwold's villas protest the most at his "two conditions: that the houses be bought complete with every last thing in them, that the entire contents be retained by the new owners; and that the actual transfer should not take place until midnight on 15 August" (95). But the wives are unprevailing in the face of such insidious colonial pressures as those of Methwold's stipulations. Allowed two months to live in these villas before "actual transfer"–symbolic of acclimatization to colonialism's most inner workings–the new Indian owners take on the attitudes and habits of their departing colonizers the British:

> Now there are twenty days to go, things are settling down, the sharp edges of things are getting blurred, so they have all failed to notice what is happening: the Estate, Methwold's Estate, is changing them. Every evening at six they are out in their gardens, celebrating the cocktail hour, and when William Methwold comes to call they slip effortlessly into their imitation Oxford drawls; and they are learning, about ceiling fans and gas cookers and the correct diet for budgerigars, and Methwold, supervising their transformation, is mumbling under his breath. Listen carefully: what's he saying? Yes, that's it. "Sabkuch ticktock hai," mumbles William Methwold. All is well. (99)

The novel has noted of Methwold "that beneath this stiff English exterior lurks a mind with a very Indian lust for allegory" (96). Methwold is hence a chip off the old Rushdie block. For the "lust for allegory" is Rushdie's own and nowhere more apparent than hereabouts in the novel. Methwold's wish to have his smaller transfer of power reflect in detail that of the nation's as a whole is symbolic of the grander British design of leaving on this postindependence society the indelible imprint of colonial habits and attitudes. His final "All is well" registers that the intention is daily being fulfilled, in the countdown to independence. On Rushdie's part the episode allegorizes also the *post*colonial dilemma, of having Indians themselves in the mimic roles.

And there is one final twist to the allegory, which exposes the cheat behind the whole colonial seduction process. Methwold's greatest attraction has been his slicked-down, center-parted, brilliantined black hair. The hair is what fascinated Wee Willie Winkie's wife Vanita and so led to her conceiving by Methwold the child who is in fact Saleem (later switched in the cradle with Shiva, the true offspring of the Sinai parents). But at the last going down of the sun on British rule Methwold's "long tapering white fingers twitched towards centre-parting." Seizing his hair, he pulls off what proves to have been a deceptive hairpiece all along. If, as the narration convincingly establishes, "William Methwold's power had resided in his hair" (114) – do we have an embedded reference here to the biblical Samson? – then, in openly ripping it off, he is as it were obscenely taunting his colonial dupes, the Indians, for having been taken in. Methwold's – or rather, at bottom Rushdie's – "very Indian lust for allegory" is telling us in terms as fantastical as they are also, and nevertheless, unmisreadable that the last British act is an unmasking device, a laying bare of their own meretricious power, by which they have seduced and ruled. With those they have ruled *over* now securely locked into their mimic roles, it is as though the British generally at this penultimate moment were taunting the Indians for their hard-won independence and saying: "Look at this power which you now laboriously know how to go through the motions of wielding. You didn't realise – and we deliberately didn't reveal until too late – the grand deception upon which it was all based. What good to you is such power, now that you know its hollowness? But of course – jolly good show this one – you cannot forgo using it, since it is *all* that we bequeath you!"

I have tried by these words to sum up some of the nuances at this point in the novel, nuances that constitute Rushdie's unmistakable historical allegory on the nature of India's independence. Naturally, the way that allegory works is more all-pervasive – more "lusty," to use a Rushdian term – than analysis can easily do justice to. And, of course, at one important level the entire novel is a historical allegory, on the deception of the inheritors of India's independence, the Children of Midnight.

Rushdie has always been interested in migration in the strict geographical sense, as *The Satanic Verses* was later to demonstrate. But Rushdie's mind, thinking figuratively as always, had early on perceived history itself as a movement of persons from another place: "the past is a country from which we have all migrated."[30] There is a major problem, however, in recuperating past reality, namely the fallibility of

memory, from which he makes his character Saleem Sinai a notable
sufferer ("In my India, Gandhi will continue to die at the wrong time"
[166]). But recognizing the fallibility of memory is not to invalidate
the historical enterprise. On the contrary, Rushdie contends in many
places (in both fiction and nonfictional writings) that it is a gross mis-
representation to suppose that the pastness of the past can ever be
accurately re-exhumed. Neither memory nor any other historical activity can reconstitute past reality. All that can be done is to engage in
activities of mind which quicken the historically charged meaningful-
ness of the present.

Failure to begin to see this is what makes carping critics such as
Richard Cronin, with his ascription of an "absence of intelligent political thinking" in Rushdie, so dully uncomprehending of what is going
on in a novel such as *Midnight's Children*. Cronin mistakes the protagonist Saleem for the novelist Rushdie, when with plodding literal-
mindedness he remarks that the novel is "committed to fantasy, because its premise is the fantastic claim of one individual to embody
the impossible diversity of India." He calls the book a "children's history of India" for the reason that it is "the product of fantasy rather
than historical research,"[31] quite failing to respond to any of the multitudinous ways that fantasy works hand in hand with realism in a historical venture of this magnitude. Above all, what Cronin fails to allow
for is the compelling modernism of the novel's form. No one has represented this in exegesis of the novel as well as the author in general
remarks, in which he makes connections between modernism as a literary mode and doubt as a philosophical frame of mind, both of them
unavoidable and interrelated aspects of our age.[32] The link is drawn in
two particular passages—one from 1982, the other from 1989—in both
of which there is anything but an absence of "intelligent political thinking." After *Midnight's Children* comes this:

> Human beings do not perceive things whole; we are not gods
> but wounded creatures, cracked lenses, capable only of frac-
> tured perceptions. Partial beings, in all senses of that phrase.
> Meaning is a shaky edifice we build out of scraps, dogmas,
> childhood injuries, newspaper articles, chance remarks, old
> films, small victories, people hated, people loved; perhaps it is
> because our sense of what is the case is constructed from such
> inadequate materials that we defend it so fiercely, even to the

death. . . . Those of us who have been forced by cultural displacement to accept the provisional nature of all truths, all certainties, have perhaps had modernism forced upon us.[33]

As an account of a state and a process, this closely describes a reality such as that realized in *Midnight's Children*. And this makes the novel better history rather than not; "fractured perception" is recognized as inevitable and, hence, deployed as the catalyst of the novel's comic-modernist form.

This line of thinking was to be extended into a fundamental philosophy of the relationship of doubt to modernism by the time, in 1989, that Rushdie was reflecting on the implications and impact of *The Satanic Verses*:

> Doubt, it seems to me, is the central condition of a human
> being in the 20th century. One of the things that has happened
> to us in the 20th century as a human race is to learn how certainty crumbles in your hand. We cannot any longer have a
> fixed certain view of anything—the table that we're sitting next
> to, the ground beneath our feet, the laws of science, are full of
> doubt now. Everything we know is pervaded by doubt and not
> by certainty. And that is the basis of the great artistic movement
> known as Modernism. Now the fact that the orthodox figures in
> the Muslim world have declared a jihad against Modernism is
> not my fault. It doesn't invalidate an entire way of looking at
> the world which is, to my mind, the most important new contribution of the 20th century to the way in which the human race
> discusses itself. If they're trying to say that this whole process
> has gone out of the window—that you can't do that, all you have
> is the old certainties—then yes, I do argue.[34]

This spirited attack on "the old certainties" is fundamental to Rushdie's ways of dealing with history—nowhere more so than in *Midnight's Children*, with its vast emphasis on "meaning as a shaky edifice," built precisely from such partial matter as "scraps, dogmas, childhood injuries, newspaper articles, chance remarks, old films, small victories, people hated [and] people loved." Two fundamentals of how a world so fissiparous and always already fragmented can be held together in a single fictive vision are use of the leitmotif and use of fantasy. Neither works against history, both strenuously for it.

Consider his use of leitmotifs. At the start of the novel the young "Europe-returned chappie" (23), Dr. Aadam Aziz (whom we've already seen in relation to the Amritsar massacre), Heidelberg trained, is ferried by the "watery Caliban," Tai the boatman, backward and forward across the lake of Srinagar in Kashmir, from home to the house of Ghani the landowner, to attend to the multiple bouts of hypochondria of the landowner's daughter Naseem. Major and abiding leitmotifs of the novel are launched in this first chapter. Tai the illiterate boatman of unspecifiable years represents an age-old India, little if at all influenced by Europe, signs of which, such as Dr. Aziz's same medical attaché bag from Heidelberg, he mistrusts absolutely: "To the ferryman, the bag represents Abroad; it is the alien thing, the invader, progress"; "Sistersleeping pigskin bag from Abroad full of foreigners' tricks" (21, 20). Tai's discourse, the "chatter" of an "old soliloquist" is described as "fantastic, grandiloquent and ceaseless" (15, 14). These words characterize at once Tai and the entire oral tradition (alternating narrative with commentary) which he represents and which is so important to the novel's own onward progress.

Many Western critics have concentrated on Rushdie's Western influences—Sterne, Swift, Dickens, Márquez, Grass—but in the figure of Tai an entirely other and oral mode of keeping historical tradition alive (one that the novel itself mimetically adopts) is immediately launched. Tai early and pointedly scolds Aziz for his (and, as it might be, our) skepticism: "Smile, smile, it is your history I am keeping in my head. Once it was set down in old lost books. . . . Even my memory is going now; but I know, although I can't read" (16). Interestingly, oral literature is seen here in the total run of history as surviving when written modes are by definition defunct. This overturns our easy Western assumptions, both of historical progression from oral to written and of the greater durability of written over oral traditions.

Moving toward a conclusion, let me stress the following: *Midnight's Children* has so much to say about the representation of history that it would be impossible in this brief analysis to include all of even the telling instances. So, instead of trying to overcome the digressions, fantastical and grotesque, of this inventive narration, in some deluded attempt to put back together a more strict "what-happened-nextism," which it has itself programmatically subverted, let us take a direct look at Rushdie's main point about India.

First, India is so multifarious and diverse that no single-stranded narration, and certainly no one person, can comprehend the whole of it. As the author has claimed: "The story is told in a manner designed to echo, as closely as my abilities allowed, the Indian talent for non-stop self-regeneration. . . . The form—multitudinous, hinting at the infinite possibilities of the country—is the optimistic counterweight to Saleem's personal tragedy."[35] "Buffeted by too much history. . . . we are a nation of forgetters," remarks Saleem (37). And elsewhere: "No people whose word for 'yesterday' is the same as their word for 'tomorrow' can be said to have a firm grip on the time" (106).

This "condition of India" theme is the basis for a phenomenology that interlinks fantasy with history, as I have earlier sought to establish. The multifarious and fantastical Children of Midnight first of all represent an infinitude of possibilities for modern India. But then, as the nation's history darkens, they have spelled out in their individual lives a closure of that infinitude and a turning instead toward its opposite: annihilation. Whereas childhood had at first been posited as an optimistic "third principle," by the middle of the novel we have reached the chilling realization that childhood "dies; or rather, it is murdered" (256), and the concomitant speculation that "the purpose of Midnight's Children might be annihilation; that we would have no meaning until we were destroyed" (229). History here takes on the configuration of a malign force that first of all distorts the purer realities of childhood— "life has been transmuted into grotesquery by the irruption into it of history" (57)—and then kills it stone dead.

That is the novel's most pessimistic perspective about India. But one other reality, the teeming inventiveness of consciousness and hence of narration, constantly lightens that burden, which would otherwise be intolerable. And India itself is always drawn in on this point too, so that the nation is not solely linked to the fate of its individuals, with their inevitable tendency to grow beyond childhood and then, like Saleem, eventually "crack up." It is equally embodied in any and all racy vagaries of consciousness and, hence, with the positive growth of the text. When Saleem, for instance, describes his "pell-mell tumble of a brain, in which everything ran into everything else and the white dot of consciousness jumped about like a wild flea from one thing to the next" (214), he is giving a very good approximation of comic narrative tendencies of the book.

But not only that. In the notion of things running into other things we have the principle of blur or leakage, which does so much to subvert anything like Western notions of individualism in the first place. "Things – even people – have a way of leaking into each other" (38), the novel early establishes as a phenomenological principle; and later, "other people's lives . . . blur . . . together" (171). This is partly a consequence of India's very population density, so great that one of the preconditions that we imagine for individualism, "deep solitude," is accounted as being an extreme rarity in this "overcrowded country" (202).

And yet, for all my qualification, there *is* a notion of the individual – and of India as a single entirety – which survives this text, despite all the pressures of crack-up. To hold onto such a vision is admitted to be a kind of overweening madness. As Saleem asks himself: "Am I so far gone, in my desperate need for meaning, that I'm prepared to distort everything – to re-write the whole history of my times purely in order to place myself in a central role?" (166). We are even told a memorable vignette, of a painter who had, like Saleem/Salman, what in another place is thought to be "an Indian disease, this urge to encapsulate the whole of reality" (75): "As a young man he had shared a room with a painter whose paintings had grown larger and larger as he tried to get the whole of life into his art. 'Look at me,' he said before he killed himself, 'I wanted to be a miniaturist and I've got elephantiasis instead!'" (48). The painter's problem is a comic analogue for the unstoppable growth of Rushdie's own work, and, no doubt, intended as such. (We know from interviews that the original draft for *Midnight's Children* was a blockbuster, four times the length of the published novel!)

But that such people as the painter exist in the way they do is itself a sign of the survival of individuality, in the face of the tyrannies of historical and cultural blurring. Furthermore, Rushdie would have it that the lives of the nation's multifarious persons can, for all that makes for unrepresentability, through enormous effort of historical will, somehow get represented. They can get represented just as they can get born because the nation, India, is not solely (in the old cliché) a teeming begetter of peoples but, also, a begetter of teeming narrative: "The children of midnight were also the children *of the time:* fathered, you understand, by history. It can happen. Especially in a country which is itself a sort of dream" (118). What we have is a profoundly useful breakdown of categories – not unlike a falling of walls between disciplines in our own world of academia – whereby history is no longer a solid edifice of what-happened-nextism (no more than this novel is) but is itself allied with dream, invention, myth, and prophecy. Above all, it is ultimately not a polar opposite of fiction but its mirrored other, as Saleem Sinai is of India.

NOTES

1. Stephan R. Clingman, *The Novels of Nadine Gordimer: History from the Inside* (London: Unwin Hyman, 1986).
2. Friedrich Nietzsche, "The Uses and Disadvantages of History for Life" (1874), *Untimely Meditations*, trans. R. J. Hollingdale (Cambridge: Cambridge Univ. Press, 1983), 67.
3. In Timothy Brennan's *Salman Rushdie and the Third World: Myths of the Nation* (London: Macmillan, 1989) there is a searching first chapter on the relationship between nations and fictions, "National Fictions, Fictional Nations," exploring these issues in terms of far more writers and contexts than I deal with here.
4. Nadine Gordimer, *Burger's Daughter* (London: Jonathan Cape, 1979); Salman Rushdie, *Midnight's Children* (London: Jonathan Cape, 1981); all page references from these two texts will be to these editions.
5. Nadine Gordimer, "Living in the Interregnum," *New York Review of Books*, 20 January 1983, 21.
6. Christa Wolf, *A Model Childhood*, trans. Ursule Molinaro and Hedwig Rappolt (London: Virago, 1983), 332; original German title *Kindheitsmunster* (Berlin: Aufbau-Verlag, 1976).
7. Stephen Greenblatt, "Towards a Poetics of Culture," in *The New Historicism*, ed. H. Aram Veeser (New York: Routledge, 1989), 4.
8. Walter Benjamin, "Theses on the Philosophy of History" (1940), *Illuminations*, ed. and intro. Hannah Arendt, trans. Harry Zohn (1970; reprint, London: Fontana, 1982), 259.
9. Gordimer, "Living in the Interregnum," 26.
10. Ibid.
11. Nadine Gordimer, "What the Book Is About," in *What Happened to "Burger's Daughter," or How South African Censorship Works*, ed. Nadine Gordimer et al. (Emmarentia, R.S.A.: Taurus, 1980), 19.
12. Ibid., 17.
13. Nadine Gordimer, "The Fischer Case," *London Magazine* 5 (March 1966): 21.
14. Ibid.
15. Ibid., 22.
16. Ibid., 29–30.
17. Gordimer, "Living in the Interregnum," 21.
18. Nadine Gordimer, introduction to her selection of short stories, *No Place Like* (Harmondsworth: Penguin, 1978); quoted in Margot Heinemann, *"Burger's Daughter:* The Synthesis of Revelation," in *The Uses of Fiction: Essays in the Modern Novel in Honour of Arnold Kettle*, ed. Douglas Jefferson and Graham Martin (Milton Keynes: Open Univ. Press, 1982), 182.

19. Gordimer, "What the Book Is About," 17.

20. Report on the Directorate of Publications, 18 July 1979; quoted in Gordimer et al., *What Happened to "Burger's Daughter,"* 6.

21. Gordimer, "Living in the Interregnum," 22.

22. Reprinted in English translation in Gordimer et al., *What Happened to "Burger's Daughter,"* 15.

23. Gordimer, "What the Book Is About," 19.

24. Most convincingly in a passage from "Living in the Interregnum," 27.

25. Salman Rushdie, *Imaginary Homelands: Essays and Criticism, 1981–1991* (London: Granta, 1991), 194.

26. Salman Rushdie, "*Midnight's Children* and *Shame,*" *Kunapipi* 7, no. 1 (1985): 10.

27. From an interview with Sean French, reprinted in *The Rushdie File,* ed. Lisa Appignanesi and Sara Maitland (London: ICA, Fourth Estate, 1989), 8.

28. Salman Rushdie, interview of 27 January 1989 by Banding File, broadcast on 14 February 1989 on channel 4; transcript from Appignanesi and Maitland, *Rushdie File,* 30.

29. Interview with Salman Rushdie in *Kunapipi* 4, no. 2 (1982): 26.

30. Salman Rushdie, "Imaginary Homelands," *London Review of Books* 4, no. 19 (1982): 18. This essay is reprinted in Rushdie's *Imaginary Homelands.*

31. Richard Cronin, "The Indian English Novel: *Kim* and *Midnight's Children,*" *Modern Fiction Studies* 33, no. 2 (1987): 210–11.

32. Other critics have not shared Cronin's views but have, on the contrary, written illuminatingly on modernist literary form in Rushdie's fiction. One of the best treatments of it is to be found in Timothy Brennan's already noted *Salman Rushdie and the Third World;* see, in particular, 37, 52, and chap. 4, "The National Longing for Form."

33. Rushdie, "Imaginary Homelands," 18.

34. Rushdie, interview of 27 January 1989 by Bandung File, 30–31.

35. Rushdie, "Imaginary Homelands," 19.

9   Reading Travel Writing

Jim Philip

This essay offers a reader's report on recent travel writing, and clearly some initial definitions and descriptions are in order. By travel writing I mean texts concerned with journeys and written by authors who are themselves frequent, if not continuous and compulsive, travelers. By the use of the term *recent* I mean to suggest not only that this particular mode has its own distinct history that has yet to be fully investigated but also that its revival, adaptation, and popularization has been one of the more significant literary events of the past ten years. In a sense, of course, we are dealing here with a larger economic and cultural history. As we move toward the twenty-first century, the lives of more and more human subjects have a thread of travel woven into their fabric. Our encounters with "foreign" places and peoples, in the forms either of tourism, study, or work, are increasingly frequent. Even when we are "at home," because of technological advances in global media the rest of the world is always with us, albeit in speedy, packaged, or unresolved forms. If this is the future of all of us, then it is certainly the future of literature and its associated discourses in their efforts to make sense of our local and translocal relationships. Indeed, whether I like it or not, and in ways that as yet I only half-understand, a new internationalism inhabits these words that I write and is also evident in the work that I shall be considering. It is latent in not unconnected ways in the commercial activities of the publishers who have undertaken to produce this volume and in the conditions under which it will be received by its projected audiences. Travel writing and the issues that it provokes are perhaps best understood, then, as the first instance, the first skirmish, in a coming full-scale international battle of the books that will involve in new ways writers, publishers, and audiences of new kinds. And one might be allowed to hope, in vain probably, that this battle of the books might be widespread and absorbing enough to replace those other degrading and divisive conflicts that have been the inauspicious openings of the "new world order."

These broad contextual issues are inevitably a part, then, of reading travel writing. But what of the texts themselves? Perhaps the first recognition to be made is that of the sheer variety and idiosyncrasy of the writings that are marketed under this bland brand name. Travel writing is more or less developed and more or less acknowledged in various parts of the globe. As one might expect, it is most practiced and most read among those peoples who, for the longest time, have exercised commercial or political power over others and whose cultural relations have therefore been most widespread and most problematical. In this sense, it might be argued, travel writing is European and has been involved in one way or another with the history of colonialism. Yet this volume has in itself been evidence of a significant body of writing in which, if one were not to put it too lightly, "the Empire strikes back," and the inclusion of a Pole among the authors considered here should in itself be a reminder of the variety of empires and the variety of resistances amid which we have lived. After only a brief survey, then, one would have to conclude that most cultures are in the process of evolving their own modes of travel and that the recognition, indeed the reading, of these differences is an intricate but necessary task.

Yet if diversity and relativity are among the new conditions to which the reader must find ways of responding, then so also is an increasing historicity. Several studies of travel writing in its previous phases have drawn attention to its fixing and essentializing tendencies, its proposal of "timeless" differences of race, character, and culture. Yet in a world as unfixed and volatile as our own it is hardly likely that such modes could survive for long. Indeed, it would be true to say of most of the writers that we shall be considering that their concern is now with the time-ridden, rather than the timeless. We are asked to consider such matters as the differences between then and now, the processes of revolution and modernization, the impact upon both landscapes and human lives of rapid and interactive change. And it would be fair to say that, if in such works a "time of arrival" is evident, then so also is a "time of departure," a moment within the culture of origin that is inscribed, albeit in less obvious ways, in the nature and direction of the commentary. But, if there is more history to be observed in the making of these texts, there is also, as an inevitable corollary perhaps, more textuality. Indeed, we should not forget that, despite the unique elements of each journey, the telling of it reaches us only by means of a range of available discourses. News reporting, anthropology, sociology, ecological science, the writings of previous travelers–these all contribute to the making of that apparently singular voice that acts as our interpreter and our guide. If the richness to which we are responding is one of experience, it is also one of writing. Relativity, historicity, textuality–these are the themes, then, that I shall endeavor to sustain.

I should like to preface my account of some particular writers with a brief, hopefully instructive, traveler's tale of my own. The journey from Colchester to Cambridge is not a long one, but recently I undertook it in such a way and with such consequences that I have never entirely returned home. The purpose of my visit was to interview, on behalf of a local arts review, the editorial staff of *Granta*, a publication that describes itself as "a paperback magazine of new writing" and that has been heralded by *Newsweek*, among others, as "a stunning contribution to contemporary literature."[1] This was an assignment that I approached with curiosity rather than with the expectation of major intellectual change. Yet what occurred in the course of my conversation was that the map of something I thought I knew well began to dissolve and to reform itself in surprising ways. Literature was business, I discovered, to be conducted on a world scale and with a certain entrepreneurial panache. Literature was news, involving the discovery and promotion of "the freshest international writing of the decade."[2] But, if literature was these things it was also crusading and committed: it was a matter of people talking to people; its enemies were power, privilege, prejudice, and cruelty. I was left wondering how *Granta* might manage to reconcile its various intensities, but one thing seemed clear: *Granta* had a deep skepticism about what it saw as the increasingly arcane and sidelined practices of academic literary criticism; there were more important things to be done. What follows is a consideration, in the main, of writers first promoted by *Granta*. It is offered as a tribute to my enlightenment on that occasion but also in the hope of suggesting that criticism does still have something constructive to say.

If there is one figure above others who can be taken as emblematic of *Granta*'s enthusiasms and the redefinitions it proposes, it is surely Ryszard Kapuściński. Brought up amid the shifting realities of wartime and postwar Poland, Kapuściński spent much time during the 1960s and 1970s as a press agency correspondent in India, Africa, the Middle East, and Central and South America. In these arenas, to put it in his own words, he "personally witnessed twenty-seven revolutions,"[3] and it is some of these experiences that are recorded in *The Emperor, Shah of Shahs, Another Day of Life,* and *The Soccer Wars,* texts that are now read worldwide, but particularly in the West. With his credentials of mobility and courage, his familiarity with first, second, and third worlds, he has achieved an almost legendary status as the writer whose hoard of stories, not yet fully disclosed, contains an unparalleled account of our times.

Yet, if Kapuściński's career is in some senses prophetic and representative, it is also historically specific. In an interview with Kapuściński conducted by Bill Buford, the editor of *Granta,* it is possible to discover something of the origins and development, in his particular case, of the linked imperatives of travel and writing. He recalls an early occasion when he wrote, and managed to publish, a controversial article concerning maladministration and corruption at Poland's showcase steel factory, Nowa Huta. He comments: "The experience was an exciting one for me. It illustrated that writing was about risk—about risking everything. And that the value of the writing is not in what you publish but in its consequences. If you set out to describe reality, then the influence of the writing is upon reality."[4] To write, then, is to risk, to overcome and expel the introjected anxieties of life in a bureaucratic society and to demand such recognition and such courage from others. As Kapuściński later suggests, though, what had to be written out was not simply the threatening apathy of Polish life but also that network of ideas that, in their rigidified and Stalinist forms, were its ultimate policing and legitimizing agency: "It was in the nineteenth century that faith in science invited an analogous faith in history: that history had laws, that it could be known, that it followed a pattern. What we believe now—certainly what I believe—is very different. History is impossible to penetrate, and that is its great richness."[5] It is instructive to discover, then, that Kapuściński's pursuit of experience has as its context the unresolved suspension, if not the total abandonment, of Marxist perspectives.

So much to write out, but much also to be written in. Kapuściński records his pressing at the limits of a discovered ignorance. "You mustn't forget that for my generation the outside world did not exist. There was no outside world, or, if there was, we knew little about it."[6] He records his dissatisfaction at the constraints of "straightforward journalism" which enabled him to record only "the political event."[7] Toward the end of the interview, when challenged to define the qualities of his own writing, he has the following to say:

> *Kapuściński:* I don't know. I'm not forming a manifesto and certainly don't want to appear dogmatic. But I do feel that we are describing a new kind of literature. I feel sometimes that I am working in a completely new field of literature, in an area that is both unoccupied and unexplored.
> *Buford:* The literature of political experience?
> *Kapuściński:* The literature of personal . . . no, that's not right. You know, sometimes, in describing what I do, I resort to the Latin phrase *silva rerum:* the forest of things. That's my subject: the forest of things, as I've seen it, living and travelling in it.[8]

There is a revealing hesitation here between the terms *political* and *personal*, as if Kapuściński were unwilling or unable to relinquish either to the other. Perhaps what is glimpsed here is that ultimately Utopian hope inscribed in his writings – namely, that the two terms might on some future ground be fully reconcilable; that an informed, exploratory personal life might find new ways of contributing to political debate; that a new politics, a new global politics perhaps, might be based more fully upon the personal, participatory expressions of its citizens. Yet, if the space of disaffiliation opened in Kapuściński's writing is occupied partly by these hopes for the new, it would be fair to say also that there are contradictory aspects of reversion, of return to older models for confirmation and support. One might point in this context to the undeniably Conradian elements in his work: the wry, almost hopeless, sense of the paradoxes; the slowness; the injustices of history; and the ambiguities of most personal efforts within it. Conradian also is the pride in authorship, the conviction that, at least in the selection and crafting of particular incidents, a kind of integrity is to be found.

These remarks have been designed to prepare the reader for what is to be experienced in Kapuściński's short but concentrated texts. In an overall sense these books record and celebrate the fall of tyrannies and pay tribute to the often anonymous acts of personal courage which have set these events in motion and sustained them. Yet there are constant crosscurrents of ironic response, and we are left always with the feeling that the future is far from secure, that it remains hostage to forces of barbarism or exploitation from the past which still have a role to play, in whatever transformed guises. In *The Emperor* efforts, of an increasingly unhinged kind, to "modernize" Ethiopia take place amid the atavism of an ancient conspiratorial state. In *Another Day of Life* decolonization struggles against recolonization in an arena still decimated by the traumatic and divisive legacy of the slave trade. Of the places and moments, the play of hopes and fears, to be found in these texts, one example must suffice. It comes from the latter of these two books:

> Balombo is a little town in the forest that keeps changing hands. Neither side can settle in for good because of the forest, which allows the enemy to sneak to within point-blank range under cover and suddenly attack the town. This morning Balombo was taken by an MPLA detachment of a hundred people. There is still shooting in the surrounding woods because the enemy has retreated, but not very far. In Balombo, which is devastated, not a single civilian remains – only these hundred soldiers. There is water, and the girls from the detachment approach us freshly bathed, with their wet hair wound around curling papers. Carlotta admonishes them: They shouldn't behave as if preparing to go out for the evening; they ought to be ready to fight at all times. They complain that they had to attack in the first wave because the boys were not eager to advance. The boys strike their foreheads with their hands and say the girls are lying. They are all sixteen to eighteen years old, the age of our high school students or of the fighters in the Warsaw uprising. Part of the unit is joyriding up and down the main street on a captured tractor. Each group makes one circuit and hands the wheel over to the next one. Others have given up contending for the tractor and are riding around on captured bicycles. It is chilly in Balombo because it lies in the hills; there is a light breeze and the forest is rustling.[9]

Here, then, is *silva rerum*, the forest of things. The utopianism is evident and irresistible. For a space of time peace has replaced war; it is a moment of infectious hilarity, of spontaneous play. Yet, if the play is about anything, it is about the glimpsed potentialities of the revolution itself; the reordering of relationships of power and gender, the reclaiming of technology, the rebuilding of distinct local communities. It is into this moment that the narrator also is drawn, his hard-boiled account of yet another skirmish transforming itself into the intricacies of personal and sensual detail and the involuntary movement of memory. To recall "the fighters in the Warsaw uprising" in the context of this other group of young people is to honor both and to unite them under the banners of courage and hope. And yet, if there are currents of feeling of these kinds recorded in the passage, there are also their undermining opposites. Everything is temporary. This is not a revolution but a caricature of a revolution, a ritualized and repeated maneuver in a minor and confusing war. The Warsaw fighters rose against one tyrannical force only to be cynically abandoned to their fate by another. We are left to speculate on whether the fate of Carlotta and her companions may be any less perilous.

With Kapuściński we have traveled from Poland to Angola. Let us now, by way of contrast, travel from England to the Philippines in the company of James Fenton, a younger writer also favored by *Granta* and a self-confessed admirer of Kapuściński's work. The scene is Malacañang, the Marcos's palace, and the time is the evening of 25 February 1986:

> One of the Filipino photographers just walked past the guard, then another followed, then Bing went past; and finally I was the only one left.
>
> I thought: oh well, he hasn't shot them, he won't shoot me. I scuttled past him in that way people do when they expect to be kicked up the backside. "Hey, man, stop," said the guard, but as he followed me round the corner we both saw he had been standing in the wrong place: the people in the crowd had come round another way and were now going through boxes and packing-cases to see what they could find. There were no takers for the Evian water. But everything else was disappearing. I caught up with Bing, who was looking through the remains of a box of monogrammed towels. We realized they had Imelda's initials. There were a couple left. They were irresistible.

> I couldn't believe I would be able to find the actual Marcos
> apartments, and I knew there was no point in asking. We went
> up some servants' stairs, at the foot of which I remember seeing
> an opened crate with two large green jade plates. They were so
> large as to be vulgar. On the first floor a door opened, and we
> found ourselves in the great hall where the press conferences
> had been held. This was the one bit of the palace the crowd
> would recognize, as it had so often watched Marcos being tele-
> vised from here. People ran and sat on his throne and began
> giving mock press-conferences, issuing orders in his deep voice,
> falling about with laughter or just gaping at the splendour of
> the room. It was all fully lit. Nobody had bothered, as they left,
> to turn out the lights.[10]

One way to read this is surely as a wickedly funny parody of the "I was
there" mode of Kapuściński himself. Our intrepid reporter braves danger, in this case that of being shouted at; he joins the people, who are
not engaged in heroism but, rather, in the combined activities of loot-
ing and fooling. Together they approach the central lair of power, but
that power has already fled, leaving the lights on. If there is an element
of absurdity to be descried in the events themselves, so also is there in
Fenton's self-presentation. Trying, in Evelyn Waugh fashion, to preserve his dignity and his taste, he is at the same time the gaping tourist
and the frantic souvenir hunter. At the center of this forest of things is
to be discovered no culminating experience but, rather, the cherished
prize of Imelda's immaculate, "irresistible" towel.

Fenton's willingness to replay events, and his own participation in
them, as farce, as carnival, can be enjoyed for its own sake, but perhaps its more important role might be to remind us of the sheer variety
of scenes and of ways of apprehending them to be found in his text,
The Snap Revolution. If the Philippine revolution is comedic, it is also
intensely conversational. No one seems to know what is happening,
but everyone is talking about it. Fenton seeks out representatives of all
political factions and engages them in debates during which he partly
learns and partly adds to the chaos through a determination to pro-
pound his own pragmatic, English, democratic socialist vistas. And, if
the Filipinos are heard, or rather half-heard, as they talk their way into
a different future, so also they are observed as, with real courage and
cooperation, they take to the streets to block and to confront the mili-

tary forces that the increasingly inept Marcos intended to unleash upon them after the exposure of his electoral fraud. Signs here of a return to the Kapuściński mode, despite previous disavowals. It would be fair to say, then, that this journey is one that offers interesting, if provisional, reconsiderations both of destination and of origin. What is written in, in all its confusing complexity, is that new, largely peaceful kind of people's revolution, of which we have since seen other comparable examples. What is written out is that aggressive cultural chauvinism, those delusions of grandeur, those refusals of ironic self-awareness, which were the international mode of Thatcherism during the mid-1980s.

These remarks on *The Snap Revolution* have been designed in part as a response to a highly critical account of it – and, by implication, of the whole mode of travel writing out of which it emerges – by Benedict Anderson in the *New Left Review.* Here Fenton is pilloried as the worst example of a new kind of writer, the "political tourist." "He is a creature of the media, and his travels to exotic politics are aimed at the acquisition of slides which will be saleable on the mass market for the vicarious *frissons* they offer to consumers."[11] On the passage quoted above and what follows it Anderson has the following to say:

> Our tourist steals a couple of Imelda's monogrammed towels,
> and strums Bach's Prelude in C on one of her pianos, while, as
> *Granta* burbles ineffably, "the population of Manila rioted."
> After all this excitement, no wonder that "like Helen, I was rev-
> olutioned out." . . . What better way to rest up than to hold a
> *Granta*-funded beach-party for the dragonman, the "boys," and
> their girl-friends, especially as one of the girls brings along a
> last whiff of the mysterious Orient in the form of a body-
> guarded Chinese lover.[12]

One begins to wonder whether the luckless Fenton hasn't here found himself caught in the crossfire of yet another power struggle, this time between the editorial boards of the two magazines. It must be said, though, that there is something sadly unperceptive and programmed about Benedict Anderson's response. In his failure to recognize the reflexivity, the heterogeneity, the self-mockery, of Fenton's text, in his puritan condemnation of both media sharks and gullible masses, there are indications of a certain elitist intellectual ghetto within which the

British Left is in danger of incarcerating itself. Read accurately, these books do have more to offer than the mere exploitative riding on the currents of recent events which he proposes. They certainly have as much to contribute to our exploration of the globe as the lectures and history lessons that the *New Left Review* will no doubt continue to offer us.

Yet there remain, perhaps, some further questions. Given the distinct interests and itineraries of each journey, why is it, after all, that so many are now being made? And is it possible, beyond the relativities, to discover some common topic, some common juncture of history, which has called forth the revival of the mode and is making new demands upon it? For assistance on these grounds we might turn to Fredric Jameson, another leftist critic, equally high-minded, but certainly more flexible and more exploratory in his analyses than Anderson. In his justly renowned article "Post-modernism, or the Cultural Logic of Late Capitalism" Jameson has drawn attention to the rapid development of international capitalism as the determining instance of our times and has traced a series of responses to what he describes as this new "sublime" across a range of cultural productions. All of them – forms of writing, of architecture, of filmmaking, and others – give evidence, so he claims, of "the incapacity of our minds, at least at present, to map the great global multinational and decentred communicational network in which we find ourselves caught as individual subjects."[13] In an interesting, if somewhat vatic, passage at the end of the essay he seeks out the dialectic of this situation and offers some clues about the transformation of a reactive, bemused, and often cynical postmodernism into a more purposive cultural challenge:

> An aesthetic of cognitive mapping – a pedagogical political culture which seeks to endow the individual subject with some new heightened sense of its place in the global system – will necessarily have to respect this now enormously complex representational dialectic and to invent radically new forms in order to do it justice. This is not, then, clearly a call for a return to some older kind of machinery, some older and more transparent national space, or some more traditional and reassuring perspectival or mimetic enclave: the new political art – if it is indeed possible at all – will have to hold to the truth of postmodernism, that is, to say, to its fundamental object – the world space of multinational capital – at the same time at which it

achieves a breakthrough to some as yet unimaginable new mode
of representing this last, in which we may again begin to grasp
our positioning as individual and collective subjects and regain
a capacity to act and struggle which is at present neutralized by
our spatial as well as our social confusion. The political form of
postmodernism, if there ever is any, will have as its vocation
the invention and projection of a global cognitive mapping, on a
social as well as a spatial scale.[14]

One cannot help feeling that there is a certain Californian exaggeration and haze in these formulations, both in regard to the pervasive,
mystifying impenetrability that is attributed to capitalism itself and in
regard to the new art that is to emerge apparently out of nowhere to
encounter it. Yet there is no doubt that Jameson's comments must be
of interest to us in the present context, for, in proposing "an aesthetic
of cognitive mapping," he must surely be proposing a travel writing of
some kind as a model for the future. One further line of inquiry, then,
begins to open up. Perhaps it may be possible, after all, to read these
texts as a site of the emergence, however tentatively, of a new kind of
international *society*, with its own groups, its own alliances, its own
agendas, capable both of figuring and of opposing those forces of capital which have preceded it upon the global scene.

Of this kind of analysis three brief examples will have to suffice. We
shall begin by considering a short story by Bruce Chatwin, a Scottish
writer capable of sentimentalisms and exploitations but also, as we
shall see, of curiously haunting concentrations. In "The Albatross" he
recalls an earlier encounter with this bird on a trip to Patagonia and
continues:

> A year and a half later, when *In Patagonia* was in press, I went to
> the island of Steepholm in the Bristol Channel. My companion
> was a naturalist in his eighties. The purpose of our visit was to
> see in flower the peony that is supposed to have been brought
> here as a medicinal herb by monks from the Mediterranean.
>
> I told my friend the story of how, in the nineteenth century, a
> Black-browed albatross had followed a ship north of the Equa-
> tor. Its direction-finding mechanisms had been thrown out of
> line. It had ended up on a rock in the Faroe Islands where it
> lived for thirty-odd years and was known as "The King of the
> Gannets." The Hon. Walter Rothschild made a pilgrimage to see

it. Finally, it was shot, stuffed and put in the Copenhagen
Museum.

"But there's a new Albatross," the old man said. "A female
bird. She was on Bass Rock last year, and I think she's gone to
Hermaness."

Hermaness, at the tip of Unst in Shetland, is the ultimate
headland of the British Isles.

From my flat in London, I called Bobby Tullock, the Shetland
ornithologist.

"Sure, she's on Hermaness. She's made a nest among the Gannets and she's sitting proud. Why don't you come and see her?
You'll find her on the West Cliff. You can't miss her."

Chatwin joins the night train to Aberdeen and has the following
encounter:

The man jumped into the upper bunk. I tried to talk. I tried
English, French, Italian, Greek. Useless. I tried Spanish and it
worked. I should have guessed. He was a South American
Indian.

"Where are you from?" I asked.

"Chile."

"I have been in Chile. Whereabouts?"

"Punta Arenas."

Punta Arenas on the Straits of Magellan is the southernmost
city in the world.

"I was there," I said.

"I come from Punta Arenas. But that is not my home. My
home is Navarino Island."

"You must know Grandpa Felipe."

"*Es mi tio.*" "He is my uncle."

Having exceptional powers of balance, the young man and
his brother found work in Punta Arenas as refuellers of the
light-buoys at the entrance to the Magellan Strait. In any sea
they would jump onto the buoy and insert the fuel nozzle. After
the fall of Allende, the brother got a job with an American oil
company, using his talent on off-shore rigs. The company had
sent him to the North Sea oil field. He had asked for his brother
to join him. They would each earn £600 a week.

I told him I was traveling north to see a bird that had flown
from his country. The story mystified him.

Two days later I lay on the West Cliff off Hermaness and watched the Albatross through binoculars: a black exception in a snow field of Gannets. She sat, head high and tail high, on her nest of mud, on her clutch of infertile eggs.

I too am mystified by this story.[15]

One might begin to elucidate the mystery by pointing out that what we have here, under the protective aegis of that ultimate global traveler, the bird itself, is the meeting of two kinds of new world citizens. Chatwin is the traveler from the North. Behind his infectious enthusiasms we are aware of the not inconsiderable efforts of a range of botanists, ornithologists, ecologists, and anthropologists. Here, as elsewhere in his work, he presents himself as a gleeful networker, enjoying, popularizing, that other, more acceptable mode of modern science in its attempts to preserve and enhance, rather than to destroy, the variety of the created world. His companion is the traveler from the South, the migrant worker, whose mobility is partly a voyage of discovery and assessment but partly also at the behest of a multinational company. The story is enigmatic, of course; we are offered only the possibilities, the latencies, of conversations and alliances that have yet to make their full appearance upon the historical stage. But at least the implications are clear that we might think of that future not as the uncontested site of the spectacles of international capitalism but as a ground upon which science might find ways of redeeming its critical and life-enhancing potential and upon which poverty might find ways of expressing itself as never before.

In Primo Levi's fascinating book *The Wrench* this conversation is continued, but with the new energies and emphases of a reversed format. It is now the narrator who listens, and Libertino Faussone, the Italian rigger whose skills have taken him far from the village of his origin, who speaks. In the following passage he is recalling his response to the moment when his work on an Alaskan offshore oil project reaches its culmination:

> It tilted more and more; the top of the platform rose, until finally, with a lot of foam, it was on its legs. It sank just a little, then stopped abruptly, still like an island, but it was an island we had made. . . .
>
> Now don't go telling this to anybody, but at that moment I felt like crying. Not because of the derrick, but because of my father. I mean, that metal monster anchored there in the midst

of the water reminded me of a crazy monument my father
made once with some friends of his, a piece at a time, on Sun-
days after their bowling, all of them old geezers, a bit loony, and
a bit drunk. They had all been in the war, some in Russia, some
in Africa, some God knows where, and they'd had a bellyful; so,
since they were all more or less in the same line of work – one
could weld, another could file, another could beat metal plate,
et cetera – they decided to make a monument and give it to the
town, but it was going to be a monument in reverse: iron
instead of bronze, and instead of all the eagles and wreaths of
glory and the charging soldier with his bayonet, they wanted to
make a statue of the Unknown Baker, yes, the man who invented the loaf.[16]

Faussone's repressed tears and the intensity of his memories are powerful signs of a demand for justice and liberty which has yet to make
its way fully into the world. In comparison with the enforced and unrecorded traveling of his father's generation, his own recasting of the
world (if I may put it that way) has a meaning and a dignity to it. Yet
here, as throughout the book, it is not only by a compulsion to build
that he is gripped but also by a compulsion to talk – to discover, through
recollection and conversation, the outlines of a communal, as well as
an individual, project.

Primo Levi's unstated suggestion in *The Wrench* that, for the sake of
a more interesting future, we should often be content simply to attend
to what is being said to us, is one that should not go unheeded. At the
risk of being accused of last-minute tokenism I should like, as a final critical act, to transform myself into a listener. If the underlying purpose of
travel writing is to seek out the hopeful manifestations of our age, then
we should do well, claims Martha Gellhorn, in her collection *The View
from the Ground,* to recognize the women of Cuba and the contributions
they also have made to the emergence a future world citizenry.

I like the government's decision in favour of pleasure: Cuba's
Revolución is not puritanical. Outlawing drugs, gambling and
prostitution eradicated crime as big business, hardly a bad idea.
. . . But I think that the main cause of a different, open, pleasurable life-style is the change in women. The old Hispanic and
Catholic custom of the women at home – isolated, the daughter
guarded, the stiffness of that relation between men and

women – is truly gone. Women are on their own at work, feeling equal to men, and showing this new confidence. Girls are educated equally with boys and chaperonage is dead. There is a feeling that men and women, girls and boys are having a good time together, in a way unknown before.[17]

NOTES

1. Quoted on back cover of *Granta* 21 (Spring 1987).
2. Quoted on back cover of *Granta* 18 (Summer 1986).
3. *Granta* 21, 90.
4. Ibid., 88.
5. Ibid., 92.
6. Ibid., 89.
7. Ibid., 94.
8. Ibid., 96.
9. Ryszard Kapuściński, *Another Day of Life* (London: Pan Books, 1988), 58.
10. *Granta* 18, 141.
11. Benedict Anderson, "The Snapshot Revolution," *New Left Review* 158 (1986): 82.
12. Ibid., 88.
13. Fredric Jameson, "Postmodernism, or the Cultural Logic of Late Capitalism," *New Left Review* 146 (1984): 84.
14. Ibid., 92.
15. Bruce Chatwin, *What Am I Doing Here?* (London: Pan Books, 1990), 344–45.
16. Primo Levi, *The Wrench*, trans. William Weaver (London: Sphere Books, 1988), 73–74.
17. Martha Gellhorn, *The View from the Ground* (London: Granta, 1990), 430.

Contributors

Patrick Fuery, Lecturer, Department of English, Macquarie University.

Peter Hulme, Professor, Department of Literature, University of Essex.

Sally Keenan, Department of Literature, University of Essex.

Neil Lazarus, Associate Professor, Department of English and Center for Modern Culture and Media Studies, Brown University.

Carolyn Masel, Lecturer, Department of American Studies, University of Manchester.

Jim Philip, Lecturer, Department of Literature, University of Essex.

Jerry Phillips, Associate Professor, Department of English, University of Connecticut at Storrs.

Dennis Walder, Senior Lecturer in Literature, Open University.

Jonathan White, Lecturer, Department of Literature, University of Essex.

LIBRARY OF CONGRESS CATALOGING-IN-PUBLICATION DATA

Recasting the world : writing after colonialism / edited by Jonathan White.
  p.   cm. – (Parallax : re-visions of culture and society)
  Includes bibliographical references.
  ISBN 0-8018-4605-6 (hard : alk. paper). – ISBN 0-8018-4606-4 (pbk. : alk. paper)
  1. Commonwealth literature (English) – History and criticism.   2. Literature
and society – Commonwealth countries.   3. Decolonization in literature.
4. Colonies in literature.
I. White, Jonathan.   II. Series: Parallax (Baltimore, Md.)
PR9080.R42   1993
820.9'9171241 – dc20
                                                                    93-22456